LITERACY IN MULTIMEDIA AMERICA

CRITICAL EDUCATION PRACTICE
VOL. 25
GARLAND REFERENCE LIBRARY OF SOCIAL SCIENCE
VOL. 1096

CRITICAL EDUCATION PRACTICE
SHIRLEY R. STEINBERG AND JOE L. KINCHELOE, *Series Editors*

LITERACY IN MULTIMEDIA AMERICA

INTEGRATING MEDIA EDUCATION ACROSS THE CURRICULUM

LADISLAUS M. SEMALI

FALMER PRESS
A MEMBER OF THE TAYLOR & FRANCIS GROUP
NEW YORK & LONDON
2000

Bib: 40558

Published in 2000 by
Falmer Press
A member of the Taylor & Francis Group
29 West 35th Street
New York, NY 10001

10 9 8 7 6 5 4 3 2 1

Library of Congress Cataloging-in-Publication Data is available from
the Library of Congress

Semali, Ladislaus M.
    Literacy in multimedia America : integrating media education across the
curriculum / Ladislaus M. Semali
        p.   cm. — (Garland reference library of social science ; vol. 1096)
(Critical education practice ; vol. 25)
    Includes bibliographical references and index.
    ISBN 0-8153-2295-X

Printed on acid-free, 250-year-life paper.
Manufactured in the United States of America

To My Students

Contents

Preface

Understanding how media bias confines and defines public discourse on diverse issues is a key concept of media literacy education and the primary goal of this book. *Literacy in Multimedia America: Integrating Media Education across the Curriculum* challenges students to take a critical stance when they read, view, or think about textual or media representations prevalent across the school curriculum. As defined in this book, critical media literacy, also know in other countries as media education, is not an antidote to help students learn how to liberate themselves from texts that are designed to dupe them. Rather, the broader goal is to cultivate systematic methods of inquiry, models of critique, and analytical ways of reading visual images and messages embedded in both print and electronic texts. Such a process seeks to get at the deeper meaning of texts as well as enhance the pleasures that students may derive from them. By questioning texts, students will learn more and thus produce knowledge of their own. As will be explained in the chapters of this book, this approach encourages students to question what they see on television and the Internet, ponder what they listen to daily on the radio and in songs, and recognize bias or misrepresentations when they perceive them in any other textual form.

Integrating critical media literacy across the curriculum is an under-researched topic in literacy education. In the seven chapters of this book, I explore several themes: technology, integration, critical pedagogy, critical viewing, representation, and values. In some of the chapters I have also included a vignette of anecdotes intended to help teachers reflect on examples from their own practice in order to gain insights to further strengthen integrative curriculum. The themes I take up in *Literacy in Multimedia America: Integrating Media Education across the Curriculum* encourage students to challenge the authority of readings and text, and challenge the opinions of all educators, including the new educator of choice, television. By engaging in authentic questioning, students will actively deconstruct prepackaged knowledge that is found in textbooks, films, songs, Web pages, and other media texts.

The main focus of this book is to provide a guide to teachers on how to integrate critical media literacy across the curriculum. It also draws students' attention to how powerful groups define their own particular meanings, values, experiences, and forms of writing and reading as the valued ones in society. Through critical media literacy, students will better understand the inequalities and violations of social justice the media continue to peddle through multiple forms of imagery, found in the entertainment programs and culture products that students consume every day. However, in writing this book, it is not my intention to promote a false notion of consensus of teaching that erases difference and ignores alternatives. Doing so would negate the whole purpose of this volume. Rather, I wish to emphasize the development of multiple ways of knowing within all students in order to encourage them to see life as a process of creations and negotiations rather than as linear steps toward a universal and final goal.

In the course of writing this book, I received several inquiries via e-mail from teachers who were trying to design a critical media literacy curriculum for their schools. Where would they start? they asked. What resources are available to novice teachers to help them think about curriculum planning? These teachers realized that media literacy was important to their students, but they were unsure where to put it. Where does it fit in the overall curriculum? How does one integrate it without adding yet another course in an already overloaded curriculum? These were legitimate concerns.

As I respond to these concerns in this volume, I am convinced that we need to promote integration more seriously. I advocate integration because, as a teacher, I believe that students' lives are not disconnected, and when we engage them and encourage them to make sense of the world around them, especially the world of media, we in fact support, though sometimes not openly, a classroom practice that advocates a holistic approach to life and learning. Integration is an important concept in this regard because the overall intent of critical media pedagogy is to seek ways to integrate the world of the classroom with the world of the child and society as a whole. Thus, integration is at the center of the critical media literacy project.

Furthermore, integration as an educational goal has been valued and advocated by nationwide organizations, such as the Association for Supervision and Curriculum Development and the International Reading Association. At their annual conferences and in their journals these and other organizations have advised teachers and other educators that processes and abilities do not grow in isolation from content. They insist that students acquire these processes and abilities through observing, listening, reading, talking, and writing about science, mathematics, the arts, and other aspects of our intellectual, social, and cultural heritage. Their prevailing rationale is inspired by the belief that the separation of school from the "real world" only increases when the arts and media remain marginalized and extracurricular. Likewise, efforts to increase literacy learning are rendered incomplete and irrelevant when they fail to acknowledge the meaning-making capabilities of extracurricular media messages and information.

Integration is one of three major concepts that run throughout this book. The other two concepts are curriculum and critical pedagogy. The notion of curriculum is taken up as a broad theory of curriculum design that encompasses particular views about the purpose of schools, the nature of learning, the organization and uses of knowledge, and the meaning of educational experience. The third concept in this book centers on critical pedagogy and the perspective it offers teachers and students to use in analyzing human experiences as lived by members of a culture. I believe the usefulness of critical pedagogy as a classroom practice lies in its ability to generate skepticism through its inquiry methods. Once we are skeptical, we can begin to investigate the questions that arise from such skepticism, the unquestioned assumptions, and uncertainty of the veracity of events, ideas, or the rendering of a popular story. Such critical analysis undermines the intellectual certitude that gives some educators the intellectual authority to dismiss some classroom practices as culturally deficient and to accept others as academically sound.

It is through such analytical explorations that we discover the origins of the myths we hold so dear to us, the stereotypes we have believed were true for so long, and the culture of denial that has become so much a part of our routine. The practice of critical pedagogy as envisaged in a critical media literacy project, and as I have conceptualized it in this book, is a critical framework for unpacking assumptions underlying cultural practices as legitimized by the many texts that surround us in multiple forms—print, visual, and electronic. These three concepts—integration, curriculum, and critical pedagogy—form the three legs of the metaphorical stool that buttress the critical medial literacy program that I describe in this volume.

Whereas educators and their national organizations are excited about the pedagogical gains offered by curriculum integration, students in many public schools haven't developed the habits of mind necessary for academic inquiry appropriate for genuine integration. In Chapter 1, I argue that the acquisition and mastery of such habits expected in the students of the twenty-first century is a necessary condition to survive in a multimedia society. In this multimedia world, technology and the media have become part of the texts of students' everyday lives. This is the reality and it is not going away soon. In Chapter 2, I take up the issues related to integration of critical media literacy across the curriculum in detail.

Chapter 3 examines the origins of critical pedagogy and the foundations of critical media literacy. The chapter notes that what is missing in many schools is the methodology to read, question, and understand the new languages of media and examples of ways to produce meaning that enhances lives and rejects the oppressive nature of texts that privilege some students and deny other students' voice. The concepts of integration, curriculum, and critical pedagogy dominate the first part of this book. The second half of the book outlines frameworks teachers could use to analyze cultural texts.

The habits of mind that a critical media literacy curriculum might provide students include the ability to imagine and value points of view different from their own. These new ways of seeing and knowing can strengthen, refine, enlarge, and reshape students' ideas of cultural context in light of those other perspectives gained from inquiry. Such critical habits also include openness to new ideas combined with a skepticism that demands testing those ideas against previous experience, reading, and belief. They include a desire to see things as a whole and to integrate specific knowledge into larger frameworks.

After conducting a survey of media literacy books in print in the United States, I found that few authors have seriously explored the issues of integrating critical media literacy across the curriculum. Because critical pedagogy is still new to many teachers and because there is a fear of introducing its methods into classrooms on account of its emphasis on literacy as political, the integration of critical media literacy has failed to impress veteran teachers. My goal in this book is to show that as adults, teachers, and parents, we need to confront our own beliefs about teaching, learning, and democratic citizenship. As a cross-disciplinary study, critical media literacy provides the missing link between curriculum and institutions; representations of people and events, and systems of beliefs and communicative practices.

To begin an authentic questioning of our beliefs is a complex matter. Few examples exist in this vein to model such critical inquiry. Few models or frameworks can be found in the United States to illustrate how we can integrate the critical pedagogy of media literacy across the school curriculum, K–12. Even though there is a growing interest to integrate media education across the curriculum in Canada, Australia, and England, efforts like these have not become common practice in the United States. But to date, we can observe some isolated references emerging slowly in standards-based education and experiments with media literacy found in several states.

Perhaps these developments are a move in the right direction. But still, taking on a critical pedagogy approach in curriculum practice—particularly a pedagogy that gives students the technical skills and analytical frameworks with which to dismantle and dismiss ideologically biased or stereotyped messages, such as racist and sexist content—is still rare in most public schools. My hope is that veteran teachers will read the aims outlined in this volume as important and worthy of trial in their classrooms. I believe that from these experiences, teachers can glean some insights that will summon their creativity and imagination to construct a classroom that promotes the development of critical perspective within their students and themselves. I also hope that through the chapters of this book I have communicated my passion for critical media literacy curriculum and that such enthusiasm can radiate to influence veteran and prospective teachers to think about the insight that media literacy can nurture within their students.

LITERACY IN
MULTIMEDIA AMERICA

CHAPTER 1

Media, Technology, and Schools

When the world crashes in, into my living room
Television made me what I am
People like to put the television down
But we are just good friends
I'm a television man.
—DAVID BYRNE'S REFRAIN, "TELEVISION MAN," p. 603

Multimedia—the integration of sound, text, graphics, and full-motion video—is enriching the way in which users interact with computer technology. Technology developers are creating multimedia-driven applications. Areas include interactive television, distance learning, telemedicine, corporate presentations, electronic publishing, video conferencing, video broadcasting, Web marketing, and electronic commerce. At the same time, technology innovators are scheming to find ways to meet the challenges of achieving the fast delivery of rich multimedia Internet content to users using communications media that include the plain old telephone system, satellite communication and even the electrical power supply.

Furthermore, instead of flying scores of students across the United States from Colorado to attend a lecture at a University on the East Coast or to chat with peers, it is now possible to place a camera at the function so that they may participate "virtually" by visiting a Web site, or via videoconference and e-mail. Today, this is possible through the continuing convergence of different media technologies—radio, TV, Internet, books on compact discs or tape, and so on. The use of video streaming technology, which takes up less bandwidth by allowing the user to watch part of the presentation while the rest of it is being streamed across the communications medium, has opened up many possibilities not possible before. This phenomenon has in turn impacted learning, behavior, and individual attitudes.

Kids in school have grown up with multimedia software, VCRs, the Internet, and a host of electronic gadgetry—games and toys—since infancy. College students are now able to have a conference call set up so that they can discuss the subject matter with peers at another location and ask questions at the same time. What might be the implications of these new developments to learning and instruction? What role can schools and teachers play to facilitate this new way of constructing knowledge and disseminating information? How are our lives affected by multimedia technologies?

Over the past quarter century, communication technologies have spawned an explosion of possible ways in which "text" is part of the out-of-class curriculum, both written and electronic, from photographs to film to videotext. One major irony is that American education has failed to develop a philosophy or pedagogy based on the role of visuals in instruction while it has spent an increasingly large share of its budget on iconic technologies such as computers, VCRs, video cameras, and interactive video. These technologies are much more than electronic envelopes for delivering the old curriculum in a marginally new way. But as made clear by Bennett (1995), an important question lies just beneath the surface of the much glorified electronic superhighway: How will democracy cope with news/information that is ever more standardized and politically managed at its source, while becoming ever more personalized and socially isolated at its destination? The answer awaits not only the input of citizens but also of teachers and students themselves.

This book engages teachers in new forms of inquiry using the pedagogy of critical media literacy to integrate the new forms of visual and electronic "texts" across the curriculum in the multi-subject learning environments found in the United States. The technologies of reading, writing, and viewing have outpaced our pedagogy, our curriculum and instruction methods, and the definitions of what it means to be literate in multimedia America. Moving into the twenty-first century, print no longer dominates our lives as it did in the nineteenth century. The fundamental question that this chapter attempts to answer is: With recent advancement of multiforms of media, can kids learn anything from the multimedia and multiform screens—television screen, video screen, computer screen, and from other media environments that modern multimedia technology has to offer? A response to this question aims to expose the emerging literacies and to bridge the widening gap between the curriculum of the classroom and the emerging curriculum of the screen.

My task in this chapter is to show that American schools can no longer continue to define literacy in terms of print or the classics alone. Students in many public high schools today find the classic works of

Shakespeare, Milton, Brontë, and other revered writers remote and disconnected from their experiences, whereas they find contemporary film to be connected and near. Just as the debates have focused on the canon of acceptable literary works, so too is it time for the debate to broaden the canon and the curriculum to include the expanding technologies of television, film, video, and computers.

CHALLENGES FACING SCHOOLS
IN MULTIMEDIA AMERICA

Many new challenges will face teachers in the years to come: How does a teacher teach reading or language arts, science, or social studies to today's students who are constantly exposed to multimedia and technological advances in a world of virtual intelligence and electronic communities? Can these multimedia technologies be integrated in the K–12 curriculum as a critical project without conflict or competition with other courses? Would students and teachers want American schools to create a politicized citizenry capable of fighting responsibly for various forms of public life, equality, and social justice? Are teachers willing to struggle and make sacrifices necessary to put critical content into democracy? These rhetorical questions provide a broad and important area of inquiry that this book attempts to address.

The rationale for integrating critical media literacy education is based on the notion that if we are to provide students with media skills for today and tomorrow, we must help them comprehend and communicate through both traditional and emerging technologies of communication. This means making them understand (1) the programs themselves —how they produce meaning, how media language forms are organized, and how they construct reality; (2) the contexts in which the programs are transmitted; (3) the organizations or culture industries that produce them; (4) the technologies of production, distribution and reception— how they represent individuals and groups; and (6) the different ways in which audiences use and respond to the mass media, especially television. These important aspects of understanding media are the central tenet of this chapter.

Drawing upon the work of Jürgen Habermas and other critical theorists, who have executed epochal "learning turn" in social theory, I introduce media literacy that is revamped by a critical learning theory, and which takes its direction from Habermas. Moreover, by situating the discussion of media literacy in this volume around critical literacy education, the reader gains a deeper understanding and appreciation of contributions from cultural studies on representation, popular culture, the construction of youth, subjectivity, positioning, and perspectives of critical consciousness that have been made possible by the work of theorists like Stuart Hall, Henry Giroux, Paulo Freire, Doug Kellner, Alan Luke, Joe Kincheloe, and others. In this discussion, the emerging discipline of cultural studies provides an interdisciplinary approach for the study of subjectivities that views popular culture as a site of social differences and struggle. This view is of theoretical and practical importance within the literacy community because the popular culture forms we set out to analyze in this book are connected to economic and social relations, power and oppression, particularly in terms of gender, class, race, sexuality, and age.

When I discuss critical media literacy within such a broad theoretical framework, I hope to engage the reader and challenge him or her to find a more sustainable analysis of popular culture and other media texts, and eventually make sense of examples of a classroom practice that is anchored in critical pedagogy. In this book, I propose analytical frameworks that use a critical pedagogy approach. As will become clearer in the following chapters, the term *pedagogy* simply means the realities of what happens in classrooms. Conceptualized as critical pedagogy, media literacy education hopes to provide the necessary theoretical opening for understanding how an educative process might enable students and their parents to give up bias, myths, clichés and illusions largely created by mass media constructions. Furthermore, because of its cross-disciplinary approach, media literacy education moves to cross-disciplinary borders. Using critical pedagogical tools, media literacy helps students to interpret the layered meanings embedded in the stories they read and the characters they encounter in media texts. Also, it enables learners to question the intentions of the producer, writer, distributor, as well as the larger social context—such as history, social economic status, familiarity and comfort with the subject matter, benefits, and one's privileged position in the culture—within which the story is created, read, and interpreted, to uncover the oppressive spaces in which difference and unequal power exist in relations of inequality and resistance.

The notion of media literacy suggests a process of understanding and using different media (including the mass media) in an active and nonpassive way. This process involves analyzing, comparing, interpreting, and finding meaning that is different from the usual, routine, and preferred meaning. Typically, preferred meanings are found in texts that insist on the existing dominant interpretation or ideology, that explain why things are the way they are. When such texts are read or viewed in this particular way, their interpretation or meaning tends to coincide with mythical beliefs, clichés, and stereotypical or hidden bias. By applying critical media literacy strategies to read these texts, the reader or viewer is able to read against the grain, and to evaluate the texts using multiple frameworks that go beyond the myth, cliché, and stereotype. In this sense-making process, the reader/viewer can make an informed decision to either question the proposed premise/explanation of the media text, or to partially accept it, or even to reject it completely. Such critical reading of media texts is part of the active and nonpassive reading, viewing, and listening that individuals can acquire from the critical pedagogy of media literacy education.

Critical pedagogy, however, introduces something more to the classroom. As will be further developed in Chapter 2, the notion of critical pedagogy stresses that the realities of what happens in classrooms not only instruct students as recipients of knowledge. But rather, (1) it stresses how teachers work within an institutional context; (2) specifies a particular version of what knowledge is of most worth; (3) clarifies in what direction we should desire; (4) explains what it means to know something; and (5) shows how we might construct representations of ourselves, others, and our physical and societal environment. Critical pedagogy is practiced not only in schools, but also in the family, public discourse, the church, the media, and so on. A critical pedagogy must address these spheres in its explication of education, as well as "what happens in schools" (Kincheloe & Steinberg, 1995, p. 5).

In his book, *Teaching Media Literacy,* Masterman (1985) argues that it is only a matter of time before schools realize that they must teach students to critically analyze media texts and visual images. The increased use of video and other visual materials will require students to "assess visual evidence" and "will be a cross-curricula skill which will need to inform teaching and learning in all subjects" (p. 14). For Masterman (1985), the gulf between the heavily print-based education in the classroom and education outside of school continues to grow and there is no likelihood of narrowing this gap any time soon. He adds:

> Schools continue to be dominated by print. To have difficulties in decoding print is, in school terms, to be a failure. Outside of school the most influential and widely disseminated modes of communication are visual (or oral).
>
> As we have seen, television is probably the most important source of political information in our society and is regarded by most people

as the most reliable sources of news, perhaps because of its ability to present a visual record of events. Even print is coming to be regarded as a visual medium. Layout, design and typography are widely understood to be a significant part of the total communicating process, whilst even the term "print media" is frequently a misnomer, since in most texts print is rarely accompanied by visual images. (p. 13)

As we enter a new millennium, Masterman urges us to take a closer look at the new media technologies. They provide our children with new language forms that need to be evaluated, learned, and taught. Olson (1988) is even more convinced that media literacy is a skill that one learns just as one learns to read the written word. "For all new media, new categories for interpretation and criticism, must be developed and taught to children so that they will have interpretive skills that are as powerful as those exploited in the literate tradition" (p. 34).

Development in communication technology has provided some important questions regarding the literate tradition, the nature of education, learning, and thinking. For Davies (1996), a school administrator in Florida, the mass media are ushering in a new period of learning, which he refers to as "the new learning." The advent of this new but rapidly evolving learning of literacy turns the world into a big classroom. Based on the mass media and the fast growing Internet as the dominant force in this country, learning depends heavily upon visual imagery outside the walls of the schoolhouse. What can we as educators do about it? Do we have the material as well as academic resources to deal with these new forms of knowledge production? McLaren and Hammer (1995) clearly point out the new dynamics playing into contemporary classrooms and how literacy is taught and acquired.

In the current historical juncture of democratic decline in the United States, ideals and images have become detached from their anchorage in stable and agreed-upon meaning and associations and are now beginning to assume a reality of their own. The self-referential world of the media is one that splinters, obliterates, peripheralizes, partitions and segments social space, time, knowledge, and subjectivity in order to unify, encompass, entrap, totalize and homogenize them *through the meta-form of entertainment.* [Emphasis in original.] What needs to be addressed is the way in which capitalism is able to secure this cultural and ideological totalization and homogenization through its ability to insinuate itself into social practices and private perceptions through various forms of media knowledges. (p. 196)

McLaren and Hammer urge us to take a hard look to realize the new situation brought upon us by multimedia technologies. Teachers, students, parents, and school administrators need to think carefully about the implications of the looming self-referential world of media. McLaren and Hammer raise the following critical questions:

- How are the subjectivities and identities of individuals and the production of media knowledges within popular culture mutually articulated?
- To what extent does the hyperreal correspond to practices of self and social constitution in contemporary society?
- Do we remain "sunk in the depressing hyperbole of the hyperreal," encysted in the monologic self-referentiality of the mode of information?
- Or do we establish a politics of refusal that is able to contest the tropes that govern Western colonialist narratives of supremacy and oppression?
- What isn't being discussed is the pressing need within pedagogical sites for creating a media literate citizenry that can disrupt, contest, and transform media apparatuses so that they no longer possess the power to infantilize the population and continue to create passive and paranoid social subjects (p. 196).

These rhetorical questions also urge teachers and students to consider alternative definitions of literacy and go beyond print literacy. A lack of critical pedagogy in schools creates passive citizens. Time has arrived to broaden the canons of traditional education and the curriculum to include the expanding technologies of television, film, video, and computers. Using critical pedagogy to integrate the new forms of visual and electronic "texts" represents a curriculum requiring new competencies and a new definition of what constitutes learning as well as how and when it takes place. Making these changes requires that teachers be trained in the emerging literacies.

By forging connections between these emerging literacies, the learning process is no longer disconnected from institutional, legal, cultural, political, and economic factors that surround the texts students read, whether from textbooks or from the screen. These contexts of media "text" are crucial to making meaning and lead to many questions: Who produces multimedia texts? Visual images? For whose consumption? For what purposes? What alternative images are thereby excluded? Questions like these form the core of critical media literacy. Through media literacy, the classroom is transformed from a rote memorizing of neutral and value-free materials to a struggle over multimedia texts. Instead, students must interpret and understand how meaning is made and derived from all texts found in textbooks, photographs, and other electronic visuals, images, and messages. Media literacy brings to bear the analysis of connotative messages embedded in the text of the visual as well as interaction of pictures to words, the context of the viewer, and relayed messages obtained from the maker of the image. This new way of looking at curriculum extends the sphere of pedagogical practice beyond school to include the modern media as a powerful institution that occupies a large portion of students' time.

TEACHING CRITICAL MEDIA LITERACY IN MULTIMEDIA AMERICA

While attending an International Reading Association conference in Washington, D.C., I heard a literacy educator complain to an audience that many students graduating from high school do not read books for the sake of enjoyment anymore! This educator was quick to point out that the reason for the situation was that so many students in high school do not have comparable literacy skills that would make reading enjoyable. Print literacy, that is! What this educator failed to appreciate is that the dimensions of literacy have changed drastically with the onset of the new communication technologies. It is as if these students are now living in a cultural environment that is in effect split in two. In this situation, adolescents will tend to read less print and use more new age technology to obtain the information they need to survive in multimedia America.

The new age technology within reach of many middle-class adolescents has changed the learning space. For example, when I was doing research for this book, I met Norma, a student in eighth grade at a neighboring high school. In a conversation with Norma, I learned with great surprise that every night Norma goes to bed with an electronic book. Sold at local bookstores, "books" on tape have become a common innovation like the electric toothbrush. Norma feels comfortable and happy with this new type of "mind page," not only for its convenience but also because it is the only way she can enjoy literature in a horizontal position. Troubled with her eyes for the longest time, Norma has found a way to enrich her life with literature while trying to fall asleep and when traveling in the car with her parents and siblings. She says that because of her sight problems, she gets tired of reading very quickly and that made her hate reading. Voice books or electronic books have saved her situation. As will be shown in this book, these new technological inventions have revolutionized print the way we know it, have liberated and freed text from its locked position of print, and made literacy a new word-perfect vocabulary.

Unfortunately, Norma lamented that the electronic books she can enjoy at home are rarely available to her at school as textbooks. But I told Norma that it would not be long before this will be a reality in every school. Of course, I was thinking of Web-based teaching and the many courses now available on the Internet. I assured her that we are experiencing an irreversible movement away from paper-printed forms to electronic forms of reading and writing as we approach the twenty-first century. The information superhighway and the advancing Internet are examples of exciting contemporary technologies that students will need to access as they become literate and as they surf the Internet to search other topics in social studies, math, and science. The proposal of President Bill Clinton, developed by Vice President Al Gore to "give every American the chance for the best education on the superhighway" through universal cabling, is an important step in helping students like Norma to make their dreams come true and to acknowledge the cruel fact that the Internet is not yet available to all students due to financial and technical problems that sometimes seem insurmountable to many teachers, students, and parents. The problem is clear: Students are growing in a split environment, a world of two cultures.

TORN BETWEEN TWO CULTURES

In the preface of their book *Visual Messages*, authors Considine and Haley (1992) describe the phenomenon of split environments as widespread in the United States. On the one hand, they mention the classroom culture that is text-based, logical, sequential, and linear by nature, and imbued with values that stress hard work and long-term goals. On the other hand, they perceive that there is a "wired world that is mediated by the pervasive and persuasive vehicles of the communications revolutions"

(p. ix). This "wired world culture" is characterized as being "mosaic, imagistic (image-laden), fluid, impressionistic, and profoundly capable of influencing children's feelings as well as their thoughts" (ibid.). It is a consumer culture that promotes short-term goals and instant gratification.

Postman (1993) describes the "wired world culture" as the world of television, which because of its technological powers changes what "we mean by 'knowing' and 'truth'; alter those deeply embedded habits of thought which give to a culture its sense of what the world is like—a sense of what is the natural order of things, of what is reasonable, of what is necessary, of what is inevitable, of what is real." Postman continues:

> . . . children come to school having been deeply conditioned by the biases of television. There, they encounter the world of the printed word. A sort of psychic battle takes place, and there are many casualties—children who can't learn to read or won't, children who cannot organize their thought into logical structure even in a simple paragraph, children who cannot attend to lectures or oral explanations for more than a few minutes at a time. They are failures, but not because they are stupid. They are failures because there is a media war going on, and they are on the wrong side—at least for the moment. (p. 15)

In short, Postman warns that a vibrant, vital, and inclusive literacy has emerged outside the walls of the school, while the narrow view of literacy valued within the school remains, for many, inaccessible, irrelevant, and alienating.

The argument that Postman (1993) and Considine and Haley (1992) put forward in response to the apparent conflict experienced by young high school students is that in order to bridge the gap between these two different and often conflicting cultures, educators should recognize that technology has brought about an "iconic information system that communicates most powerfully and persuasively through pictures" and must consequently deploy a pedagogy that demystifies that technology, while teaching students to understand and create alternative visual communications (Considine & Haley, 1992, p. 4).

Perhaps what teachers and students seem to see in the world of media is a precursor of a much larger technological revolution. We are poised to enter what Marshall McLuhan (1962) and others predicted to be the post-typographic era. The media bombardment we are experiencing outside the walls of the school has the potential of increasing in schools commercial initiatives like "Channel One" sponsored by corporations like the Whittle Educational Network. This program has been reported to be a controversial news program that is broadcast into classrooms each morning nationwide in more than 1,200 schools. These schools in turn receive television equipment for use in classrooms in exchange for daily broadcast of current events programming for adolescents. These broadcasts include two minutes of advertising. Such initiatives are more likely to expand to engulf many schools. Likewise, cable programming is expanding through PBS, the Discovery Channel, and a host of independent cable programming companies into classrooms and other places to which they have never been introduced before. Very soon, many television programs will be offered to students that hold the real promise of providing rich educational experiences that have the potential to expand and enrich their lives. These initiatives also point to fundamental changes in the way we communicate and disseminate information, the way we approach the task of reading and writing, and the way we think about helping people become literate in their communities.

BEYOND McLUHAN'S TYPOGRAPHIC WORLD

As summed up by Reinking (1995, p. 19), the term *post-typographic* has been used to mark an intellectual and cultural watershed with a significance that extends beyond the question of whether we compose with a stylus, a typewriter, or a computer. To highlight different effects of electronic communication, various writers have used the term *post-typographic* spuriously. For McLuhan (1962), it meant cultural effects. But for some critical social theorists it has suggested a time when postmodern views of meaning will be operationalized. Such contemporary critical theorist positions—associated with Jacques Derrida, Michel Foucault, Gilles Deleuze, and Felix Guattari—broaden the notions of reading, writing, and textuality to a variety of cultural notions ranging from philosophical treatise to novels, newspaper advertisements, visuals, and films. However, for Walter Ong (1986) post-typographic meant a cognitive shift toward a "second orality." In sum, the term *post-typographic* points to the fact that electronic texts are increasingly becoming a destabilizing influence, requiring students and teachers to examine the assumptions about literacy, books, and what we know and what we think we know about classroom teaching.

Inasmuch as today's children come to school from homes and communities that provide them with wide exposure to nonprint media, it is crucial that literacy education teachers draw upon this background, both to recognize the students' knowledge and to develop the students' critical thinking about nonprint media. As described earlier, Norma's experience in a culture dominated by media messages and visual images is similar in many ways to the experience of adolescents in America today, which is only a forewarning of the impending post-typographic era and of signs of new literacies emerging within the walls of the classroom at a time when print is waning. The technology of reading and writing has outpaced our pedagogy and definitions of literacy. The challenge is: How do you teach reading to today's students who are barraged with multimedia and technological advances in a senseless world of intelligence and virtual communities? (See Vignette 1 at the end of this chapter.)

MASS MEDIA AS INSTRUMENT OF SOCIALIZATION

Preparing students to become good citizens has traditionally been one of the goals of American education. Socialization theorists argue that the media, like the family, church, school, and peer groups, function as an instrument of socialization (Burger & Luckmann, 1972; Danzinger, 1971). As aptly noted in a discussion of the socialization effects of television, Kellner (1982) argues that television has replaced fairy tales and myths as the primary producer of children's tales. Even in present-day programming, television continues to be one of the most important producers of myths and symbols in the society. Kellner insists that television has become a powerful socializing machine. "Both television entertainment and information may well gain in power precisely because individuals are not aware that their thoughts and behaviors are being shaped by the ubiquitous idea and image machines of their homes" (Kellner, 1990, p. 126).

Fontana (1988) echoes much of Kellner's concerns when he claims that media and particularly television are a major determinant of what citizens know about history, economics, political systems, social issues, and interpersonal relationships. It is no wonder anymore that television personalities and movie stars provide gender and role models for children and young adults with a powerful impact on their fantasy lives and actual behavior. Long before the explosion in electronic media, Lambert and Klineberg (1967) found that much of what American children learned about other nationalities came from the media. Sometimes learning is formal, at other times informal. What is often forgotten in these studies is that the media shape our cultural understanding of others and the world around us. Media critics like Stuart Hall (1977) warn that the media are consciousness industries that provide not simply information about the world, but ways of seeing and understanding it.

In the broadest sense, all this means that the media in general, and television in particular, provide continuous education throughout life, offering a popular day and night school for the nation. Backed by many Gallup surveys, these remarks tend to be widely accepted by audiences as a true depiction of the extent of media influence in America today. It is now commonly known that children start watching television several years before they begin reading. By the time they graduate from high school, they have spent 18,000 hours in front of the television as opposed to 13,000 hours in school. In the inner city, estimates for media exposure are higher, up to eleven hours per day.

These statistics from the Nielsen Company are daunting. For example, the A.C. Nielsen Company claims that the television set is turned on an average of 7 hours and 38 minutes a day in American households. The Gallup Poll claims about the same. The "average" American will spend in excess of seven years watching television (Kubey & Csikszentmihalyi, 1990, p. xi).

A study conducted by the American Academy of Pediatrics in 1987 claims that children between the ages of two and twelve spend an average of twenty-five hours a week watching television. By the time six-year-olds enter first grade, they will have seen over 100,000 commercials on television; by the time they graduate from high school, they will have spent 11,000 hours in classrooms and 15,000 hours watching television, during which time they will have seen as many 350,000 advertisements on television. By the time an average American dies she or he will have spent one and one-half years of their lives watching television commercials (Lutz, 1989, pp. 73–74).

Between seventh and twelfth grades, adolescents spend about 10,500 hours listening to rock music, only 500 hours less than the amount of time they spend in classroom instruction in twelve years—and many songs contain lyrics that have been identified as sexist and violent (Leming, 1987).

In their 1990 Cartoon Study, the National Coalition on Television Violence (NCTV) reported that cartoons have three times as many acts of violence as found on prime-time television. More recent studies have indicated that cartoons average twenty-six acts of violence per hour, while adult prime-time television averages five violent acts per hour. In 1990, major network programming on Saturday mornings depicted twenty violent acts per hour; FOX recorded an average of thirty-four violent acts per hour, the highest network rating since 1980. Television advertisers spend over $800 million a year on commercials directed at children under age twelve.

These statistics from the Nielsen Company do not include the time children and adults spend watching films and videos, working with computers, communicating through networks, playing electronic games, or the exposure to other communication forms—magazines, billboards, books, comics, and the popular cultural events in shopping malls, theme parks, or of daily life. Research points out that people use mass media variously throughout their lives. Children and the elderly are often, for example, the heaviest consumers of television, and adolescents are heavy users of radio but light viewers of television (Silverblatt, 1995). Adolescents are also frequent patrons of movies and purchasers of music recordings. Adults are more likely than youngsters to read newspapers. Boys are heavier computer users than girls.

Simply put: These statistics speak to one important fact—teachers cannot afford to dismiss or ignore the opportunities offered by new technology and the language it brings with it. They must strive to forge connections and meaningful metaphors in students' everyday living. It may well be necessary to use materials that, while potentially controversial, need to be examined so students can confront the stereotyping, propagandizing, and editorial gatekeeping so prevalent in the media. No doubt, such classroom study allows students to discover that nonprint media products are constructions of reality that have commercial, ideological, and value messages. However, two questions persist: How do you teach these media literacy concepts in the classroom? Where will a teacher begin? How will he or she do?

A BROADER DEFINITION OF LITERACY

Perhaps a good place to start is to encourage teachers to examine their classroom practice and the definition(s) of literacy. It appears to me that rather than adhering to print-based definitions of literacy, contemporary theories extend reading and meaning-making processes of literacy (reading, writing, speaking, and listening) to other texts including visuals. Current American definitions of literacy continue to ignore the electronic evolution of print and fail to recognize the need for an expanded vision of what it means to function effectively in a culture dominated by media images and messages. The concept of literacy is expanding and it is so far-reaching that we have yet to fully know how far it can go. With the advance of the new electronic forms, a new language has emerged making it necessary to allow the broader definition of literacy to include the media forms and electronic texts. For this reason, the new nonprint media, especially those that are part of students' everyday lives, cannot be considered anymore as isolated phenomena in schools.

In a 1991 issue of *Educational Leadership*, Elliot Eisner said: "School programs ought to develop literacy, that is, the ability to secure meanings from the wide range of forms that are used in culture to express meaning. This surely includes far more than the literal use of language, or the ability to write precise 'Standard English'" (1991, 14–15). In his subsequent writings, Eisner (1994) has consistently argued for a conceptualization of literacy that would allow for multiple forms of representation. His argument is closely related to Gardner's (1993) theory of multiple intelligences. Gardner contends that different cultures value different intelligences and consequently develop specific forms of literacy within their cultural contexts. In this case, it means we no longer can talk about a universal notion of literacy, but perhaps multiple literacies or multicultural literacies. However, the intent is not to look at Gardner's notion of "multiple intelligences" as a deficit or lack of the right cognitive skills. This is not about recognizing or privileging one type of intelligence over another, but rather about multiple ways of knowing. As individuals, students come to school from multiple environments, cultures, and racial, gender, and class positions that influence what they consider important or of value to them. It is these kinds of positionalities or contexts that interest many theorists in defining multiple literacies as multiple ways of constructing and producing multimedia texts. Within this approach, it means we no longer can talk about a universal notion of literacy that is fixed and applicable to all times and situations, but perhaps multiple, multilevel, or multicultural literacies.

Clearly, our interactions with and through modern technology and media comprise a large part of our lives. Due to their accessibility, frequency, content, and processes, modern communication media are perhaps the most powerful tools humans have ever created. Because they form such a large part of modern experience, the processes, forms, and outcomes of these communicational events must be examined and understood. We are being urged to consider a broader conceptualization in which literacy is defined as the ability to function competently in the cultural media context we live in today—which include the language arts as well as the media: film, art, video, and television. The need to expand

and explore a more extensive notion of literacy has been propelled, in part, by the proliferation of a variety of communication technologies that have become integral parts of daily life in the 1990s.

Consider, for example, how many kitchens in America today are wired and equipped with electronic gadgets—from microwave ovens, coffee makers, air or climate control timers, fancy cooking appliances, and dishwashers, to simple electric can openers. Most of these electric equipments are equipped with electronics of the highest order—without which such gadgets would not appeal to the baby boomers. Some of these new generation kitchen appliances are equipped with a demo program that runs on a small screen display that can be turned off when not desired. What has revolutionized American kitchens is the microcomputer chip now present in almost everything electric and which has made it possible to replace the tedious equipment and appliance manuals that used to accompany them. Instead, many of these manuals are now designed with drawings, pictures, a moving cursor, or flashing lights, a sort of imitation of the iconic graphics and symbols prevalent in many versions of Windows software now part of most word processing programs. Such iconic and graphic presentations of information have not only replaced print but also have made it unnecessary. As will be made clearer in subsequent chapters, nonprint media, including television, music, video, videotape, film, radio, compact disk, and hypertext for personal computers, have increasingly become primary sources of information and recreation, as well as sources of emotional and artistic experiences for many adolescent Americans.

CHALLENGES ON THE HORIZON

What can we conclude from these new trends? What lessons can we learn from the new dynamics of multimedia technology? I think that today, America faces a challenge that will require tremendous resilience. Sophisticated technology is rapidly changing virtually every aspect of the way Americans work and live. As rightly argued by Postman (1993) in his media and technology books, the uses made of any technology are largely determined by the structure of the technology itself. That is to say, its functions follow from its form. In our own time, we have consciously added thousands of new words and phrases to our language having to do with the new technologies—"VCR," "binary digit," "software," "modems," "hardware," "hard drive," "Walkman," "e-mail," "multimedia," "bytes," "cursor," and so on. New things require new words. The new words not only enrich our language but also alter the way students learn. Postman teaches that technology imperiously commandeers our most important terminology. It redefines "freedom," "truth," "intelligence," "fact," "wisdom," "memory," "history"—all the words we live by. Postman concludes that new technologies change what we mean by "knowing" and "truth"; they alter those deeply embedded habits of thought that give to a culture its sense of what the world is like—a sense of what is the natural order of things, of what is reasonable, of what is necessary, of what is inevitable, of what is real (p. 45).

It was not so long ago that there was a time when any high school graduate with a basic mechanical aptitude could expect to find a meaningful employment in industry. Those days are gone. In the workplace of today, employees on the factory floor must be highly literate and computer competent. Skill requirements are changing dramatically and increasingly require independent judgment as well as analytical and interpersonal skills. But current trends suggest that our public schools are not producing graduates capable of meeting today's workplace demands, let alone the pressures of the looming economic globalization. By now, the disturbing statistics on this country's youth are all too familiar. In the past decade, several reports point to this discrepancy. More specifically, *Turning Points* (Carnegie Council on Adolescent Development, 1989), *A Portrayal of Young Adolescents in the 1990s* (Scales, 1991), *A Matter of Time* (Carnegie Council of Adolescent Development, 1993), and *Fateful Choices* (Hechinger, 1992) underscore the at-risk nature of today's adolescent. The U.S. national dropout rate continues to hover around 30 percent, and exceeds 50 percent in many inner cities. Of those students who graduate, roughly 700,000 cannot read their diplomas and only half compute well enough to use decimals and fractions or recognize geometric figures. Barely 7 percent of high school students can claim any sophistication in science (Davies, 1996).

As if these were not enough problems for an overburdened educational system, there are even more outcries about shortcomings in moral education. With recent school shootings in Colorado, Georgia, Arkansas, and Kentucky, family values and parental accountability are once again popular topics with politicians and talk show hosts. The Association for Supervision and Curriculum Development (ASCD) devoted an entire issue of *Educational Leadership* (November 1993) to moral education. In this decade alone, I can identify several of such outcries demanding that schools take up moral education more seriously. For example: *Why Johnny Can't Tell Right from Wrong* (Kilpatrick, 1992), *Moral Character and Civic Education in the Elementary School* (Benninga, 1991), *Reclaiming Our Schools: A Handbook on Teaching Character, Academics, and Discipline* (Wynne & Ryan, 1992), as well as *Educating for Character: How Our Schools Can Teach Respect and Responsibility* (Lickona, 1991). These study reports call for the need to return character education to the classroom.

In all this disquiet, the role of the teacher in educating the youth is being challenged from many quarters. These challenges emanate from changes brought upon us by the onslaught of new technologies and the mass media. Some educators and parents agree that the schools are not working, they are not delivering what they were designed to do. In the early 1980s, the prescribed solution was "back to basics"—getting the youngsters to work harder. In the late 1980s, the prescription was the professionalization of teachers and the dismantling of the central bureaucracy. In the early 1990s, the solution seems to have been endless choices and "break the mold" schools including innovations like: creating multi-age classrooms, inclusive classrooms, acknowledging multiple intelligences, challenging gifted children, raising math and science standards, creating a technologically literate classroom, block-scheduling, year-round schools, school choice, inviting corporations to run schools, and more.

Despite all the disquiet, however, I believe that teachers in public schools are working hard in very difficult and changing classrooms. I also believe that our schools must undergo fundamental changes, a paradigmatic shift, and that any successful American education must involve the family, the institutions of the community, and the mass media. Such a coalescence of educators and parents must acknowledge that the scope of classrooms is shrinking as the learning environment expands beyond the walls of schools to include media knowledges and virtual reality. For most adolescents, the media, particularly television, has become the teacher of choice. Students spend many of their waking hours learning from the media: cartoons (Ninja Turtles, Batman), electronic games (Nintendo), comics, television programs, and the Internet. This is the reality. What can we do about it? How can a learning process that begins at home and continues through the community and school be conceptualized and taught as a holistic, lifelong enterprise? Although progressive teachers know that many examples exist, they continue to be shielded and prevented from access to these innovations by conservative school districts, misinformed parents, and a tax system that favors affluent school districts. It is important to note that tinkering with school reform has been a contested phenomenon since the 1800s and, of the numerous reports over the years, few have been kind to the results on the report card (see, for example, Bracey, 1997, pp. 39–52).

Most of the education reports, including the *Wall Street Journal* and *USA Today*, published in the past decade, emphasize that if America is to maintain its economic vigor and preserve its standard of living into the twenty-first century, we must embark on an intensive campaign to reinvigorate school systems and meet the training needs of the current work force (Bracey, 1997). If we are to provide students with communication skills for today and tomorrow we must help them to comprehend and communicate through both traditional and emerging technologies of communication. Making these changes requires that teachers, principals, superintendents, and administrators recognize, value, and respect the relationship between the literacies: media literacy, print literacy, school literacy, computer literacy, and so on.

The notion of expanding literacy to include many different knowledge representations, as explained by Eisner (1991), has been embraced by some educators and rejected by others from a variety of fields. There seems to exist a wide range of ambivalence about the value and consequences of broadening our conceptualization of literacy to include the mass media—that is, widespread television and film viewing in our classrooms. Many parents have serious ambivalence about mass media in schools. Educators are just as ambivalent about media in the classroom as the rest of society. Most teachers worry about the effects of mass media on children. Parents and teachers want to be absolutely sure that the mass media will play a helpful role in the educational process. Even though we realize that many of our students have a tremendous amount of knowledge and the interest in media, we are still reluctant to embrace media without serious research efforts that unequivocally demonstrate its efficacy. These concerns are legitimate.

But we cannot stop here and look on. Many educators have urged investigation into mass media because they fear that media educators sometimes mistakenly think they are expanding the student's concept of literacy when they use television, computers, video, and film to teach. This expanded notion of literacy does not augur well with traditional teachers and parents. In his findings, Bianculli (1993) came up with five major concerns that parents have about television/media: (1) violence in film and television desensitizes children and alters their conception of the social world; (2) television has damaged the process of elections;

(3) mass media organizations disrupt the private lives of individuals; (4) values of sensationalism that are created by mass media have reshaped culture and the arts; and (5) television will displace reading. Other reports seem to echo Bianculi's findings. For example, a report on moral education from the Association for Supervision and Curriculum Development (1988) identified the disturbing trends in increased homicides, suicides, and out-of-wedlock births as contributing to the increasing concern about moral education in schools. The ASCD panel on moral education names the mass media as one of those factors that has heightened concerns about the moral life of students today. With these concerns in mind, how can researchers and scholars advocate for more television in the classroom?

CONCLUDING COMMENTS

This introductory chapter provides an overview of the important dimensions of teaching media literacy across the curriculum. It would be easy to blame the mass media for the value crisis that confronts society today; however, this would not only be unfair, but counterproductive. On the other hand, it would be shortsighted to pretend that the media not only help shape our culture but our values as well. It appears that what seems to elude educators who are appalled by the negative effects of television is the narrowly defined dimensions of literacy and, consequently, the pedagogies that frame and inform the way literacy is taught in the classroom. The literacies of the twenty-first century can no longer be limited to skills used to understand only a single medium like printed text or oral communication. They must include the critical literacies of our times. The critical literacies of our times are much more than merely processes of decoding a text, writing a five-paragraph essay effectively, or reading a limited canon of classic literature. Teaching about media in classrooms is part of critical literacy education. The goal of critical media literacy is to cultivate a systematic inquiry method and models of critique and of reading visual images and messages embedded in both print and visual texts. As will be developed in subsequent chapters, this approach encourages students to question what they see, to ponder what they hear on the radio and in songs, and to recognize bias or misrepresentations when they view them on television or the Internet. As a pedagogical practice, critical media literacy is not preaching about how violent or evil the media have become. It is not protecting children because they cannot fend for themselves from the dangerous media. Rather, it is a curriculum and instruction that goes beyond preaching and protecting children from the shows they would rather watch when an adult is not looking over their shoulders; it is critical viewing and critical reading of all media texts, including print. Critical media literacy stimulates critical thinking and guides students away from rote memorization. Critical media literacy expands the notion of school literacy, which is principally the ability to read the printed text and to include a critical reading of media texts as well. Critical media literacy encourages students to challenge the authority of readings and texts, and challenge the opinions of all educators, including the new educator of choice, television. Critical media literacy therefore becomes a pedagogical tool for examining media messages and its institutions.

In a survey of Pennsylvania schools from 1993 to 1995, I examined among other questions the use of media in classrooms. The results showed that few teachers teach about media. Most teachers used media as a teaching tool, namely as audiovisuals to illustrate instruction. Teaching about media as a source of information, messages, or "texts" was rarely done. To many educators media are entertainment, not for serious study. But when the students' viewing habits after school were surveyed, I learned that television was not entertainment, but a far-reaching tool. Adolescents learn from it all the time. Besides, some schools in this sample had very elaborate equipment including satellite dishes, e-mail connections, videocassette recorders, and film projectors. One school had full-fledged production equipment. Two schools were among the classrooms across the United States hooked up to Whittle Educational Network's "Channel One."

The results of this study on the use of media in classrooms presented nothing we did not already know. We know children spend lots of time with television. Statistics on television viewing, for example, suggest that children today spend more time watching television than they spend in school. If we add to this amount the time spent watching films, reading comics, and magazines, and listening to music, we arrive at figures beyond belief. These results only affirm what other educators already knew, that is, American education has failed to develop a philosophy or pedagogy based on the role of visuals in instruction. At the same time, schools have spent an increasingly large share of their budgets on iconic technologies such as computers, VCRs, video cameras, and interactive video. At least one thing was clear from this study, that a real expansion of literacy will require teaching *with* as well as teaching *about* television, computers, video, and film. The goal is to ensure that all students, kindergarten through grade 12, acquire media literacy in the arts and media programs that are very much a part of our culture by studying challenging material in every grade. Indeed, I do not deny that the "media" are comprised of a variety of media forms each with its own unique vocabulary and conventions. What I attack is the elitism postulated in the conservative model that canonizes great books, complex literacy skills, and the artifacts of high culture. Through such elitism, contrary to the popular belief that traditional high culture provides unique pleasures and enticements, its high regard and canonization also serves as an instrument of exclusion, marginalization, and domination by oppressive gender, ethnic, disability, sexual orientation, race, and class forces (Kellner, 1991). I am convinced that what we are missing from the school canon are examples of the new literate interactions and virtual communities that students are engaged in after school. My hope is that critical media literacy can fill this widening gap. With its focus on critical pedagogy through clear writing, lucid explanations, and numerous examples of real classroom work, this book will appeal to all those who are looking for ways to introduce critical media literacy into learning. In its critical pedagogic strategies, media literacy can make an important contribution toward those ends.

VIGNETTE ONE

My brother is an excellent example of today's average adolescent. He works hard in school and studies as much as he has to in order to do well; but most of his learning comes from sources other than American history textbooks. After he comes home from school, his minimized homework time is sandwiched between two large slices of watching *Married with Children* reruns and playing WWF Wrestling on his Sega system. On his way to basketball practice, he drives past billboards that advertise "cool" Camel Joe cigarettes, and when he does read outside of class he chooses baseball card price guides or professional wrestling magazines with a pumped-up, greased-down Hulk Hogan on the cover.

Though traditional schooling looks down upon these alternative forms of texts as inferior, my brother has learned more from these other media about how to be a man, a citizen, and a consumer than he has from memorizing the Bill of Rights from his textbook. Because our schools have dismissed my brother's most influential "teachers" as mere entertainment, he has uncritically acquired racist, sexist, and homophobic attitudes that our schools are supposedly trying to uproot. To better accomplish our schools' ambitions of molding our students to be productive members of a democracy, we need to expand our notions of literacy and text, introduce these ideas and media into the classrooms, and teach our children to penetrate the embedded layers of the messages that currently surround them everywhere except their schools. As a result, we will be producing a community of critical thinkers.

My brother is currently going through the same educational system that I went through, which ignored the importance of media literacy. Though the upper-track classes of my high school did at times try to push us toward higher-order thinking skills and to critically analyze the novels that we read, my teachers had limited notions of which texts should be analyzed critically and through what type of perspectives these texts should be viewed.

For example, we watched *Hamlet* starring Mel Gibson in concordance with our reading of Shakespeare's play. We attempted to dissect the author's written words as they appeared on the page, but we paid little attention to breaking down the film that we watched. The film was seen as a mere attention grabber that hoped to sell a sixteenth-century play as entertaining and relevant to resistant Generation X-ers. We never explored the fact that Gibson's presentation of the character is only one interpretation of Shakespeare's lines.

We also should have analyzed this film in conjunction with other presentations, whether they were other films or theater presentations, to see how different meanings and ideas were created by different actors and historical periods. In the process we would (or should) have answered such important questions as: What words or scenes were left out to convey these messages? How did lighting and camera angles help convey the intended messages? Why was Mel Gibson chosen for the part as opposed to a more accredited actor such as Kevin Spacey? Was the presentation molded by or resistant toward the social and political climates of the times? Whose view of the world (i.e., expressionism) wins out—the actor's, the director's, or the production company's? Whom does this winning view/ideology benefit?

Even when we examined the written text of *Hamlet*, we did it through a limited perspective. We pretty much followed the teacher's construction of meaning through her own perspective. The teacher should have assumed the responsibility of introducing different readings of the play such as feminist, Marxist, and/or psychoanalytic critiques. The students should then have been asked to evaluate these different perspectives, see how they corroborate with their personal responses to the same material, and analyze the reasons for any differences. First understanding what the "experts" have to say and then applying and evaluating such concepts would have pushed us beyond a simple affirmation of our personal responses to thinking more critically and theoretically about how meaning is constructed by our affiliations with different subcultures within text of the dominant about important (e.g., how female stereotypes pervade Shakespeare's creation of Ophelia and how society's current view of women shaped the students' reactions to her). Such readings would also have addressed the communicative problems of selective exposure, selective perception, and selective retention that most uncritical thinkers suffer from, as well as legitimatized different and often marginalized voices; this would further our quest for democracy within and outside the classroom.

Before we watched these presentations or even read the first scene, however, the students should have been forced to question why we were reading *Hamlet* in the first place. Why has Shakespeare weathered the test of time? Is it because he confirmed and reinforced the dominant ideology, or is it for the seemingly apolitical reason that he was simply a great writer? This would have forced us to not blindly accept what we were exposed, to and spurred us to struggle and resist a seemingly concrete canon.

If my high school expands the range of voices heard in the classroom and engages the students in inquiry, my brother will enter college as a better critical thinker than I was. Teaching critical thinking along with media literacy will arm him against a pervasive and manipulative media and other weapons of intellectual resistance to combat the embedded messages.

—*Brian*

- What are your reactions to Brian's thoughts, situation, frustrations, predicaments, and questions?
- How is this approach to content knowledge different from an emphasis on knowledge as facts?

REFERENCES

Aronson, D. (1994). Teachers are asking students to take a hard look at what TV tells them about the world. *Teaching Tolerance,* Fall, 7–12.

Bennett, T. (1995). *Outside literature.* London: Routledge.

Benninga, J. S. (1991). *Moral character and civic education in the elementary school.* New York: Teachers College Press.

Bianculli, D. (1993). *Teleliteracy: Taking television seriously.* New York: Continuum.

Bracey, G. W. (1997). The dumbing of America? The truth about how schools have changed. *American Heritage,* November, 39–52.

Broadcast/Cable Yearbook. (1989) New York: Broadcasting.

Brown, J. A. (1991). *Television "critical viewing skills" education: Major media literacy projects in the United States and selected countries.* Hillsdale, N.: Lawrence Erlbaum.

Burger, P., & Luckmann, T. (1972). *The social construction of reality.* Garden City, NY: Doubleday.

Carnegie Council on Adolescent Development (1993). *A matter of time: Opportunities in the nonschool hours.* Washington, DC: Carnegie Council on Adolescent Development.

———. (1989). *Turning points: Preparing youth for the 21st century.* Washington, DC: Carnegie Council on Adolescent Development.

Considine, D. M., & Haley, G. E. (1992). *Visual messages: Integrating imagery into instruction.* Englewood, CO: Teachers Ideas Press.

Danzinger, L. (1971). *Socialization.* Baltimore, MD: Penguin.

Davies, J. (1996). *Educating students in a media saturated culture.* Lancaster, PA: Technomic.

Eisner, E. (1991). Rethinking literacy. *Educational Horizon, 69*(3): 120–128.

Eisner, E. W. (1994). *Cognition and curriculum: A basis of deciding what to teach.* New York: Longman.

Fiske, J. (1987). *Television culture.* New York: Methuen.

———, & Hartley, J. (1989). *Reading television.* New York: Routledge.

Fontana, L. A. (1988). Television and the social studies. *Social Education, 52*(5): 348 –350.

Freire, P., & Macedo, D. (1987). *Literacy—Reading the word and the world.* Westport, CT: Bergin & Garvey.

Gilbert, D. (1988). *Compendium of public opinion.* New York: Facts on File.

Giroux, H., & Simon, R. (1989). *Popular culture, schooling, and everyday life.* Westport, CT: Bergin & Garvey.

Hall, S. (1977). Culture, the media and the "ideological effect." In Curran, J., et al. (Eds.), *Mass communication and society.* London: Arnold.

———. (Ed.). (1996). *Representation: Cultural representations and signifying practices.* London: Sage.

Hechinger, F. (1992). Fateful choices: Healthy choices for the 21st century. Washington, DC: Carnegie Council on Adolescent Development.

Hobbs, R. (1994). "Channel One" undone. The Billerica initiative brings media literacy to middle school. *Community Media Review,* Vol. 1, January.

Kellner, D. (1982). Television myth and ritual. *Praxis, 6.*

———. (1990). *Television and the crisis of democracy.* Boulder, CO: Westview Press.

———. (1991). Reading images critically: Toward a postmodern pedagogy. In H. Giroux. (Ed.), *Postmodernism, feminism, and cultural politics: Redrawing educational boundaries.* Albany, NY: State University of New York Press.

Kilpatrick, W. (1992). *Why Johnny can't tell right from wrong: Moral illiteracy and the case for character education.* New York: Simon & Schuster.

Kincheloe, J., & Steinberg, S. (1995). Introduction. In P. McLaren, R. Hammer, D. Sholle, & S. Reilly. (Eds.), *Rethinking media literacy: A critical pedagogy of representation.* New York: Peter Lang, pp. 1–6.

Kubey, R., & Csikszentmihalyi, M. (1990). *Television and the quality of life.* Hillsdale, NJ: Lawrence Erlbaum.

Lambert, W. E., & Klineberg, O. (1967). *Children's views of foreign peoples: A cross-national study.* New York: Appleton-Century-Crofts.

Leming, J. (1987). Rock music and the socialization of moral values in early adolescence. *Young and Society 18*(4): 363–383.

Lickona, T. (1991). *Educating for character: How our schools can teach respect and responsibility.* New York: Bantam Books.

Lusted, D. (1991). *The media studies book. A guide for teachers.* New York: Routledge.

Lutz, C., & Collins, J. (1993). *Reading national geography.* Chicago: University of Chicago Press.

Lutz, W. (1989). *DoubleSpeak.* New York: Harper Perrenial.

Lytle, S. L., & Botel, M. (1990). *The Pennsylvania framework for reading, writing and talking across the curriculum, PCRP II.* Pennsylvania Department of Education, Fourth Printing.

Masterman, L. (1985). *Teaching the media.* London: Routledge.

McLaren, P., & Hammer, R. (1995). Media knowledges, warrior citizenry and postmodern literacies. In P. McLaren, R. Hammer, D. Sholle, & S. Reilly, (Eds.), *Rethinking media literacy: A critical pedagogy of representation,* (pp. 171–204). New York: Peter Lang.

McLuhan, M. (1962). *The Gutenberg galaxy: The making of typographic man.* Toronto: University of Toronto Press.

Meyers, C. (1991). *Teaching students to think critically.* San Francisco: Jossey-Bass.

Olson, D. R. (1988). Mind and media: The epistemic functions of literacy. *Journal of Communication, 38*(3): 27–36.

Ong, W. (1986). Knowledge in time. In R. Gumpert, & G. Cathcart (Eds.), *Inter/Media* (pp. 630–647). New York and Oxford: Oxford University Press.

Pennsylvania Education, 24(5), February 1993: 3–5.

Philadelphia Inquirer, Wednesday, September 28, 1994.

Postman, N. (1993). *Technopoly: The surrender of culture to technology.* New York: Alfred Knopf.

Reinking, D. (1995). Reading and writing with computers: Literacy research in a post-typographic world. In K. A. Hinchman, D. J. Leu, & C. K. Kinzer (Eds.), *Perspectives on literacy research and practice* (Vol. 44, pp. 17–33). Chicago: National Reading Conference.

Roper, B. (1981). *Evolving public attitudes toward television and other mass media, 1959–1980.* New York: Television Information Office.

Scales, P. C. (1991). *A portrayal of young adolescents in the 1990s. Implications for promoting a healthy growth and development.* Chapel Hill, NC: Center for Early Adolescence.

Silverblatt, A. (1995). *Media literacy. Keys to interpreting media messages.* Westport, CT: Praeger.

Worth, S. & Gross, L. (Eds.) (1981). *Studying visual communication.* Philadelphia, PA: University of Pennsylvania Press.

Wyne, E. A., & Ryan, K. (1992). *Reclaiming our schools: A handbook on teaching character, academics, and discipline.* New York: Merrill.

CHAPTER 2

Integrating Critical Media Literacy across the Curriculum

Integration is not a novel concept. But integrating critical media literacy across the curriculum is new to many public schools in the United States. The integration of skills and subject matter or content has been the central concept of the essentials of education advocated and backed by nationwide organizations that include the International Reading Association, the National Council of Teachers of English, the National Council for Social Studies, the National Association of Elementary School Principals, the Association for Supervision and Curriculum Development, and the National Education Association. These organizations of educators have for the past decade advised teachers and other educators that processes and abilities do not grow in isolation from content. They insist that students acquire these processes and abilities through observing, listening, reading, talking, and writing about science, mathematics, history, and the social sciences, the arts, and other aspects of our intellectual, social, and cultural heritage. Their prevailing rationale is inspired by the belief that the separation of school from the "real world" only increases when the arts and media remain marginalized or extracurricular. Likewise, efforts to increase literacy learning are rendered incomplete and irrelevant when they fail to acknowledge the meaning-making capabilities of extracurricular media messages and information.

While these educators are excited about the pedagogical gains offered by curriculum integration, students in many schools haven't developed the habits of mind necessary for academic inquiry appropriate for genuine integration. These habits include the ability to imagine and value points of view different from their own, and then to strengthen, refine, enlarge, or reshape their ideas in light of those other perspectives. They include openness to new ideas combined with a skepticism that demands testing those ideas against previous experience, reading, and belief. They include a desire to see things as a whole and to integrate specific knowledge into larger frameworks. In more traditional terms, these intellectual habits mean to have the ability to synthesize, analyze, evaluate, and argue—to engage ideas actively and write substantively about them. Developing these desired habits form the key concepts of a critical media literacy inquiry.

DEVELOPING A "PROCESS" OF CURRICULUM INQUIRY

In this chapter, I introduce critical media literacy as a "process" of curriculum inquiry. Despite its importance, media literacy simply cannot be reduced into yet another subject we need to teach in American public schools. Rather, it must be integrated throughout the curriculum. Considine and Haley (1992) state that such "integration attempts to unify a fragmented curriculum by stressing the common themes and competencies among subjects" thereby integrating "the world of the classroom with the world of the child and society as a whole" (p. 29). How can teachers facilitate this integration process especially in the English curriculum?

As will be illustrated in this volume, the answer lies in the core concepts of critical media literacy: reading, writing, listening, thinking, and viewing of multiple texts from which multicultural, multiperspectival, and multilevel perspectives are possible (see Kellner, 1995, pp. 93–122). A perspective is simply a way of seeing, a way of knowing. In this case, I am talking about a classroom that acknowledges many points of view brought into the learning space by teachers and students. By introducing multiperspectival, multilevel, and multicultural perspectives in the English curriculum, an integrated curriculum is distinguished from a multidisciplinary curriculum by deep differences. In an integrated curriculum, students move from one activity or project to another, with each one *involving knowledge from multiple sources.* Like the separate-subject approach, the multidisciplinary curriculum still begins and ends with the subject-based content and skills, while curriculum integration begins and ends with the problem and issue-centered organizing themes (Bellack & Kliebard, 1971, cited in Beane, 1997). These organizing themes also contextualize knowledge and give it significant purpose. The task I undertake in this chapter, therefore, is to illustrate how teachers can integrate these multiple perspectives across the curriculum within the framework of critical media literacy.

Through critical media literacy, students engage in a "process" of curriculum inquiry that seeks to employ analytic habits of thinking, reading, speaking, or discussing, which go beneath surface impressions, traditional myths, mere opinions, to refine or reshape their worldview relative to their own social context. I say process, because I am not talking about a one-shot deal, a technique, or a single framework that does the trick. Rather, I focus on a process that is intermedial. Central to this process is critical, careful analysis of the meanings media transmit and the meanings viewers construct for themselves. The questions generated through this process to get to the deeper meaning of texts are not complete or accomplished by one round of questioning. The questioning is iterative, that is, questions leading to new questions. As students compare the text to their social context and notice contradictions, they are motivated to pose even further questions.

Developing a process of curriculum inquiry, therefore, involves active, varied transactions of meaning-making, not as busy work, but transactions that lead into action aimed at reshaping students' worldview relative to their own social context. With critical media literacy, students learn to become critical consumers who are aware of visual manipulation and stereotyping as an important project toward being literate. This form of inquiry involves immersing oneself in a media text or topic and taking time to explore the text in order to find questions that are significant to the learner and then systematically investigating those questions. For example, this approach to curriculum inquiry aims to help demystify the nature of media culture by examining its construction, production, and the meaning-making processes by which media imagery and popular representations of people help shape students' personal, social, and political worlds.

The teaching methods adopted by critical media literacy as a form of inquiry are built on a model of teaching as reflective practice. Teachers make collective and individual decisions about life in classrooms in order to help students develop active, knowledgeable citizens of a multicultural world. These decisions are based on teachers' understanding of self and prior experiences; their students; human development and diversity; subject matter; educational theory; curricular design; instructional methods; federal, state, and institutional regulations; and political, social, and moral relationships between education, community, and world affairs. Teachers develop their understanding through continual, systematic, intensive inquiry into these matters involving problem-posing data gathering through educational literature review, product analysis, observations, and discussion, probing the historical conditions that produced the present circumstances, and acting on this new knowledge. Critically reflecting on and taking action upon one's daily work is the hallmark of a profession engaged in self-improvement (Zeichner & Liston, 1996). As reflective inquirers, schoolteachers bring personal, social, and theoretical knowledge to bear so as to promote curriculum change and school improvement. Reflective teaching is the mortar that holds the building blocks of an integrated curriculum. In sum, this practice requires teachers to examine critically their experiences, knowledge, and values, and to bring to the classroom an understanding of the consequences of one's teaching, provide heartfelt justifications for one's beliefs and actions, and commit to equality, social justice, and respect for differences.

WHAT DIFFERENCE DOES INTEGRATION MAKE?

Veteran and novice teachers will not find the ideas discussed here totally new. But the discussion of this integration process brings together extensive research and practices of teachers who have used these curriculum inquiry methods, theories, critical media pedagogy, analytical schemes and techniques to build bridges between school and society and between students and teachers (see for example, Cazden, Green & Wallace, 1992; Fairclough, 1992; Freire, 1970; Gee, 1996; Kress, 1988). These bridges are key components of the holistic teaching and learning implicit in an *integrated* approach to education. The overall intent of critical media pedagogy is to seek ways to integrate the world of the classroom with the world of the child and society as a whole. We begin this inquiry by exploring the question: What is the role of critical teaching in a world in which culture can no longer be understood as providing the normative integration and common values that cement together democratic social life? The ultimate goal of critical media literacy is to create in schools a more media-literate cadre of teachers who are inquirers, decision makers, and creators of knowledge. Perhaps as teachers use this method of inquiry as a process toward their own learning and professional growth, they also become committed to a critical pedagogy that promotes social critique and a re-imagining of the common good in a diverse culture, and which creates classroom learning environments that support students in their own inquiries.

The immediate purpose of inquiry implied in a critical media literacy curriculum and instruction is to expand the notion of print literacy to include ability to read, analyze, evaluate, and produce communications in a variety of media texts. In pursuing this intent, I acknowledge and take note that both media people and their audiences are active makers and interpreters of meaning. In addition, this approach engages in the examination of issues of diversity the inequalities in knowledge and power that exist between those who manufacture information in their own interests and those who consume it innocently as news, pleasure, and entertainment. The general outlook of this approach is to develop systematic educational inquiry methods and models of critique, decoding, analyzing, and of reading biased media texts. An analysis and critique of texts and images of women, minorities, people from other cultures, ethnic groups, and images of other social groups is important to unpack, uncover, and recognize stereotypes, derogatory bias, and discrimination. Such exercise also helps to detect and understand how these texts and images help to structure our experience and identities.

The frameworks of critical media literacy I propose in this book lay the foundation for investigating the role beliefs and values play in our "knowing" and "doing" as teachers. I direct our attention particularly to those beliefs, actions, and values shaped by our media culture. In this analysis, I also point out that economic and other resources, advantages, and privileges are distributed inequitably in part because of power dynamics involving beliefs in racial, gender, and class divisions. This critical analysis will not be limited to TV and films only but will be extended to other multimedia forms of representation including textbooks, book covers, and other school-related materials. The frameworks of inquiry I am talking about seek to address issues such as the destructive effects of hegemonic language forms borrowed and legitimated by the mass media, particularly when they become the sole lingua franca of the classroom: the canonical provision of notions of knowledge, truth, and beauty, without regard to the grounds of their construction; the violence perpetrated by an educational practice that inadequately addresses the reproduction of sexism and racism; the representation of men and women of color in derogatory or stereotypical ways; the scientism of science that constructs a powerful and excluding ideology regarding what it means to do science; or the forms of work education that reduce valued labor to that which fits existing economic arrangements (Kincheloe & Steinberg, 1998).

CRITICAL MEDIA LITERACY
AS AN INTEGRATED PROCESS

Clearly, media literacy as curriculum inquiry is not only a method to be learned, but also a *process*, central to the entire notion of communication and construction of meaning. Thus, it cuts across all subject areas. As an integrative process, media literacy is not simply a method for rearranging lesson plans, as so many educators seem to think. Rather, it is a broad theory of curriculum design that encompasses particular views about the purpose of schools, the nature of learning, the organization and uses of knowledge, and the meaning of educational experience. Students do not come to the classroom with blank minds ready to be filled with knowledge. Rather, they bring to every topic (as we all do) all kinds of experiences including ideas, prejudices, misconceptions, and stereotypes, many of which they have picked from the mass media. How then can teachers include critical pedagogy in their practice and what resistances might they find? How do institutional structures enable/disable teachers to change their practice in ways that are more equitable? Effective teaching will need to take critical pedagogy into account, and might well begin with a consideration of media representations of the topic at hand. To bring critical mindedness to such media issues or representations (of people, events, cultural values, etc.) will be the central tenet of visual media and textual analysis I attempt to discuss in this chapter.

This critical mindedness enables teachers and students to examine all media texts in a manner distinct from traditional classroom practice. It provides a critical lens or framework to sort out media representations of people and events to find out what is at issue, how the issue is defined, who is involved, what the arguments are and what is taken for granted including cultural assumptions (Werner & Nixon, 1990). This means addressing the "naturalness" of dominant ways of seeing, saying, and doing, by provoking a consideration of why things are the way they are, how they got to be that way, in what ways might change be desirable, and what it would take for things to change or be otherwise. Through such framework of inquiry, students will be constantly encouraged to apply critical thinking skills to question the clarity and strength of reasoning, identify assumptions and values, recognize points of view and attitudes, and evaluate conclusions and actions. Such exercise also involves being aware that issues are shaped by groups who may have their own interests to protect and that the media are not merely neutral conduits for information. In the next section, I will examine (1) what integration means in a media literacy classroom, (2) why integration is important, and (3) how to integrate critical media literacy across the curriculum.

INTEGRATION OF MEDIA LITERACY IN CLASSROOMS

In writing this chapter, I reflected on my own practice in teaching critical media literacy to undergraduate preservice teachers. I pondered over the key concepts of media literacy, the aspects of media literacy that make classroom reading and viewing of media texts a critical project, and how to go about realizing a curriculum that bridges what goes on in the classroom and outside the walls of the schoolhouse. I also reflected on the many questions my students raise about my teaching every semester. I am often asked questions like: What is integration? Is interdisciplinary teaching the same as integration? If teachers use advertising to teach students vocabulary, is that integrating media literacy in the English curriculum? Since the media literacy course I teach is within a secondary English teaching methods curriculum, questions about integration are legitimate and appropriate. These questions seem to arise from the multiple and often confusing uses of the term *integration* in the educational literature. Integration means everything and at the same time nothing. It has been used and misused so often and for so many conflicting reasons. The varied uses conjure up multiple definitions and applications of the term.

A quick scan of these applications shows that integration means different things to many educators. There are misconceptions about what integration is and is not. To clarify for myself and for the students I teach, I read James Beane's book *Curriculum Integration: Designing the Core of Democratic Education*. Beane's book directed me to read Hopkins' book: *Integration: Its Meaning and Application*. I found these two books most useful in defining what integration is and is not. The first two chapters of Beane's book helped to clarify and confirm for myself what I had believed to be the rationale for integrating critical media literacy across the curriculum. Reading through the long history of the "integration" movement since the 1800s, I was surprised by the many political agendas that seem to stand in the way of implementing integration. How can such a commonsense idea be so problematic? Why would integration be so controversial in curriculum reform efforts? Why has it taken this long for teachers to grasp and embrace a method that would be so helpful to students' lives? I came to realize that what might seem to me as natural was not the same to my colleagues or to the educational reform movement in the United States. Partly this is so because as teachers, we come from different backgrounds, diverse training backgrounds, and ideological positions.

By investigating the history of the debate surrounding the notions of integration and curriculum reform, I was able to understand and determine what genuine integration might look like in a critical media literacy classroom. The irony of these debates is that they all come together in very real ways inside the classroom and that they seem to revolve around issues of content. The question of "what to teach" as opposed to "how to teach" and "whom to teach" have taken the front lines in these debates. And the debates rage on into the 1990s. For instance, in the early 1990s version of reform, teachers were faced with a variety of movements: school-based management, shared decision making, teacher empowerment, collaborative learning, and school-based accountability. These pressures were real to most teachers. With the changing demographic landscape of our schools, issues of multicultural education and inclusive curricula to accommodate the diverse student populations showing up in classrooms in American schools have not made it any easier for teachers to implement these reforms in a systematic way.

WHAT INTEGRATION IS NOT

According to Beane (1997), curriculum integration is often defined by what it is not. It is distinguished from the separate subject approach that has dominated schools for so long. It is also different from other arrangements and designs that are, to some extent, beyond the strict separate-subject approach and to which the term *curriculum integration* is often misapplied. Curriculum integration is not the same thing as interdisciplinary or multidisciplinary. For example, in some schools, the term has been used in attempts to reassemble fragmented pieces of a discipline of knowledge, such as creating social studies out of history and geography or whole language out of fragmented language arts. It has also been used with regard to addressing things such as thinking, writing, and valuing across subject areas. Although some teachers have argued that the word *integration* is technically acceptable in these situations of reassembling fragmented disciplines of knowledge, this is not what has been meant historically by "curriculum integration." Simply put by Beane (1997), integration has traditionally been seen as "a search for an integrative curriculum—one that promotes the integration of experiences, of knowledge, of school and the larger world, or self and social interests" (p. 19).

Beane (1997) warns that the greatest confusion has to do with a very different curriculum design that is often, and mistakenly, labeled as "curriculum integration" but would more accurately be called "multi-disciplinary" or "multisubject." To make the distinction between these approaches, teachers must contrast the ways in which such curricula are planned. In this context, Beane emphasizes that in curriculum integration, planning begins with a central theme and proceeds outward through identification of big ideas or concepts related to the theme and activities that might be used to explore them. This planning is done without regard for subject-area lines, since the overriding purpose is to explore the theme itself. In curriculum integration, organizing themes are drawn from life as it is being lived and experienced. By using such life-related themes, the way is opened for young people to inquire critically into real issues and to pursue social action wherever they see the need. The inquiry and action that follow inevitably add depth to the meaning of democracy in schools, which curriculum integration further underscores through its emphasis on collaborative teacher-student curriculum planning. "Such collaboration also opens the way to redefining power relations in the classroom and to challenging the idea that important knowledge is only that named and endorsed by academicians and bureaucrats outside the classroom" (p. xi).

However, in a multidisciplinary or multisubject approach, planning begins with recognition of the identities of various subjects as well as important content and skills that are to be mastered within them. A theme is then identified "often from within one or another subject and approached through the question, 'What can each subject contribute to the theme?'" In this way, the identities of the separate subjects are retained in the selection of content to be used, and students still rotate from one subject to another as content and/or skills from each are correlated to the theme. Teachers must note that even though the subjects are taught in relation to the theme, the overriding purpose is still the mastery of content and skills from the subjects involved. In this sense, the theme is really a secondary matter and not the primary focus as it would be in a genuine integration model.

Within a critical media literacy framework, the themes are drawn from life as it is being lived and experienced. One place students might start their inquiry about real-life issues could be their experiences with popular mass media. Adolescent students, for example, often find themselves immersed in popular media texts that present dilemmas to them. Notions of success, beauty, and sexuality are constantly being presented to them through advertising, the Internet, and shopping malls. They also read stories about romance, sexuality, and fashion trends. These texts manipulate their images and problematize for them issues of identity, coming of age, sexuality, love, racial discrimination, gender bias, substance abuse, and violence. Where can they find guidance to resolve the dilemmas they face? What frameworks can they use to read, deconstruct, criticize, and expose media representations and their powerful manipulative force to a critique and be able to discern the messages, values, and ideologies embedded in all these media texts? How can schools become the place of social literacy where real and frightening issues are addressed to young men and women so as to enable them to look critically upon their world and the information they are given in terms of who they are supposed to be and what they are supposed to look like? By using media issues as a place to start classroom inquiry, the way is open for these young people to inquire critically into real issues and to pursue social action where they see the need. Through an analysis of such popular genres as soap operas, talk shows, rap music, sitcoms, rock videos, pornography, made-for-TV movies, advertising, and romance novels, students are invited to engage in a critical media scholarship. This integrated method of learning through inquiry engages the examination of issues of diversity and the inequalities of knowledge and power that exist between those who write and produce the texts or information and those who consume it as they read and view to gratify their desire, pleasure, and fantasies.

The emphasis on critical media literacy, therefore, is not to establish another subject or separate lesson plans within a disciplinary unit. Genuine curriculum integration in a critical media literacy project involves applying knowledge to questions and concerns that have personal and social significance to adolescent students. In doing this, the boundaries between separate subject areas are dissolved and knowledge is repositioned in the context of those questions and concerns. Regardless of content area or subject matter, the scope and sequence of knowledge are determined by the questions and concerns collaboratively planned by teachers and students. This repositioning of knowledge to reflect questions and concerns requires flexible use of resources drawn from all texts, not only from printed texts, but from visual texts, the arts, the Internet, as well as popular media. Thus, with its emphasis on participatory planning, contextual knowledge, real-life issues, and unified organization, critical media literacy offers the possibility of integration that provides broad access to knowledge for diverse young people and hence opens the way for more academic success to many of them.

RATIONALE FOR INTEGRATING MEDIA LITERACY ACROSS THE CURRICULUM

There are many arguments for connecting curricula through critical media literacy: creating a literate, knowledgeable populace, developing critical consumers, preparing future workers, critical citizenship, and involving participants in a just democratic process. Critical analysis of diverse media, coupled with generation of new texts, promotes student empowerment, interest, active learning, and multicultural awareness (Considine & Haley, 1992; Sinatra, 1990). When students are able to relate personal, academic, and varied social experiences, their motivation and learning may increase (Reutzel & Cooter, 1992). Perhaps most importantly, educators who intervene in the cycle of isolated learning experiences may empower students, inviting them into what Frank Smith (1984) calls "the literacy club," establishing lifelong patterns of positive learning, thinking, and acting.

Scholars have long recognized that integrating critical media literacy practices across the curriculum supports and extends many instructional frameworks and curricula. These include whole language (Fehlman, 1996); multicultural curricula (Sinatra, 1986; Considine & Haley, 1992); values education (Lickona, 1991); inquiry learning (Schmidt, 1997); interdisciplinary approaches (Considine, 1987; Schnitzer, 1990); skills-based reading and writing (Moline, 1995; Cheyney, 1992); cooperative learning (Considine & Haley, 1992; Watts Pailliotet, 1997); content area reading and learning (Watts Pailliotet, 1997); constructivism (Hyerle, 1996; Evans, 1987); as well as critical thinking and viewing (Considine, Haley, & Lacy, 1994; Semali, 1994).

The purpose and desired outcome of integrating media literacy across the curriculum are grounded in the notion of praxis, "self-creative activity through which men and women . . . [c]hange (shape) the historical human world and themselves" (Sholle & Denski, 1993, p. 300). Within an integrative framework, as defined by Beane, it is not enough to simply decode or understand existing texts. Students and teachers must transform their newfound critical understandings into agency: positive acts and effects in themselves and others. This might transpire through generation of new texts and knowledge, developing ways of thinking and acting, or working toward alterations of unjust social conditions.

One classroom example of praxis at the secondary level might involve inquiry learning about a community condition, combined with direct action. As students read literature in their English classes, they will learn from stories in both historical and contemporary texts about what it is or was to live in a particular community. For example, in Crane's *Maggie: A Girl of the Streets* (1983), one would understand how the American poor live in the back streets. There are fights, rapes, and indifference to members of Maggie's family. One would learn that Crane writes about the sordid aspect of human life. The life of the lower middle class is one filled with fights, shouts, horror, seduction, and illusion. One sees, in short, a life of the inferno.

Also, in Henry David Thoreau's *Walden, or Life in the Woods* (1854), one can read about how life should be. For Thoreau, it is a pity that the modern man in a mad pursuit of material gain has become nothing but a machine. The author advises that man [sic] simplify his life so that he would have time to study, mediate, and enjoy life. Thoreau "went to the woods because I wished to live deliberately, to confront only the essential facts of life." He refuses to live what is not life. He refuses to realize that he has not lived at all at the time when he has to die. Living is very dear and nothing can take it away. In short, he refuses to live like a machine or a beast of burden. In stories such as these, the language use and the social, political, and cultural conditions of the specific times will paint a picture about "how things were or are" for the people they are reading or viewing about. Students would not stop here. They would proceed to seek deeper meaning from multiple texts that inform their understanding about the questions they might raise about the text they are reading. Some of these questions might include: Who is the author? What historical, political, or social contexts influenced the author to write the novel or story?

Students would engage in an inquiry examining varied media to gain information. They would then create public service announcements, research reports, Web sites, newsletters, and action plans to address the issues they find important. A secondary classroom application might involve critical analysis of content and point of view represented in social studies, mass media, or English/language arts texts. After identifying missing information, students could employ community interviews, oral histories, original documents, mass media, or artistic resources to build broader pictures of events or texts. They might write their own books, create a newspaper, a Web site, a mural or a dramatic presentation to convey their new understandings.

In college, preservice teachers may also apply intermedial principles and media literacy to achieve praxis. Using readings, observations, personal interviews, artifacts in their own lives, videos, list server discussions (Internet chat rooms), and written reflections, they may assess, articulate, examine, and adapt their beliefs about teaching, making professional changes, and formulating plans for future growth.

The notion of integration-based instruction, therefore, is grounded in connecting analytical skills to social or daily contexts. Because of the impending multimedia technologies, the literacies these technologies bring to classrooms will soon become part of the fabric of contemporary life, whether we like it or not. Teachers must be the first to learn to adopt the methods and practices necessary for multimedia environments (Watkin, 1994). My intention in this book, therefore, is to broaden the lens for reading all texts and describe opportunities for teachers to prepare for the new media environments and hopefully introduce integrative methods and practices necessary for multimedia classrooms as we enter the new millennium.

WHY IS INTEGRATION IMPORTANT IN MULTIMEDIA CLASSROOMS?

The 1990s were marked by a renewed interest in curriculum integration. Several factors have converged to give the idea of integration some serious momentum:

- The rise of mass media and technology in U.S. society and schools has led to new ways of looking at the world and how we construct meaning. Our worldviews are shaped and influenced by the technology we use in our schools and homes—computers, automated teller machines, fax modems, digital television, cable, and a variety of gadgetry that continue to enter our lives subsequent to the invention of computer environments and the microchip. These technologies have also impacted the way we communicate and how we receive information. For this reason, there is a growing support for curriculum arrangements that involve application of knowledge rather than mere memorization and accumulation of facts. The move away from simple accumulation has support among somewhat of a mix of advocates, including educators disenchanted with low-level learning and bored students, business leaders interested in applied knowledge skills such as problem solving, various groups calling for higher standards and more challenging content, and evaluation specialists concerned about authentic assessment.

- There is an emerging sense that knowledge is neither fixed nor universal. I refer to the postmodern poststructural fascination with multiple meanings of language and action, and with the idea that knowledge is socially constructed. All texts are constructions—that is, they involve active, varied transactions of meaning-making. Rather than receiving information in a conduit, linear fashion, people interact with ("read") and mediate ("write") texts to develop understandings (Barthes, 1974; Britton, 1985; Evans, 1987; Rosenblatt, 1978; McLuhan & Fiore, 1967; Smith, 1984). These transactions have neither a clearly defined beginning nor end. They involve complex, multiple, simultaneous, and recursive processes (Bissex, 1980; Elbow, 1985; Flower, 1989; McLuhan & Fiore, 1967). Readers/writers/audiences employ many senses (Barthes, 1974; Perl, 1980; Pike, Compain, & Mumper, 1997), intellectual processes (Britton, 1985; Calkins, 1983; McLuhan, 1964; Ong, 1986; Messaris, 1994), and emotions (Brand, 1987; Lester, 1995; McLuhan, 1964) to access, construct, and interpret textual languages. In the late twentieth century, it is getting increasingly hard to think of an answer to the question of what knowledge is of most worth when nothing is more certain than uncertainty, when yesterday's truth is repealed by today's discovery, which in turn, is clearly in danger of tomorrow's breakthrough.
- Texts, as well as processes for understanding and constructing them, are connected. Readers/writers/audiences do not create meanings in isolation. Instead they draw from experiences of other texts, connecting past and present understandings (Bhaktin, 1988; Cooper, 1986; Goody, 1978). Since all texts share common elements, processes developed in one form of communication support others. Reading, writing, speaking, listening, thinking, acting, *and* viewing are synergistic, interdependent, and interactive processes (Flood & Lapp, 1995; Neuman, 1991; Sinatra, 1986; Watts Pailliotet, 1997).
- Furthermore, there is the recognition among a growing number of scholars that problems of real significance cannot be solved out of a single discipline of knowledge and, therefore, that it is increasingly necessary to look at the world across disciplines (Klein, 1990). For example, how is it that problems in the environment, in human relations, in medical ethics, and so on can be resolved by work within a single area? The answer is that they cannot. And

what is the sense of having a curriculum that acts as though such problems are not on the minds of the young or that their consideration must begin with mastering a smattering of isolated facts from different subject areas rather than with the problems themselves? Through curriculum integration, students can find connections between subject areas and will be able to bridge the gaps between school and home, academic work and play, subject matter and daily problem solutions.

- Another factor is the continuing presence of those educators who maintain a serious interest in progressive education ideas. This group would include, for example, advocates of "whole-learning" arrangements, such as whole language, unit teaching, thematic curriculum, and problem- and project-centered methods. It would also include those who recognize the social problem focus and the instrumental uses of knowledge in curriculum integration as an aspect of democratic education (Apple & Beane, 1995). It would include also representatives of subject-area associations and projects, including those in mathematics and science, who have called for ending fragmentation within their areas and connecting them to larger problems and issues. Ironically, many educators today like to speak of change in terms of "paradigm shifts" they have made or are trying to make. Such shifts more often seem to involve things like changing the school schedule, more sharply defining outcomes of schooling, or coming up with new methods of assessment. I understand the meaning of paradigm shift to entail change in viewpoint so fundamental that much of what is currently taken for granted is now called into question or rendered irrelevant or wrong (Kuhn, 1962). So defined, I believe, therefore, what is urgent in the multimedia classrooms of the twenty-first century is a new way of conceptualizing curriculum and not making do with what exists. As educators, we must begin to ask different kinds of questions: How does the traditional curriculum of American public schools conflict with lived experiences of minority children, for example, African American and Latino students? As noted by other scholars, it is hard to take the kinds of changes just mentioned as paradigm shifts. These, like most of the changes usually associated with "restructuring," ask only about "how" we do things and leave alone more fundamental questions about "what" we do and "why" (Beane, 1997).

POSSIBILITIES OF INTEGRATING MEDIA LITERACY IN AMERICAN CLASSROOMS

The context of what students are studying has become the new focus of curriculum reform by education professionals and professional associations and foundations. Common themes found in academic standards mandated by many state education boards across the nation include integration, emphasis on thinking skills, more rigorous content for all students, and reform of learning assessment practices. More frequently than ever before teachers are challenged to become effective teachers as well as lifelong learners: They should not be dispensers of information and judges of right answers (Kimpston, Williams, & Stockton, 1992). Many teachers, however, wonder: How can instruction be adapted in response to the changing literacy landscape, and how can teachers and students exploit electronic forms of reading and writing to enhance teaching and learning?

Timothy Dohrer (1998), in an article titled, "A Textbook for Everyone: Balancing Canons and Cultures in English Textbooks," makes explicit the demands that teachers face in their classrooms and the challenges they must contend with. He states:

> English teachers in the nineties are being asked to do everything: teach the "classics" but include voices of "others," be innovative with material but use only the state adopted textbook, teach students to read and to write of course, but don't forget speech, critical thinking, collaboration, listening skills, and (computer) word processing. While teachers are continually rising to the challenge, the burden of being society's solution to everything is over-loading the current system. (p. 95)

As an English teacher, Dohrer finds himself overwhelmed at times by the philosophical debates raging outside the classroom. He is haunted by such questions as:

> Am I teaching too many works or not enough? Am I presenting a balance of voices? Did I ask the right questions in our discussion about Huck Finn or Gwendolyn Brooks's "We Real Cool?" Is it OK for me to stray away from the textbook and bring in another perspective? If I do, then which author will I leave out? (p. 96)

In each of these questions, Dohrer points out the underlying preoccupation of many teachers who worry about content and the formation of the canon. The English teacher is faced with tough choices about district demands, personal ethical issues, students' needs, and much more. How might "integration" become helpful in organizing the everyday curriculum? What approaches might teachers use to deal with the pressures of educational reform and the burden of being society's solution to everything that is overloading the current system? How might media literacy as a curriculum inquiry provide the kinds of insights that Dohrer is looking for?

MIXED MESSAGES ABOUT INTEGRATING MEDIA LITERACY

It seems to me that the same confusion I perceive pervading curriculum reform over the years in this country pervades as well the media literacy movement. Since the media literacy movement was founded in North America in 1978, there has been a big effort to introduce media education in the classroom. Since 1978, many workshops and institutes have been held in various cities to explore the languages of media and how to teach them to students in elementary and secondary schools. During this period, *Telemedium*, a journal of media literacy, was established at the University of Wisconsin, Madison, and it has been churning out scholarly articles about theory and practice of media literacy. This publication has also been useful to teachers through its offerings of lists of resource materials including textbooks, Web site addresses, new educational films, and video programs. These materials have added to the momentum already experienced in the national media literacy movement (Duncan, 1997).

However, the extent of integrating critical media literacy in American classrooms has been limited and varied. As discussed elsewhere (Semali & Pailliotet, 1999), an examination of textbooks produced in the United States during the past fifteen-year period reveals that few books have taken time to focus on the theory *and* practice of critical media literacy. The largest number of these books focus on theory. Over twenty books have been published describing the language of media, particularly popular media (see, for example, the list generated by Duncan, 1997, p. 20). Media educators have written few of these books. For the most part, authors are media critics, or cultural theorists, not classroom teachers.

Our findings also show that there is another kind of divide. Some teachers of English simply transfer over literature response techniques to visual analysis methods advocated by media educators. As noted by Duncan (1993), there is a tension between those educators who focus on *content* (what is taught) and those who are preoccupied by *form* (how media literacy is taught). In these books, there is evidence of a range of considerable disagreement among theorists. However, these theorists acknowledge the need for teaching about media and they also acknowledge some benefit to be realized by students who engage in some type of media analysis. These books also have systematically dodged the practical questions of integrating media across the curriculum. Many authors offer frameworks that support teaching about media but fall short of methods illustrating openly how to do it.

Even though recent publications discuss the need for developing critical thinking, critical viewing, and critical reading of popular media, authors do not seem to agree in practice what "critical" means. For example, in their book *Imagine That: Developing Critical Thinking and Critical Viewing through Children's Literature,* Considine and colleagues (1994) provide student activities and strategies at many opportunities: Writing and drawing tasks, verbal connections, and manual and emotional experiences are some of the many suggestions. Both veteran and prospective teachers are left to wonder and ask: How can teachers take up a critical stance in their daily teaching? How can teachers' reflective and teaching practices develop a critical stance to generate a critical authoring, reading, and viewing of texts? How can teachers enable students to navigate the seas of multiple texts, especially those represented in multimedia formats currently flooding their learning environments through the Internet, video, CD-ROM, and so on, at a time when literacy education is no longer confined to paper-and-pencil technologies? How can reader/viewer response analysis stimulate and help students develop critical reading, critical viewing, critical listening, and critical thinking for lifelong learning? How does a critical pedagogy of representation as envisaged in a media literacy project fit the lessons teachers will take up on Monday morning in a language arts or social studies class? How do they fit with the requirements of academic standards and assessment prerogatives?

These are difficult questions for teachers, and although I have outlined them elsewhere, I find it appropriate to raise them here again. These questions are especially difficult when we consider that most teachers operate in school districts where the curriculum is already full. There is no room to add on another stand-alone course in media literacy, yet some of the books we examined have suggested or implied that teachers do just that—add another course. Others have indicated that language arts and social studies are the best place for teachers to begin integrating media literacy, and thus mistakenly insinuate that these subjects are closely related, which could be a condition for integration. In this case, the *subject* would drive integration, and not, as explained earlier by the *themes* that call for a media literacy framework of analysis.

Our analysis of the North American textbooks reveals, however, the reason praxis has been so difficult to model or illustrate has to do with teachers' attitudes about integration. When teachers encourage learning as an integrative process, they shift the focus to the students' social context in order to expand and develop students' current awareness. Why are certain curriculum organizations or approaches more likely than others to assist young people with the processes of personal and social integration? How can learning become an integrative process? As noted by Beane (1997), one response suggests that the process of integration can be facilitated by a child-centered curriculum that draws its direction and organization from the child's interests, experiences, and "development." An example may well be an "activity curriculum" in which children are encouraged to draw their own conclusions from activities that involve observation, hands-on experimentation, and the like (Kilpartick, 1934). Another example could be the "experience curriculum" in which teachers and students cooperatively plan activities around real-life situations with skills and concepts learned from carrying out the activities (Hopkins, 1941). In this endeavor, the teacher and students are engaged in an inquiry aimed not only at understanding, but also at shaping the large social "reality" that in turn shapes the possibilities of their lives (see also Apple, 1982; Giroux, 1981).

In the next section, I will discuss the possibilities and the extent to which teachers might integrate critical media literacy in American classrooms. How might multimedia technology facilitate this process of integration in American classrooms? What might some examples of best practices look like? Using Beane's (1997) levels of integration, the next section outlines the possibilities of integrating critical media literacy across the curriculum at the experiential, social, knowledge, and curriculum levels.

Experiential Level

I concur with Beane (1997) that most of the ideas that young people have about themselves and their world—their perceptions, beliefs, values, and so on—are constructed out of their experiences. What we learn from reflecting on our experiences becomes a resource for dealing with problems, issues, and other situations, both personal and social, as they arise in the future. These experiences and the schemes of meaning we construct out of them do not simply sit in our minds as static, hardened categories. Instead they are fluid and dynamic meanings that may be organized one way for dealing with one issue, another way for a second issue, and so on. This kind of learning involves having constructive, reflective experiences that not only broaden and deepen our present understandings of ourselves and our world but that also are "learned" in such a way that they may be carried forward and put to use in new situations (Dressel, 1958).

Within this perspective, the teacher and students seek the opportunity in this project to take further the process of critically questioning themselves and their interpretation of the world. Students and teachers strive to capture or demystify the media in order to reveal the ideological messages embedded in its message and its possible impact on society or individual lives (see Freire, 1985; Illich, 1971; Neill, 1960). This perspective therefore distinguishes media literacy as a "content." Shifting away from a content approach, this critical stance also encourages students to examine their positions in society and the multiple layers of text to discover the embedded meanings. Thus, this approach to critical literacy stands in contrast to the practice of teaching the classics and a canon of acceptable literary works far removed from the students' experiences to be memorized for exams. Such learning involves integration in two ways: first, as new experiences are "integrated" into our schemes of meaning and, second, as we organize or "integrate" past experience to help us in new problem situations. As noted by Beane, the critical issues with regard to this theory are, of course, how to organize curriculum experiences and the knowledge they engage in such a way that young people may most easily integrate them into their schemes of meaning and carry them forward. In too many cases, the notion of learning that schools seem to promote is quite different from this. Instead of seeking meaningful integration of experience and knowledge, both are treated as a kind of "capital" for accumulation and cultural ornamentation. Knowledge is dispensed with the idea that it is to be stored away for future use, either to hand back in the form of test answers or displayed when the occasion suggests.

Because impending multimedia technologies and the literacies they bring to classrooms will soon become part of the fabric of contemporary life, whether we like it or not, teachers must take frontline positions and learn to adopt new methods and practices necessary for multimedia environments (Watkin, 1994). The intention in this volume is to broaden the lens of reading all texts and describe opportunities for teachers to enrich the possibilities of communication with students—thus bridging the gaps between home and school. As readily acknowledged by media educators, connecting home and school environment has been the most important and yet the most challenging to teachers.

Many media educators already suspect that this challenge has hindered the media literacy movement from reaching many teachers in U.S. classrooms. For example, Barbara Dobbs (1988) surmises that some early media literacy curricula "died a slow death because they were not global in their approach. The visual literacy skills that were taught in those isolated classes were not transferred to other curricula and more importantly, were not transferred to students' world outside the classroom" (p. 12). This lack of articulation of the social context prompted McMahon and Quin (1993) to undertake systemwide study in their home state in Australia called *Monitoring Standards in Education.* They rightly argue that the time has come for evaluation of the aims, content, and strategies of media literacy. They insist that unless students are given the skills to apply their classroom analysis skills to the world in which they live, there is the danger that this knowledge will remain in the classroom and will not achieve the aim of producing media-literate, empowered students.

The results of McMahon and Quin's study indicate that although students are adept in deconstructing a given image, and competent in textual analysis, they are often unable to make the conceptual leap between the text and its context. They point out that students' problems with linking textual analysis to wider issues of representations, on one level, is perhaps a question of maturity. This may well be true because students do not have a worldview or a sense of themselves as part of a wider society. For some, society is something "out there" that they will deal with outside the school classroom after three o'clock or when they graduate from high school. In their eyes, that time is a long way from now. For others, the time for critical examinations may occur after they graduate from college. McMahon and Quin identified the first problem of current media literacy instruction: not furnishing students with the skills to apply their analysis skills to a wider social context.

Some of the strategies outlined by McMahon and Quin include broadening the students' worldview, and our notion of integrating media across the curriculum coincides with their aim. They view texts as polysemous, that is, informed by various preexistent discourses. This is another way of looking at multiple texts, multilayered visuals, and multi-literacies. McMahon and Quin also suggest that media literacy strategies include inquiry, reflection, and action. They suggest that teachers encourage students to: (1) ask different questions about the issue; (2) analyze the institutions that produce the prevailing views; and (3) seek alternative images that may provide a different view, such as those found in radical texts. One important point they make that is relevant to multimedia classrooms is that if teachers continue to ask the same questions on social issues, they will simply recycle prevailing views. McMahon and Quin list "alternative questions" that could be asked around any social issue raised by the text (literature or visuals related to them): (1) Through whose eyes or perspective do we get the information? (2) What assumptions are being made in the view presented? (3) What representations are there of the group concerned? (4) Whose voices are not being heard? (5) If a key piece of information were changed, how would the meaning change? (6) Why has this group been singled out for depiction in this manner? Who gains from this representation? (7) What would be the effect if the various depictions were reversed? These questions form the basis of intermediality and integration—the core concepts of a critical media literacy program. Through questioning, reflection, and action, students get to know their social context, evaluate it, and plan action to take to make changes. This volume offers both a way of thinking about and negotiating through praxis the relationship among classroom teaching, the production of knowledge, the larger institutional structures of the school, and the social and material relations of the wider community, society, and the nation-state.

High school students in the present-day United States recognize the significance of technology to their lives—even if their teachers do not—and come to school expecting to see technology integrated into education. What may have seemed far-fetched remarks by Marshall McLuhan in 1960 may now have come to face our generation of high school students. McLuhan said: "In the 19th century, the knowledge inside the classroom was higher than the knowledge outside. Today it is reversed. The child knows that, in going to school, he is in a sense interrupting his education" (McLuhan, 1978). McLuhan warned that schools may be irrelevant and boring for students if they do not open up their curriculum and instruction to include today's technologies and media with the accompanying learning styles individuals bring to classrooms. A high school that responds inadequately to the current technological imperative is out of touch with its students and runs the risk of making their education appear irrelevant to them. As educators, we know we must harness the power of emerging technologies like the Internet, but we have a lot of catching up to do. Now that "TV" is more than broadcast and cable, merging with the telephone and the computer, it is becoming even more pervasive and more powerful. Even before we have fully comprehended the nature of this force being ushered in by the information age, the scope of its effects, or the economics of its multi-billion-dollar outreach, a tidal wave of new technologies has hit us, delivering even more information. Unavoidably, with such delivery comes a new set of ethical, moral, and social consequences that now present dilemmas in new terms. Despite these challenges and transformations, surprisingly little academic research has been undertaken around the study of media, culture, and education and how they have come to shape the agendas of literacy research and practice in U.S. classrooms (Reinking, 1995).

Social Level

Beane (1997) talks about social integration. When teachers take up curriculum integration at the social level, they engage students with the curriculum on life itself rather than on the mastery of fragmented information within the boundaries of subject areas. By curriculum of life, Beane means to emphasize the view of learning as a continuous integration of new knowledge and experience so as to deepen and broaden our understanding of our world and ourselves. This approach to learning focuses on life as it is lived now rather than on preparation for some later life or grade level of schooling. It serves the young people for whom the curriculum is intended rather than the specialized interests of adults, academicians or textbook publishers. In those classrooms where the curriculum of life takes place, meaning is a contested phenomenon. Students engage in the social struggle over meaning and strive to navigate today's classrooms, sifting through the multiple layers of competing texts presented in intermedial environments of Web sites, videos, sound bytes, and electronic bulletin boards. This process involves the active analysis and construction of meaning rather than merely assuming the validity of others' meanings. It brings the idea of democracy to life. Through its method of inquiry and problem-centered focus, this approach engages students in multiple ways of knowing, and elicits from them social action plans germane to their social context.

Perhaps the most important aspects of integration at the social level is the acknowledgment of the political function that schools perform.

Schools in a democratic society strive to provide common or shared educational experiences for young people with diverse characteristics and multicultural backgrounds. The assumption is that they will grow to be responsible citizens with common values of participatory democracy, justice, and hard work. The ideas of such experiences has long been tied to the common concept of integration through emphasis on a curriculum that promotes some sense of common values or a "common good" (Smith, 1927; Childs & Dewey, 1933). This way of looking at the curriculum has been mistakenly appropriated by some conservative educators to promote the notion of national culture or what E.D. Hirsch (1987) calls "cultural literacy" to be learned by all Americans. This monocultural "melting pot" view of an all-encompassing curriculum is now widely contested as unrealistic and unpopular, and as a curriculum of illusion in a nation that is divided by race and ethnicity, and which is diverse and growing demographically and multiculturally (Banks, 1993).

However, in this book we acknowledge the opportunity and possibilities that a critical media literacy can offer across the curriculum. In the inquiry approach of media literacy, students, particularly future teachers, must constantly question representational attempts to establish such monocultural visions of America. Are the visions of America represented in history books, in secondary English textbooks, in documentary films, in newspaper articles, in television genres, and so on, a fair, accurate representation of all Americans? American curriculum theorists and sociologists of education have been more forthcoming in their examination of how the variables of class and more recently those of gender, homophobia, disability, and age have informed the organization and selection of school knowledge and the production and reproduction of subcultures among school youth than they have been in their examination of race (McCarthy, 1988). Critical social theory provides the inquiry methods that make it possible to examine more closely the portion of the school program devoted to this purpose of "social integration," often referred to as "general education." It is this general education that is the site of debates over what ought to be required of all students or what all young people should "know."

While most people seem to think general education should amount to a collection of required subjects (and to which media literacy ought to be added), many educators and activists committed to social reform have called for other types of arrangements. Most prominent among these has been a curriculum organized around personal and social issues, collaboratively planned and carried out by teachers and students together and committed to the integration of knowledge. These kinds of arrangements are promoted not simply because they make knowledge more accessible for young people but because they help to create democratic classroom settings as a context for social integration.

For example, as explained by Beane (1997) the use of a problem-centered curriculum follows from the idea that the democratic way of life involves collaborative work on common social issues. The participation of young people in curriculum planning follows from the democratic concept of participatory, collaborative governance and decision making. The inclusion of personal issues alongside social problems follow from the democratic possibility of integrating self- and social interest. The sad fact is that both social integration and democratic practice have largely eluded the schools. Worse yet, the schools and their traditional curriculum organization have often been among the persistent sources of inequity and "integration" found across the whole society.

It is my desire that teachers use this method of inquiry to initiate a process for their own learning and professional growth. I also hope they will become committed to a critical pedagogy that promotes social critique, re-imagining the common good in a diverse culture, and that creates classroom learning environments that support students in their inquiries about personal, as well as social, issues. The immediate goal of inquiry implied in my media literacy curriculum is to expand the notion of literacy to include the ability to read, analyze, evaluate, and produce communications in a variety of media texts. Included in the analysis is the democratic possibility of integrating the self with social interests.

Knowledge Level

When Beane talks about integration of knowledge, he calls our attention to how knowledge is constructed in real-world situations and urges educators to look beyond the individual subject and discipline to learn what is around us. When used in relation to curriculum, therefore, *integration* also refers to a theory of the organization and uses of knowledge. Beane gives the example: Imagine for the moment that we are confronted with some problem or puzzling situation in our lives. How do we approach the situation? Do we stop and ask ourselves which part of the situation is language arts, or music, or mathematics, or history, or art? Instead we take on the problem or situation using whatever knowledge is appropriate or pertinent without regard for subject-area lines. And if the problem or situation is significant enough to us, we are willing and anxious to seek out needed knowledge that we do not already have. In this way, we come to understand and use knowledge not in terms of the differentiated compartments by which it is labeled in school, but rather as it is "integrated" in the context of the real problems and issues.

As acknowledged by many educators, including Beane, the isolation and fragmentation of knowledge is part of the deep structures of schooling. This is evident in the subject-specific curriculum documents, schedules, and other artifacts of middle and high schools and in the separate subject/skill schedule in so many elementary school classrooms. This latter point is important because it is too often assumed that the elementary school curriculum is not as subject-defined as that of the middle and high schools. Yet the structure of a self-contained elementary school classroom, like the structure of "interdisciplinary" teams in middle and high schools, too often hides a schedule in which the first hour is for language arts, the second for arithmetic, the third for another area, and so on.

When the integration of knowledge is advocated in schools, it is usually argued on grounds that it makes knowledge more accessible or more meaningful by bringing it out of separate subject compartments and placing it in contexts that will supposedly make more sense to young people. A growing body of research evidence suggests that such *contextualizing* of knowledge *does* make it more accessible, especially when those contexts are linked to the life experiences of young people.

Important as this is, however, it is not the only argument for the integration of knowledge in curriculum organization. Foucault's work informed my insistence on grasping power-knowledge nexus. Knowledge is a dynamic instrument of individuals and groups to use in approaching issues in their lives. In that sense knowledge is a kind of power, since it helps give people some measure of control over their own lives. When knowledge is seen simply as a collection of bits and pieces of information and skill organized by separate subjects or disciplines of knowledge, its uses and its power are confined by their boundaries and thus diminished. For example, the definition of problems and the means of addressing them are limited to what is known and deemed problematic within a particular subject or discipline. When we understand knowledge as integrated, we are free to define problems as broadly as they are in real life and to use a wide range of knowledge to address them.

In this connection, I have discussed elsewhere the notion of intermediality. *Intermediality* illustrates a broader view of "knowing" (Semali & Pailliotet, 1999). Coming to grips with this notion, I argue that conceptions of situations from one's experiences, problems, and goals help shape individuals' knowledge, agendas, desires, and actions. In addition, the rise of mass media and technology in U.S. society and schools has led to new ways of looking at the world and how we construct meaning and what we "know." Our worldviews are shaped and influenced by the technology we use in our schools and homes—computers, automated teller machines, fax modems, digital television, cable, and a variety of gadgetry that continue to enter our lives subsequent to the invention of the microchip. These technologies have also impacted the way we make meaning of our lives, predict the ways of the world we live in, and how we communicate and receive information.

In a country as diverse as the United States and as well equipped with multiple forms of media, meaning cannot assume a universal formula but rather a multiform. To understand the form of any media text is to know the codes and conventions that lie beneath its meaning. Understanding where meanings come from and how meanings are produced is a matter of complex inquiry that raises questions about the power to construct and maintain a certain pattern of meanings and with what effects. Such inquiry shifts the attention away from the individual psychology of the producer to the rules that govern the readings of those who use the codes or conventions making up the media text.

Text includes any meaning-making devices such as verbal communication, images, pictures, media messages, motion pictures, music, and computer and other iconic texts. Context is usually what is not explicitly stated, commonly referring to its social context. For example, a strictly social interpretation tends to look outside of, as well as at the work being studied: Who is the artist? How was he or she placed in society? What are the cultural forces in the society in which the artist was raised and/or is working? What is the message of the visual statement in terms of political and social import? How can this message be evaluated using the prevailing values of the culture of the artist rather than the viewer? As facilitators, teachers need to help students take an exploratory stance to probe their relationship with media. This stance encourages students to raise issues and questions in response to media texts including the textbook. Furthermore, such a critical stance also helps students to penetrate the layers when they identify the symbols and understand their meaning and functions, when they analyze the structure and understand its power, when they articulate the meaning as (and whatever) it communicates to them within our social context.

The use of media conventions and putting the power of media languages into good use is known to leave readers and viewers mesmerized and for the most part invisible. This explains why some particular media texts draw and captivate our attention completely—a television show with a wide audience appeal, or a good book that once you start reading it, you cannot put it down. How can we help students to understand what goes on? What benefits could be drawn from questioning the relation of our position in the text? Will doing such an exercise deny students the pleasure in the media text?

Media conventions form part of our cultural knowledge. That is to say, we recognize with some familiarity when we hear certain music, see certain media images produced in a particular sequence or at a particular case, or relate to familiar actors and actresses and anticipate with nostalgia the story they are about to tell. This kind of familiarity gives us the ability to participate in the assumptions, or widespread beliefs and popular attitudes that form our cultural knowledge.

When we talk about a "worldview" we mean the *values hierarchy* created by media presentations to form a mythic reality that people buy into over a period of time. For example, the construction of such a worldview may be a result of news reports about a country, an ethnic or racial group of people, or an idea. In the United States, for instance, media presentations have often been influenced by world events as well as domestic social and political agendas such as the Vietnam War, the Gulf War, the wave of church burning in the South, the Oklahoma City bombing, the O.J. Simpson criminal and civil trials in Los Angeles, and recently the school shooting in Littleton, Colorado. In sum, such a worldview is based on fiction or nonfiction stories with certain fundamental assumptions about how the world operates.

Foregrounded here is the nature of media as pedagogical machines, which function in the defining of what counts as legitimate knowledge. But most theories of schooling have ignored the manner in which cultural institutions contain pedagogical practices that are as significant for learning as institutionalized education. As Corcoran (1994) notes, we need to widen our understanding of how we are taught, and how we learn, and how we know and this involves analyzing the pedagogy of popular forms. Certainly, the dominant educational medium of contemporary culture is television and the functioning of the pedagogical in this medium has a bearing of how education in general functions in our society. Lawrence Grossberg (1996, p. 94) demarcates the effective pedagogical terrain of popular culture, seeing it as operating and producing knowledge at three levels: (1) the production of common sense—"the multi-layered, fragmented collection of meanings, values, and ideas that we both inherit and construct and which largely define our taken-for-granted interpretations of the world; (2) the determination of our libidinal and affective lives; (the production of a site where our identities and experiences are constructed)."

It is from this critical standpoint that integrating critical media literacy in American classrooms becomes a process rather than an analytical skill of decoding content. Critical media literacy challenges educators to extend their contributions to students by designing curricula that draw on the full range of human ways of knowing. This implies that instead of preparing students for eventual literate behavior, teachers engage them in genuine acts of literacy right from the beginning and throughout the school career. It also implies that the language arts curriculum will not be fragmented into separate components for reading, composing, and editing, but rather will integrate these in meaningful ways while valuing students' experiences, particularly mass media experiences. Further, it implies that skills will be taught within the context of genuine reading as separate from writing, and of isolating grammar usage, spelling, and vocabulary. Teaching them as separate subjects is, in my opinion, misguided and counterproductive.

However, this is not to suggest that content is not important. Rather, I view content as an ongoing developmental process on the part of the learner. I am suggesting that content must be relevant to the experience of the learner. This is to say that larger process-related consideration should govern the selection of content. Thus, the idea of flexibility does not mean that teachers and students are free to do whatever they please, but rather that they are able to work out specific ways of bringing that framework to life. While there may be a great diversity across classroom situations, all would be engaged with the same general curriculum. In other words, coordination would be found in the framework for the curriculum rather than the details of its implementation. Applying this kind of critical mindedness in talking texts and making this the object of media literacy alters the central tenets of the dichotomous arguments of content perspective on disjoined curriculum instead of genuine integration. That is what critical media literacy provides.

Curriculum Level

The fourth level of integrating media literacy in American classrooms is at the curriculum level. The occasion for this could not be more timely due to the looming technological and media changes impacting our society

in recent years. Today, the media, defined broadly, have replaced textbooks as one of the most important producers of myths and symbols in
our society. In the past, students read cultural stories about dinosaurs in
science books, fairy tales, plays, novels, and poems. Today, students gain
most of their knowledge from Disney movies and *Jurassic Park*. In the
printed stories, authors took time to develop these myth-making genres
with such known conventions as the plot, the characters, and also put lots
of thought to the resolution of conflict. Today, television and movies
have in fact replaced years of storytelling familiar to children with a different language and way of telling stories. Throughout this telling, media
inform every subject area of the curriculum and reinforce students' notions of history, geography, scientific knowledge, bias, stereotypes, and
truth. To this equation is now added the Internet and a wide proliferation
of Web sites. Because media are pervasive in our culture and are present
throughout the curriculum, as such, it is imperative that mass media are
studied across all subject areas. Even though most media educators
would prefer a gradual introduction of media literacy to avoid bombardment and overwhelming teachers, I advocate a total curriculum integration across all subject areas. Teachers in all subject areas must ask
students to take a hard look at what TV tells them about history, science,
geography, and people's culture.

The question that remains is where to locate the media literacy program in the curriculum. This is a major concern of curriculum developers. Agencies and proponents of media literacy across the curriculum
usually recommend that it be included in the language arts or social studies curriculum in the elementary school. On the secondary level, they
suggest that media literacy skills should be included in the social studies
curriculum or in a separate elective course. An alternative approach
would involve the integration of critical media literacy with the total
K–12 curriculum. I advocate a total curriculum integration for obvious
reasons.

As described earlier, the design named "curriculum integration" has
several features that, when taken together, distinguish it from other approaches. First, the curriculum is organized around problems and issues
that are of personal and social significance in the real world. Second,
learning experiences in relation to the organizing center are planned so
as to integrate pertinent knowledge in the context of the organizing centers. Third, knowledge is developed and used to address the organizing
center currently under study rather than to prepare for some later test or
grade level. In this approach, emphasis is placed on substantive projects

and other activities that involve real application of knowledge, thus increasing the possibility for young people to integrate curriculum experiences into their schemes of meaning and to experience the democratic process of problem solving.

James Beane adds one more, namely the participation of students in curriculum planning. If integrative learning is a serious intention, it is important to know how young people might frame the issues and concerns that are used to organize the curriculum as well as what experiences they believe might help them learn (Hopkins, 1941). It is hard to imagine how adults might find about how any particular group of young people view these matters without somehow consulting them directly. As noted by Beane (1997), since curriculum integration is tied to the larger concept of democratic education, the matter of student participation in planning their own experiences must eventually become a crucial aspect of the design.

Traditional educators have ignored involving students in curriculum planning, the critique of schooling, the analysis of social conditions, and ideological contexts for so long that it is not natural for teachers to incorporate such contexts in readings or classroom discussions. The kinds of inquiry advocated and described in this book stand apart from the objective and depoliticized analysis employed by both liberal and conservative educators who have adopted the viewer-response and active-viewer approaches in their classrooms without taking a critical pedagogy approach. Therefore, when we talk about inquiry as part of curriculum integration and classroom instruction, we refer to a holistic and interconnected process where teachers and students question, reflect, and act on what they have learned to change their social conditions. On the one hand, questioning throughout the curriculum does not mean only seeking answers. Rather, it means a pursuit of deeper meaning by asking questions that generate more questions about all texts and contexts students read, including the institutions that produce them.

On the other hand, reflection is neither separate from inquiry nor something that can be neatly packaged as a set of techniques for teachers to use. Reflection provides teachers and students with space to step back and analyze and apply meanings from texts to the social contexts they live in. When Dewey talked about the concept of reflection in his book *How We Think* (1933), he was urging educators to divorce their actions from routine, impulse, tradition, and authority. By confronting what is often taken for granted as a matter of routine, definitions of reality and traditional conventions are questioned. According to Dewey, as long as we continue to follow routine and not critique our actions or perceptions, we are likely to fall into the trap of perceiving reality as unproblematic and therefore immune to critique. Such a situation may well serve as an obstacle to recognizing valuable alternative viewpoints. As will be made evident in Vignette 2 at the end of this chapter, reflective practice is a controversial practice to some teachers. In this vignette, a teacher reflects on her teaching philosophy in which she presents very strong reservations about Dewey's notions of open-mindedness and what it means to be tolerant as a step toward finding out all the facts and avoiding to rush to judgment or subscribing to only "one" regimen of truth.

It is important to note that although conceptions of teaching as the reflective practice of a profession has historical precedence, some teachers think its framework is suspect. Often such suspicions and the underlying assumptions are not examined and there is no political will to do so systematically. I suspect that the stakes are high for those teachers who see themselves as technicians instead of reflective practitioners. I suspect that their unwillingness to try may well be embedded in a larger set of beliefs that are circumscribed by their own context—social, political, cultural, and the position a teacher occupies in the academic institution as well as the institution's relation with the larger community. Suffice it to say, therefore, that even though reflective practice has been discussed in scholarly publications since the time of Dewey, teachers are still skeptical and many are unwilling to try. (See Vignette 2 at the end of this chapter.) Some teachers have told me that they do not want to give up their authority as teachers. Students must be shown what to learn and be made accountable for what they learn. They feel that just as the authority of parents in the face of children cannot be compromised, so must teachers be in front of their students. The fear seems to hinge upon the fact that once the fundamentals of schooling—relations of power, privilege, and authority of the teacher, the assumptions of schooling, the impinging social structures, and the goals of education as well as the techniques for reaching those goals—are critiqued and criticized, such an effort erodes the institution and does more harm than enhance curriculum, instruction, and learning.

Reflective practitioners or professionals do not shy away from critical evaluation of their actions. They examine these broader issues, as well as the immediate practical concerns of classroom teaching. For example, teachers can question the goals, the effects, and the social context of schooling in a way that will allow them to make conscious their contribution to the agenda of schooling and the achievement of that agenda.

My experience in teaching preservice teachers indicates that teacher education programs often fail to prepare aspiring teachers to be reflective, or to respond—in ways that are consistent with their values—to the social, political, and educational contexts that circumscribe their work. I know faculty in our teacher education program who encourage students to examine the underlying assumptions, values, goals, and consequences of schooling rather than focus narrowly and exclusively on the most efficient means of reaching taken-for-granted ends. But I have often been frustrated by the fact that there is relatively little dialogue within or across the several disciplines that contributes to teacher education, and many courses fail to grapple with such issues, fostering a conception of teaching as a technical occupation with a concentration on ways to present the required curriculum. And this situation has become even more entrenched because of the pressures to use multimedia technology.

A more disturbing fact is that there are still those of us who still believe that the curriculum represents a regiment of truth and facts to be memorized and that science and mathematics provide the basis of irrefutable theorems and maxims that students must learn. A critique of this position has been well documented by Kincheloe and Steinberg. In their book *Unauthorized Methods* (1998), they devote a whole chapter to digging up the history and critique of modernism, reductionism, and positivism (see pp. 1–23.). In the next chapter, I will take up the arguments of some poststructuralists when they critique notions of "truth" and how it has become the central niche in curriculum development. However, teachers need to be reminded of the critique put forward by Zeichner and Liston when they discuss reflective practice. They emphatically state that teachers need to recognize that there is more than one way to frame the problem. Zeichner and Liston (1996, p. 9) list five key features of a reflective teacher. A teacher who is a reflective practitioner (1) examines, frames, and attempts to solve dilemmas of classroom practice; (2) is aware of and questions the assumptions and values he or she brings to teaching; (3) is attentive to the institutional and cultural contexts in which he or she teaches; (4) takes part in curriculum development and is involved in school change efforts; and (5) takes responsibility for his or her own professional development. In short, a reflective practitioner is one who is committed to transform the social conditions of the school and society. Zeichner and Liston sum up reflective teaching as a reflexive process that entails a "recognition, examination, and rumination over the implications of one's beliefs, experiences, attitudes, knowledge, and values as well as opportunities and constraints provided by the social conditions"

(p. 33). Even though these key features may not by any means be conclu-
sive, they offer some insights to teachers who wish to take a critical
stance in their teaching. However, we must reiterate that inquiry, reflection, and action do not consist of a series of steps or procedures to be
used by teachers. Rather it is a holistic way of meeting and responding to
problems, a way of being a teacher (Zeichner & Liston, 1996, p. 9).

INTEGRATING CRITICAL MEDIA LITERACY INTO TEACHER EDUCATION

By focusing upon our experience of media, teachers in all subject areas
can integrate media into instruction to discover how the media have
shaped students' perception and attitudes about individuals, institutions,
and issues. Integrating media literacy across the curriculum is part of a
curriculum reform designed to develop media as legitimate curricular
sites. In Pennsylvania, as elsewhere in the nation, for example, these initiatives stem from statewide efforts to promote integrated curricula to fit
current educational needs. They strive to enhance the critical experiences
in the existing *Pennsylvania Framework of Reading, Writing and Talking
across the Curriculum* in short, known as the *Pennsylvania Framework*
(Lytle & Botel, 1990).

The Pennsylvania Framework for language arts provides a resource
for integration that can be used by any teacher throughout the common-
wealth, of any subject, at any grade level, or by a group of teachers or a
group of school leaders and teachers to reflect upon, design, or redesign
their curricula and instructional practices. The Pennsylvania Framework
is based on the assumptions that meaning of "texts" is at the center of
learning, language is a social construction, the study of language arts is
interrelated, and that learning is part of human endeavor. These assumptions provide the basis for classroom practices labeled by the Pennsylvania Framework as "critical experiences." The five "critical experiences"
discussed in the Pennsylvania Framework are (1) reading, (2) writing,
(3) extending reading and writing, (4) investigating language, and (5)
learning to learn.

What is missing in these "critical experiences" is an explicit engagement of critical media literacy. Such engagement acknowledges the "intermedial" nature of the world students live in today. In this multimedia
world, technology and media have become part of the texts of their
everyday lives. What is also missing is the methodology to read and understand the new languages of media and produce meaning that enhances

lives and rejects the oppressive nature that privileges some students and denies other students voice. Collaborative and innovative processes are already underway to involve classroom teachers, educational specialists, administrators, university faculty, arts and media experts, and students in reflecting on theory and practice in order to design, develop, and implement a statewide integrated curricular framework of critical media literacy education. For example, in keeping with the Pennsylvania outcome-based education goals for communication, these media literacy initiatives recognize the need to expand the integrative model envisaged in the Pennsylvania Framework to ensure that all students, kindergarten through grade 12, acquire the ability to understand how visual media and particularly visuals represented in the mass media work to produce meanings. Eventually, the outcomes of this effort aim to produce a resource curricular framework that strives to develop a literate person who is able to read, write, listen, talk, analyze, evaluate, and produce alternative communications in a variety of media inclusive of print, television, music, video, film, radio, compact disk, hypertext for personal computers, and the arts. However, the implementation of a statewide curricular initiative will require the support of teachers and administrators because it makes sense to the overall curriculum. But then, who can deliver such a program in classrooms and fill the apparent gap in the Pennsylvania Framework or in other statewide frameworks in the nation?

One way to fill this gap is to implement critical pedagogy in teacher preparation colleges and classrooms. Educators and administrators need to become aware of media literacy in general, and must address in particular the relationship between media representation and the construction of knowledge in media. The myth that the accepted conventions of film, video, and photographic representation are mere neutral carriers devoid of content implications no longer holds ground.

The education of teachers should include integrated materials providing an education in mass information ranging from the preschool to the university and even to the adult-education age. During these courses, teacher trainees would acquire the knowledge and competencies that would enable them to teach their students, or at least familiarize them with the process of evaluating knowledge obtained through the visual arts and mass media. The process would also include systematizing this knowledge and integrating it into the knowledge obtained at school. As facilitators, teachers would help students take an exploratory stance to probe their relationship with media. This would encourage students to raise issues and questions in response to media texts, including textbooks, and to recognize statements of bias and inconsistencies and to judge the validity of evidence.

In an attempt to design curricula that integrate critical media literacy, I have initiated a media literacy course at the Pennsylvania State University for preservice teachers. Offered every semester, this course focuses on language and literacy education. The overall outlook of this course is to develop systematic educational inquiry approaches and models of critique, decoding, analyzing, and of reading visual images of women, minorities, foreign people, ethnic people, and other groups in the American society, embedded in visual and media messages, in order to recognize stereotypes, derogatory bias, and discrimination, and to understand how these images represent various groups in society. Such analysis is not limited to TV and films only but is extended to other multimedia forms of representation. Students are encouraged to examine the inequalities in knowledge and power that exist between those who manufacture information in their own interests and those who consume it as news and entertainment.

HOW TO INTEGRATE CRITICAL MEDIA LITERACY ACROSS THE CURRICULUM

For many years the accepted method of teaching English was to focus on a balance of reading literature (usually from the classic canon), writing term papers, and learning rules of spelling and grammar. In our multimedia society, it is becoming necessary to expand the definition of literature to include the vast amount of information permeating the world of students through television, magazines, computers, music, and movies. Our students' notion of text is expanding beyond the printed page to include an identifiable production or publication, an ad for Coca-Cola, an issue of *Seventeen* magazine, a billboard for Budweiser beer, pictures on a front page of the local newspaper.

In the past, textual analysis was used in the classroom to analyze the printed texts. Students analyzed stories, plays, poems, essays, and novels. But with recent proliferation of multimedia products and their different kinds of texts, this literary analysis in classrooms has remained limited to response-centered transactional approaches. Teachers using these approaches are often content in claiming that they are integrating media literacy in the classroom when they design activities involving visual media. Such activities include the design of charts, logs, and exercises to compare print and film versions of a novel and so on.

Such activities strive to ensure that content is mastered by encouraging students to take copious notes; pause to ask questions; and keep track of main events; and notable literary, dramatic, or cinematic aspects. Within this method, critical reading or viewing is confined to literary or artistic analysis. Even though this method calls for students to be active viewers—paying close attention to film details, writing down immediate responses, discussing interpretations with fellow students and supporting opinions with evidence from the film—such analysis rarely moves beyond the content of the visual imagery or beyond the ability to simply remember and understand visual information. Media texts are treated like pieces of literature; students typically spot themes, do a chart, fill out a log, complete worksheets, make a list, or write a response, neglecting a critical analysis of media with greater understanding of ways to build students' critical, reflective connections between the world of the school and the media culture that they experience in their daily lives. Unfortunately, this approach is far from what I have described in this chapter as genuine integration.

A genuine integration of critical media literacy in the classroom must enable students to bolster skills and knowledge they need to be able to consciously reflect on their interactions with media. It will enable them to address injustices; become critical actors committed to combat problems of youth apathy, violence, substance abuse, and rampant consumerism; and generate a strong commitment to develop a world free of oppression and exploitation. Linking critical media literacy with social concerns affirms what it means to be educated and to be media literate in an increasingly multimedia world in which information gathering and circulation processes thrive on the distortion, stereotyping, and manipulation of media spectacles. However, the question remains: How do you integrate critical media literacy across the curriculum? in your classroom? in the unit you are teaching this week? Many authors have attempted to respond to this question. In recent years, there have been several books that attempt to forge frameworks that address integration. In the chapters that follow, I will try to provide examples of such frameworks to illustrate this process. However, first and foremost, I need to address what I call inappropriate or misconceived notions of integration. I do this not to be reckless but to show how some of the examples fall short of what could otherwise be an enriching curriculum experience of media literacy. In this regard, I will discuss two books by John Davies (1996) and Teasley & Wilder (1997), which specifically address the issue of integration. For example, Davies (1996) talks about integrating media literacy into the content areas by giving an example of language arts, and he states as follows:

> Studying media literacy in language arts is a natural. The National Council of Teachers of English has been at the forefront of promoting media studies for decades. Many of the books included on reading lists for students of all grade levels are also available on video. Language arts teachers can approach movies from any number of angles by combining the use of literature and film. With modest background reading, teachers can be ready to provide an overview of the formal features of film. The most direct approach is to compare these two media. Before viewing the films, some basic formal features of films can be explored. Students can then decide how these features affect the message and impact the film. This kind of lesson can be a powerful tool for helping students to understand visual imagery, which is such an important part of today's culture. One of the goals of language arts is to help students appreciate and use the power of the written word. As noted previously, advertisers are very adept at using language and, therefore can provide still another avenue for exploring the power of language.

The ideals expressed by Davies on integration seem to focus on content rather than process. To operationalize his thinking about "integration," Davies provides examples in Chapter 10 of his book. His analogy of curriculum as a "suitcase" explains the difference from a genuine integration. Davies follows a content rather than a process approach to media literacy. His choice of language also makes his "suitcase" model and content-based curricular approach explicit. For example, when he says:

> . . . a careful evaluation of existing curricular objectives will yield opportunities for those "teachable moments" where introducing media literacy into a lesson can be done in such a way that teaching other curricular objectives can be accomplished more creatively. At the middle and high school levels media literacy can even be taught as an elective or an exploratory as well. (p. 205)

Even though Davies cautions that he has no intention to present a detailed media literacy curriculum, but rather to identify the basic components of a media literacy program at the elementary, middle, and high school levels, it is important to point out here that what he presents as his own and as ideas borrowed from Lloyd-Kolkin and Tyner confirm his basic idea of what media literacy in the classroom ought to be. For example, he explains in the introduction of his book:

> The media then provide a vast laboratory of helping students to become thinkers in the deepest sense and all that means in terms of character, responsible citizenship, and the other aims of education. Only by recognizing that media literacy represents both a responsibility, as well as an opportunity for educators, will these much needed skills find their way into the curriculum. (p. xvi)

The ideals expressed by Davies in this introduction and throughout his book fail to provide a framework of how to go about integration. How do you do it? How can the curriculum help students become responsible citizens? How can the curriculum assume a greater role in the development of moral character in today's youth, youth who will resist racial and gender bias and stereotyping, and youth who will reject the manipulation and distorted view about racial relations that the media consistently portray in its infotainment? Learning how to learn, understanding and respecting people of other cultures, appreciating the arts and their contributions to our daily lives, learning to resolve conflicts, and valuing learning for learning's sake are central to a critical media literacy project.

Elsewhere, I have expressed my thoughts about this approach (Semali & Hammett, 1999). For example, Davies provides a media activity chart by grade level. I find this very useful to make students aware of what goes on in the construction of media messages, visuals, symbols, signs, and genres (pp. 207–208). He also advocates including in a media literacy curriculum issues such as family relationships (as in TV soaps), minority and ethnic groups, gender portrayals, social problems, sexuality, and various professions such as teaching, law enforcement, medicine, and politics. We agree with Davies that it is a good thing for students to explore which groups are rarely seen on television, for example, the handicapped and the elderly, and discuss why this is so. We find this to be problematic if these activities are to be understood as an end in themselves. Unless the teacher is able to integrate these activities and ideas with what else is going on in the classroom or school in terms of race or gender relations or inequity, and unless the media program is part of diverse texts that students are introduced and challenged to grapple with, critical literacy, which is the core reason for media literacy, is not likely take place in the curriculum. What is likely to occur is that such activities will remain isolated, fragmented, and unlikely to help students connect what they learn in class with the social, political, and cultural realities around them.

Conceptualized this way, media literacy will be simply an add-on subject matter or busy work. It will not be different from what is taught in some media studies, workshop, or introductory communication courses. We do not object to helping students acquire a basic understanding of the media. Students should be encouraged to seek this in out-of-school programs as well. However, we are concerned whether teachers can meaningfully integrate media literacy as a process of reading texts—all kinds of texts—across the school curriculum. How do teachers begin to talk about "the privatization of information" as suggested by Davies, in an English literature or language arts class? Where does this fit in the lesson they will deal with on Monday morning? How does a teacher bring a critical pedagogy across the curriculum? How does a teacher begin the process of integrating critical media literacy? Where does this critical media literacy fit in today's curriculum?

Even though Davies assures his readers that all of the activities present in this chapter can be translated into instruction "in such a way that objectives in the core curriculum are not compromised," he does not go far enough to show how this can be done (p. 206). A list of media to be explored within the context of media literacy—television, film, radio, popular music, music videos, advertising, newspapers, the news media, and magazines—is appropriate but not enough. And we should not give teachers the false impression that it is easy to accomplish integration. In fact, what Davies suggests might inhibit teachers instead of encourage them. For example, his comparative list of the different disciplines of language arts, social studies, and math reiterate what we call the content-based approach (pp. 253–256). Suggesting an interdisciplinary curricular approach might help to establish the interconnectedness of the subject matter and bring to view real-life situations. Casting "what to do" in such general terms, as suggested by a middle school administrator like Davies, illustrates further how the school curriculum continues to be fragmented. A curricular framework that integrates critical media literacy prompts students and teachers to take a critical stance when they *read*, *view*, and *think* about textual or media representations by applying the following process: (1) scrutinize their initial understandings of textual and media representations; (2) engage in a critique of their own ideologically-mediated perceptions of the situation described or inscribed in the text in question; and (3) sort out "truths" from half-truths, accuracies from inaccuracies, facts from fiction, reality from myth, and objectivity from bias.

The second example I consider important to look at is Teasley and Wilder's book: *Reel Conversations*. In their chapter "Film across the Curriculum," they attempt to illustrate how to integrate film analysis in the classroom. In this regard, I think they failed to articulate a critical approach, opting instead to repeat the "active viewing strategies (p. 115) advocated in earlier chapters of their book, even though they criticize current practices of using films in content areas only as fillers and rewards to students' work. They effectively argue a number of reasons for developing effective strategies for using films, and occasionally suggest such critical activities as discussing "the filmmaking techniques used to convey the information and . . . whether the makers of the film are themselves expressing opinions or biases, whether they are openly or subtly persuading the viewer to believe the truths they are expressing" (p. 117). Such suggestions for the study of documentaries are not consistently added to questions about other films. For example, the guide questions "What information or characters are presented in a close-up?" and "Which characters or objects are viewed with high- or low-angle shots?" (p. 119) are not followed by questions that ask why viewers are being thus positioned in relation to these characters or what is the political/power project here. In other words, explicitly critical questions are not always being asked. (See a more detailed discussion of this point in Chapter 4.)

When I suggest that teachers integrate media literacy across the curriculum, I hope they will make the effort to develop the connections between disciplines, bridging gaps and crossing borders between disciplines. As acknowledged by educators who advocate a critical pedagogy in classrooms (Mantsios, 1992; Rose, 1992), the fragmented curriculum of most schools inhibits dialogue or a critical examination of social, political, and cultural realities around students. Few courses ask students to connect what they learn in class with the social, political, and cultural realities around them, and fewer still try to link these realities to students' personal experiences (Colombo, Cullen, & Lisle, 1992, p. vii). By embracing and integrating critical media literacy across the curriculum in every subject, students will be challenged to find meaning in what they learn and make sense of the world, rather than seeing school as an empty exercise or cynical game played for grades.

WHO WILL IMPLEMENT INTEGRATION
OF MEDIA LITERACY?

The first step in the implementation process focuses on those who will be
the vital link between the curriculum and the children, and the curriculum
and the parents, namely the teachers. Staff development is paramount.
Attempts to bring together preservice and in-service teachers during the
summer for workshops every year are important initiatives to initiate dialogue between the new and veteran teachers. Workshops that engage
teachers in media literacy activities are deemed essential in the interim.
Teachers are encouraged to be wise users of television themselves, or, at
the very least, aware of the languages of media and the principles underlying the discriminating use of television. They need to be informed of
the ways in which critical uses of television and other media can enhance
their curricular goals in the classroom, and of the necessary skills involved. Above all, a strong and enthusiastic commitment to such a program is required of those who will be the leaders in this endeavor.

Second, administrators, curriculum specialists, and teachers must
judiciously examine the many different program thrusts and formats that
are currently on the market labeled "media literacy." A careful selection
of these programs is important. Not all media literacy advocates would
like to see the integration of critical media literacy in classrooms. Some
of these educators are afraid of a politicized cadre of students within the
walls of their classrooms. Furthermore, curriculum integration is still
seen as busy work, not worth more than that label. Several books and
curriculum materials out there talk about promoting critical thinking
skills but never address the basic idea of what it means to be "critical."
These kinds of contradictions are confusing at best to novice teachers.

Third, strong parental involvement is dictated. Critical media literacy will have little chance of success if parents do not endorse and embrace it wholeheartedly. They need to be aware of, for example, some of
the devastating effects of indiscriminate television use on children and
adolescents. At the same time, they need to be made conscious of the potential of television for enhancing learning. They will need to understand
the programs that the school has adopted and be knowledgeable about
ways in which they can be "implementers" in the home. Since most television viewing is done at home, an active and cooperative relationship
between home and school is crucial. In the final analysis, creating a
classroom environment that encourages discussion, questioning, probing, and pondering will go a long way toward fostering critical minded-

ness. And, media literacy offers that opportunity. Schools that do not integrate media into the curriculum abandon motivated children and adolescents to potential media manipulation and fail to provide them with skills necessary to understand the impact of media in a multimedia society like the United States.

To become a literate person in America today calls for new ways of teaching to allow students the ability to solve day-to-day problems in the home and workplace and to access and understand the world around them from the multiple and changing perspectives. The new concept of critical media literacy challenges the traditional definition of what it is to be literate by emphasizing the importance of all forms of texts and broadening students' ability to analyze and communicate information effectively. It is important, therefore, to keep in mind that the texts that students read in classrooms, as well as processes for understanding and constructing them, are interconnected. Readers/writers/audiences do not create meaning in isolation. Instead, they draw from experiences of other texts connecting past and present. This synergy of texts and meaning makes the case for us to embrace curriculum integration that cuts across the individual's experiential, social, and knowledge construction levels. Incorporating multiple media representations and multiperspectives provides that integration that students are seeking—to bring together many parts of their lives into a whole.

CONCLUDING COMMENTS

In this chapter, I have defined critical media literacy as a viable means of introducing students to critical reading and critical thinking skills. I have also explained why media literacy can be a valuable pedagogical site to carry out genuine curriculum integration. Although educators in many schools recognize the gains offered by curriculum integration, the majority of students have not developed the needed aptitudes and habits for genuine curriculum integration in which they find easy connections between schoolwork and everyday solutions for their problems. A genuine curriculum integration in a critical media literacy project involves applying knowledge to questions and concerns that have personal and social significance to adolescent students.

I have discussed that essentially news events, advertising, talk shows, MTV, and the interactive nature of network computers, brought to students by the Internet, form a significant portion of their media knowledge. Their daily talk, thoughts, use of language, and experiences manifest this new phenomenon. These media knowledges have made it possible for some teachers to be freed to explore and access borderless knowledge that was unreachable decades ago, and enables students in one state to link up conversations with other students in other states and in other disciplines or countries. As we enter the twenty-first century, teachers must realize that we live in a world of multiple literacies in which knowledge can be understood as a form of meaning-making. Such knowledge production consists of both our cognitive engagement with affective investment in various media forms that represent the multimedia nature of our culture. In spite of these advances in technology, we must recognize that media knowledge constitutes possibilities for human agency as well as textual barriers placed on teachers as individuals who deal in the printed text, codes, social texts, and the "semiotic circuitry" of classrooms and everyday life. As individuals, teachers constantly play the role of meaning-manufacturers making cultural life in terms of understanding whose stories are visible and whose stories lie buried in established archives of history read in classrooms every day by our students.

We must take a hard look at what the media tell us about education, about teachers, about learning, and about students' learning habits. Because the media are no longer windows of the world, nor objective representations of our world, they have become legitimate pedagogical sites of critique, analysis, and learning for most adolescents in American living rooms. The materials presented by the media are subjective and sometime loaded with social biases, regarding race, class, sexual orientation, gender, and ethnic differences. They have become significant areas for educating viewers. For this reason, media literacy needs to be counted as a critical pedagogical tool for examining media messages and institutions. By the same token, teachers can no longer divorce their subject matter from the world in which their students live. Teachers cannot rely on decontextualized "skills" and "activities" that have no relevance to large issues. Teacher must strive to recognize and encourage links between their curriculum and historical events, political events, cultural traditions, and popular media forms.

Teachers must encourage students to question, reflect, and take action on the issues that emanate from the readings and viewing they undertake every day at school and at home. A story on slavery cannot be understood as frozen in the past, but rather as a topic that stimulates thinking about slavery in the past and slavery today, and leads to some actions that address what students can do about it in their context. Slavery is a term avoided in school curricula because for many educators it conjures up a sense of discomfort on account of our past history with slavery. Progressive teachers have seized the opportunity to use slavery as a metaphor for the variety of oppressive situations still prevalent within different sectors of this society, particularly within contexts of racial relations. It is bold to speak of these relationships, since silence and compliance are so critical in maintaining them. But it is in the course of speaking about oppression that we learn even more about how and why oppression persists in a civilized and democratic country like ours. Oppressive relations serve the exploitative needs of oppression and maintenance of privilege—to appropriate or exploit the resources of those they oppress, whether it be land, minerals, water, taxes, or people. While force is often applied to impose these oppressive relations, ideology (through the means of mass media) attempts to convince people of the appropriateness of their respective roles.

Ideology also functions to reinforce unequal or oppressive relations of power. Detecting the ideology of oppressive social relations is a critical step toward changing them. And critical media literacy takes that critical step seriously. Action must be distinguished from activities. Action is what students do to change an oppressive situation. Activities are enterprises they engage in to understand the dimensions of a situation. It is clear from the summary of these examples and arguments advanced in this chapter that media literacy stands out as an alternative approach to integrated learning formulated within a postmodern framework and agenda suited to our multimedia environment and as an appropriate response to the looming information superhighway.

VIGNETTE 2

According to John Dewey, the definition of reflective teaching includes open-mindedness, responsibility, and wholeheartedness. As a future educator, I disagree with Dewey's perspectives, as I do not fall under the category of a reflective teacher based on his terms. First and foremost, I refute Dewey's beliefs because the Bible challenges me as a believer "so that [my] faith might not rest on men's wisdom, but on God's power" (1 Corinthians, 2:5). Therefore, I subscribe myself to the "Sophisticated believer" of Dewey's categories, who "are interested in knowing opposing points of view, but only for the purpose of refuting them. Sophisticated believers are still not open to the possibility that their own belief system might be flawed" (Zeichner & Liston, 1996, p. 10). In other words, if an opinion does not match up with the Word of God, I will not support it in my classroom.

I am not as open-minded as Dewey is or my college professors would like for me to be, but I bear the responsibility that Dewey projects. Dewey states that "responsible teachers ask themselves why they are doing what they are doing in a way that goes beyond questions of immediate utility to consider the ways in which it is working, why it is working, and for whom it is working" (Zeichner & Liston, 1996, p. 11). I know that my actions in the Christian school classroom will stand for the Glory of God. In the gospel of Matthew (28:18–20), "Jesus came to them and said, 'All authority in heaven and on earth has been given to me. Therefore go and make disciples of all nations . . . and teaching them to obey everything I have commanded you.'" I believe it is my responsibility as a Christian and as a teacher to accept this commission to advance the kingdom of God. I know without a doubt the motivations for which I will lead my Christian classroom.

Finally, Dewey defines the wholeheartedness of the reflective teacher and how it impacts the class. He says "that open-mindedness and responsibility must be central components in the professional life of the reflective teacher" (Zeichner & Liston, 1996, p. 11). I will not be a wholehearted teacher because I lack the open-mindedness that Dewey claims to be crucial. However, I will have more love for my students than any non-Christian teacher will in a secular classroom. First Corinthians 13:2 states, "If I have the gift of prophecy and can fathom all mysteries and all knowledge, and if I have a faith that can move mountains, but have not love, I am nothing." The Bible does not preach wholeheartedness as essential, but love! Therefore, I believe I qualify as a reflective teacher regardless of Dewey's philosophies because God's word says that if I lack love, then I have nothing. I believe love is defined by 1 Corinthians chapter thirteen.

I hope this provides a greater insight as to why I will not rely on Dewey's wisdom so that I may be a "critical believer" or a reflective teacher. The creed of the reflective teacher opposed my faith in God that daily impacts my life. I believe that by instilling these beliefs in my students, I will be fulfilling the Great Commission as stated in Matthew (28:18–20) above by Jesus Christ himself. I will simply be conveying to them the importance of obeying God's commands. After all, this is a Christian environment, which means that students will attend my class with an understanding of what is to be expected.

I believe that I may enlighten my students with advice for issues such as racial and gender bias by using the Bible as texts in class. According to the Word of God, we are all viewed equally, but it is society that tells us otherwise. Psalm 96:10 proclaims: "say among the nations, 'The Lord Reigns.' The world is firmly established, it cannot be moved; he will judge the peoples with equity." In order to remind my students that we are all equal in God's sight, I think Psalm 96:10 exemplifies the virtues they should live by. The verse begins with an address to the nations, or all people regardless of race, class, or gender. It concludes by saying that we are all equal. A lesson from the Bible will give students a point of reference to base their beliefs upon and eliminate biases.

—Laura

- How would you respond to this teacher about her idea of reflective practice?
- Can reflective practice be taught? How do you teach someone to be open-minded? To imagine and value points of view different from his or her own?
- How might you show her that a critical pedagogy approach to literacy is multiperspectival, multicultural, and multidimensional?
- How could her ideas be different from a critical perspective?
- How could she help her students gain those critical perspectives needed for the twenty-first century, even in a Christian school?

REFERENCES

Apple, M. (1982). *Education and power.* Boston: Routledge.

Apple, M., & Beane, J. (1995). *Democratic schools.* Alexandria, VA: Association of Supervision and Curriculum Development.

Banks, J. (1989). *Multicultural education: Issues and perspectives.* Boston: Allyn and Bacon.

Barthes, R. (1974). *S/Z* (Miller, Richard, Trans.). New York: Hill and Wang/The Noonday Press.

Beane, J. (1997). *Curriculum integration. Designing the core of democratic education.* New York: Teachers College Press.

Bellack, A., & Kliebard, H. (1971). Curriculum for integration of disciplines. In L. C. Deighton (Ed.), *The encyclopedia of education* (pp. 585–590). New York: Macmillan.

Bhaktin, M. M. (1988). Intertexuality. In T. Todorov (Ed.), *Mikhail Bakhtin: The dialogical principle* (pp. 60–74). Minneapolis: University of Minnesota Press.

Bissex, G. (1980). *Guys at work.* Boston: Harvard University Press.

Brand, A. G. (1987). The why of cognition: Emotion and the writing process. *College Composition and Communication, 38*(4), 436–443.

Britton, J. (1985). Viewpoints: The distinction between participant and spectator role. *Research in the Teaching of English, 18*(3), 320–331.

Calkins, L. (1983). *Lessons from a child*. Portsmouth: Heinemann.

Cazden, C., Green, J., & Wallace, C. (1992). Critical language awareness in the EFL classroom. In N. Fairclough (Ed.), *Critical language awareness* (pp. 52–92). London: Longman.

Cheyney, A. B. (1992). *Teaching reading skills through the newspaper* (3rd ed.). Newark: International Reading Association.

Childs, J., & Dewey, J. (1933). The social-economic situation and education. In W. H. Kilpatrick et al., *The educational frontier* (pp. 32–72). New York: Century.

Colombo, G., Cullen, R., & Lisle, B. (1992). *Rereading America: Cultural contexts for critical thinking and writing*. New York: St. Martin's Press.

Considine, D. M. (1987). Visual literacy and the curriculum: More to it than meets the eye. *Language Arts, 64*(6): 34–40.

———, & Haley, G. E. (1992). *Visual messages. Integrating imagery into instruction*. Englewood, CO: Teachers Ideas Press.

———, Haley, G. E., & Lacy, L. E. (1994). *Imagine that: Developing critical thinking and critical viewing through children's literature*. Englewood, CO: Teacher Ideas Press.

Cooper, M. (1986). The ecology of writing. *College Composition and Communication, 36*(3): 364–375.

Corcoran, B. (1994). Balancing reader response and cultural theory and practice. In B. Corcoran, M. Hayhoe, & G. Pradl (Eds.), *Knowledge in the making: Challenging the text in the classroom*. Portsmouth, NH: Boynton/Cook/Heinemann.

Davies, J. (1966). *Educating students in a media saturated culture*. Lancaster, PA: Technomic Publishing, 1996.

Dobbs, B. (1988). Video friend or foe: How to teach the reading of seeing. In R. Braden et al. (Eds.), *Readings of the 21st annual conference of the International Visual Literacy Association* (pp. 12–16). Blacksburg: Virginia Polytechnic Institute.

Dohrer, T. (1998). A textbook for everyone: Balancing canons and cultures in English textbooks. In J. Kincheloe & S. Steinberg (Eds.), *Unauthorized methods: Strategies for critical teaching*. New York: Routledge.

Dressel, P. (1958). The meaning and significance of integration. In N. Henry (Ed.), *The integration of educational experiences*. Chicago: Chicago University Press.

Duncan, B. (1997). Learn more about popular culture. *Telemedium 43*(2): 20.

———. (1993). Surviving education's desert storms: Adventures in media literacy—a retrospective and a guide for tomorrow. *Telemedium 39*(1–2): 13–17.

Elbow, P. (1985). The shifting relationship between speech and writing. *College Composition and Communication, 36*(3): 283–301.

Evans, E. (1987). Readers recreating texts. In B. Corcoran, & E. Evans (Eds.), *Readers, texts, teachers* (pp. 22–40). Portsmouth: Boynton/Cook.

Fairclough, N. (Ed.). (1992). *Critical language awareness.* London: Longman.

Fehlman, R. H. (1996). Viewing film and television as whole language instruction. *English Journal 85*(2), 43–50.

Fensham, P., Gunstone, R., White, R. B. (Eds.). (1994). *The content of science: A constructivist approach to teaching and learning.* London: Falmer Press.

Flood, J., & Lapp, D. (1995). Broadening the lens: Toward an expanded conceptualization of literacy. In K. A. Hinchman, D. J. Leu, & C. K. Kinzer (Eds.), *Perspectives on literacy research and practice: Forty-fourth yearbook of the National Reading Conference* (pp. 1–16). Chicago: National Reading Conference.

Flower, L. (19＿＿). Cognition, context, and theory building. *College Composition and Communication, 40*(3): 282–311.

Freire, P. (1985). *The politics of education.* Westport, CT: Bergin & Garvey.

———. (1970). *Pedagogy of the oppressed.* New York: Continuum.

Gee, J. (1996). *Social linguistics and literacies: Ideology in discourses* (2nd ed.). London: Taylor & Francis.

Giroux, H. (1981). Ideology, culture, and the process of schooling. Philadelphia: Temple University Press.

Goody, E. N. (1978). Towards a theory of questions. In E. N. Goody (Eds.), *Questions and politeness: Strategies in social interaction* (pp. 16–43). Cambridge: Cambridge University Press.

Grossberg, L. (1996). *The audience and its landscape.* Boulder, CO: Westview Press.

———. (1989). *We gotta get out of this place.* London: Routledge.

Hirsch, E. D. (1987). *Cultural literacy.* Boston: Houghton Mifflin.

Hobbs, R. (1994). "Channel One" undone. The Billerica Initiative brings media literacy to middle school. *Community Media Review,* Vol. 1, January.

Hopkins, L. T. (1941). *Interaction: The democratic process.* New York: Heath.

———, et al. (1937). *Integration: Its meaning and application.* New York: Appleton-Century.

Hyerle, D. (1996). *Visual tools for constructing knowledge.* Alexandria, VA: Association for Supervision and Curriculum Development.

Illich, I. (1971). Deschooling society. New York: Harper & Row.

Kellner, D. (1995). *Media culture: Cultural studies, identity and politics between the modern and the postmodern.* New York: Routledge.

Kilpatrick, W. (1934). The essentials of the activity movement. *Progressive Education, 11*: 346–359.

Kimpston, R. D., Williams, H. Y., & Stockton, W. S. (1992). Ways of knowing and the curriculum. *Educational Forum 56*(2): 153–172.

Kincheloe, J., & Steinberg, S. (Eds.) (1998). *Unauthorized methods. Strategies for critical teaching.* New York: Routledge.

Klein, J. T. (1990). *Interdisciplinary history, theory, and practice.* Detroit: Wayne State University Press.

Kress, G. (1988). *Communication and culture.* Kensington, NSW: University of New South Wales Press.

Kuhn, T. (1962). *The structure of scientific revolutions.* Chicago: University of Chicago Press.

Lester, P. M. (1995). *Visual communication: Images with messages.* Belmont, CA: Wadsworth.

Lickona, T. (1991). *Educating for character: How our schools can teach respect and responsibility.* New York: Bantam.

Lytle, S. L., & Botel, M. (1990). *The Pennsylvania Framework for reading, writing, and talking across the curriculum, PCRP II.* Pennsylvania Department of Education, Fourth Printing.

McCarthy, C. (1988). Rethinking liberal and radical inequality in schooling: Making the case for nonsynchrony. *Harvard Education Review, 58*(53): 265–279.

McLuhan, M. (1978). The brain and the media: The Western hemisphere. *Journal of Communication, 28*(4): 54–60.

———. (1964). *Understanding media: The extensions of man.* New York and Toronto: McGraw-Hill.

———. (1962). *The Gutenberg galaxy: The making of typographic man.* Toronto: University of Toronto Press.

McLuhan, M., & Fiore, Q. (1967). *The medium is the message.* New York: Random House.

McMahon, B., & Quin, R. (1993). Knowledge, power, and pleasure: Direction in media education. *Telemedium 39*(1–2): 18–22.

Mantsios, G. (1992). Class in America: Myths and reality. In G. Colombo, R. Cullen, & B. Lisle (Eds.), *Rereading America: Cultural contexts of critical thinking and writing* (2nd ed.). Boston: Bedford Books and St. Martin's Press.

Messaris, P. (1994). *Visual literacy: Image, mind & reality.* Boulder, CO: Westview Press.

Moline, S. (1995). *I see what you mean: Children at work with visual information.* York, ME: Stenhouse.

Neill, A. S. (1960). *Summerhill.* New York: Hart.

Neuman, S. B. (1991). *Literacy in the television age: The myth of the TV effect.* Norwood, NJ: Ablex.

Ong, W. (1986). Knowledge in time. In R. Gumpert & G. Cathcart (Eds.), *Inter/Media* (pp. 630–647). New York and Oxford: Oxford University Press.

Perl, S. (1980). Understanding composing. *College Composition and Communication: 31,* 363–369.

Pike, K., Compain, R., & Mumper, J. (1997). *New connections: An integrated approach to literacy* (2nd ed.). New York: Longman.

Reinking, D. (1995). Reading and writing with computers: Literacy research in a post-typographic world. In K. A. Hinchman, D. J. Leu, & C. K. Kinzer (Eds.), *Perspectives on literacy research and practice* (Vol. 44, pp. 17–33). Chicago: National Reading Conference.

Reutzel, D. R., & Cooter, R. B. (1992). *Teaching children to read: From basals to books.* New York: Merrill.

Rose, M. (1992). I just wanna be average. In G. Colombo, R. Cullen, & B. Lisle (Eds.), *Rereading America: Cultural contexts of critical thinking and writing* (2nd ed.). Boston: Bedford Books and St. Martin's Press.

Rosenblatt, L. (1978). *The reader, the text, the poem: The transactional theory of the literary work.* Carbondale: Southern Illinois University Press.

Schmidt, P. R. (1997). *Exploring values through literature with inquiry learning* (presentation). Atlanta, GA: Paper presentation at International Reading Conference Institute: Exploring values across the curriculum with mass media and literature.

Schnitzer, D. K. (1990). Integrating reading, writing, speaking, art, music, and the content areas: Animation in the classroom. In P. Kelly, & W. P. Self (Eds.), *Media and technology in the English language arts* (Vol. 40, pp. 25–29). Blacksburg, VA: Virginia Association of Teachers of English.

Semali, L. (1994). Rethinking media literacy in schools. *Pennsylvania Educational Leadership, 13*(2): 11–18.

Semali, L., & Pailliotet, A. (1999). *Intermediality: The teachers handbook of critical media literacy.* Boulder, CO: Westview.

Semali, L., & Hammett, R. (1999). Critical media literacy: Content or process? *The Review of Education/Pedagogy/Cultural Studies, 20*(4): 365–384.

Sholle, D., & Denski, S. (1993). Reading and writing the media: Critical media literacy and postmodernism. In C. Lankshear, & P. L. McLaren (Eds.), *Critical literacy: Politics, praxis, and the postmodern* (pp. 297–321). Albany: State University of New York Press.

Sinatra, R. (1990). Combining visual literacy, text understanding, and writing for culturally diverse students. *Journal of Reading, 33*(8), 612–617.

————. (1986). *Visual literacy connections to thinking, reading, and writing.* Springfield, IL: Charles C. Thomas.

Smith, F. (1984). Reading like a writer. In J. Jensen (Ed.), *Composing and comprehending* (pp. 47–56). Urbana, IL: National Council of Teachers of English.

Smith, M. (1927). *Education and the integration of behavior.* New York: Teachers College Press.

Teasley A. B., & Wilder, A. (1997). *Reel conversations: Reading films with young adults.* Portsmouth, NH: Heinemann, Boynton/Cook.

Watkin, M. (1994). A defense of using pop media in the middle school classroom. *English Journal, 83*(1): 30–33.

Watts Pailliotet, A. (1997). Questing toward cohesion: Connecting advertisements and classroom reading through visual literacy. In R. E. Griffin, J. M. Hunter, C. B. Schiffman, & W. J. Gibbs (Eds.), *Visionquest: Journeys toward visual literacy* (pp. 33–41). State College, PA: International Visual Literacy Association.

Werner W., & Nixon, K. (1990). *The media and public issues: A guide for teaching critical mindedness.* London, Ontario: Althouse Press.

Zeichner, K., & Liston, D. (1996). *Reflecting teaching.* Mahwah, NJ: Lawrence Erlbaum Associates.

CHAPTER 3

Foundations of Critical Media Literacy

The theory and practice of critical media literacy is grounded in critical pedagogy. From its inception, critical pedagogy, as envisioned by critical theorists, explores the quality of the present-day social and cultural environment as the condition of development for humanity and sees education as a political enterprise. The main objective of this approach is not to propagate a fixed set of prescriptive axioms or models. Rather, it is characterized by its commitment to the sociology of knowledge and the social critique of ideology. In other words, to be critical is to assume that humans are active agents whose reflective self-analysis and whose knowledge of the world leads to action that confronts old assumptions from the standpoint of new conditions.

In practice, critical pedagogy is essentially interested in abolishing injustice and attempts to show how repressive interests are hidden by supposedly neutral formulations of science, myths, or grand narratives. This theoretical approach opposes all attempts to construct a fixed system or to identify subject with object. Critical pedagogy rejects the claim both that objectivity is possible and that only measurable entities are of interest in the field of education. Thus, the classic school textbook and test are tools, which have limited value, even in yesteryear's world. They are most often contextualized within a view of knowledge as objective, outside the individual, and beyond the shared experience of students' social community—which make textbooks a terrain of struggle in emerging theory of society in a continuing dialogue with pragmatism and other competing social theories.

The search and attempts to implement this critical pedagogy in media literacy are recent. Humanistic literary interests in language, symbols, and communication triggered the study for much of the late 1950s to the present. In fact, notions of democracy and the impact of technology have guided the history of communication theory and research in the United States that in turn have influenced the founding of the media literacy movement. As a form of curriculum inquiry, critical media literacy provides teachers and students a framework of principles around which action can be discussed rather than a set of procedures or skills. Its method is based on critical inquiry that leads to action without a preconceived idea of the exact path the inquiry (or questioning) will take. Such inquiry serves as a methodology to identify and unpack the forces that perpetuate injustice and maintain privilege among select groups and inequalities in society through media productions and classroom texts. For example, what teachers and students read and view in printed texts and visual images, respectively, are shaped by particular worldviews, values, political perspectives, conceptions of race, class, gender relations, definitions of intelligence, and so on. Since critical theory, from which critical media literacy draws its *raison d'être*, is grounded on a recognition of the existence of oppression, it stands to reason that the forces of such oppression become the objective of a critical media literacy analysis. Critical media literacy, therefore, enables students to investigate injustices; become critical actors committed to combat problems of youth apathy, violence, substance abuse, rampant consumerism; and generate a strong commitment and action to developing a world free of oppression and exploitation.

Since the late 1960s, the field of communication research reflected the conditions of a society embroiled in controversies over a war in Vietnam and experienced the emergence of a brand of social criticism strongly related to an earlier critique of American society. The history of social critique has spanned the socialist writings of political economists and sociologists during the turn of the century, the populist criticism of political and economic authority by publicists and journalists seeking out and publishing scandals in the late 1920s, and the social criticism of social scientists since the 1950s.

Throughout this development, the idea of the *critical*, stimulated by the advancement of knowledge and provoked by the social and political consequences of social change, has persisted as an example of intellectual responsibility and moral leadership, beginning with the rise of American pragmatism. (See, for example, Dewey, 1938.) Since then, the importance of communication in emerging theory of society has been a major consideration in a continuing dialogue with pragmatism and other competing social theories. However, critical theory emerged from a distinct historical context between World War I and World War II. Critical theory is often associated with members of the Frankfurt Institute for Social Research that was founded in 1923 in Frankfurt, Germany. Often referred today as the "Frankfurt School," Max Horkheimer, who coined the term "critical theory," became the director in 1930. Other members were Leo Lowental, Thodor Adorno, Erich Fromm, and Herbert Marcuse. These theorists criticized economics, materialism, and the mass media, hoping to undermine them by focusing on their ideological components. Marcuse, in particular, introduced critical theory to America. Marcuse was a harsh critic of mass media because he ascribed to an ideological dominance to media and the culture industry—a dominance that had the potential to eliminate individualism and the revolutionary potential of the working class.

Marcuse's ideas in particular influenced some radical thinkers in the United States to critique the sociopolitical and economic order to include, for instance, the dimensions of race, gender, sexuality, ethnicity, and other factors, as well as class. Furthermore, the European influence of Marxist and non-Marxist interpretations of mass culture later gained considerable attention in the United States (Hardt, 1993, p. 31). For example, feminist and multiculturalist theories of race, ethnicity, nationality, subalterneity, and sexual preference have led the way with specific critiques of oppression and theories of resistance. Their discourses root their theoretical perspectives in the struggles of oppressed people and thus politicize theory and critique with passion and perspectives from existing political struggles and personal experiences. Such perspectives continue to enlarge the political struggle of marginalized or oppressed groups.

More specifically, however, Marxism, feminism, and multicultural theory pursue a critique of boundaries, focusing on the binary system of opposition that structures class, sexist, racist, and other ideological discourses. All of these forms of critical theory are thus weapons of critique in the struggle for a more humane society that sees ideology as providing theoretical underpinnings for systems of domination.

In the past two decades, cultural studies, as an emerging discipline, has provided a new set of approaches to the study of culture and society as represented by media industries. These studies were inaugurated by the University of Birmingham, Centre for Contemporary Cultural Studies, which developed a variety of critical approaches for the analysis, interpretation, and criticism of cultural artifacts. Through a set of internal debates, and responding to social struggles and movements of the 1960s and the 1970s, the Birmingham group came to focus on how various audiences interpreted and used media culture differently, analyzing the factors that made different audiences respond in contrasting ways to various media texts.

British cultural studies demonstrated how culture came to constitute distinct forms of identity and group membership. For cultural studies, media culture provides the materials for constructing identities, behavior, and views of the world. Furthermore, theorists believe that culture and history play a major role in the construction of personality and identity. Those who uncritically follow the dictates of media culture tend to "mainstream" themselves following the dominant fashion, beliefs, values, and behavior (Kellner, 1995, p. 97). Part of this mainstreaming is played in large measure by the mass media—they significantly construct our worldview. Critical educators believe that such mainstreaming and transmitting of objectified knowledge have overridden the formation of personality and citizenship as the aim of education. Education has become a function, a means to guarantee the production of people who fit into existing societal structures. For critical educators, educational competencies might include the capacity for self-determination, participation in a democracy, and solidarity instead of objectified or instrumental knowledge. In this context, then, personal identities are produced under different social conditions, and so no such thing as a universal, ahistorical human identity is possible.

PRINCIPLES AND ASSUMPTIONS: CRITICAL THEORY AS FOUNDATION OF MEDIA LITERACY

The work I have embarked on in this volume draws its theoretical framework from perspectives that view literacy education and discourse as critical social practices and locates such practices in the interplay within and across several contexts—local, institutional, and societal. According to Bronner, current issues in critical theory deal with solidarity and the domination of nature, class and cosmopolitanism, interests and autonomy, reification and aethetics, and constraints on democracy and the need to contest arbitrary exercise of power. Within these perspectives, several assumptions are made. These principles and assumptions include the following:

- That power relations that are socially and historically constituted mediate all thought.
- That the relationship between concept and object signifier and signified is never fixed and stable, but mediated by capitalist production and consumption.
- That language is central to the formation of subjectivity.
- That certain groups are privileged over others.
- That oppression (race, class, gender, age, for example) is reproduced when subordinates accept their status or situation as natural, necessary, and/or inevitable.
- That empirical data is interrogated with the intent of uncovering contradictions and negations in objective descriptions.
- That information always involves acts of human judgment and interpretation.
- That power is the basis of society.
- That there is no such a thing as neutrality.
- That research includes political action to redress injustices found in the research process/methods; research questions focus on uncovering and providing a space for introspection, and seek out multiple realities.
- That purposes focus on facilitating change, emancipatory action.
- That conceptual context, informed by the assumptions listed above, is explicit.
- That the traditional research idea of internal and external validity is replaced by critical trustworthiness.

IMPLICATIONS FOR CRITICAL MEDIA LITERACY

The principles and assumptions listed earlier have a profound influence on the theory and praxis of critical media literacy. For media literacy, as it is the case for cultural studies, the concept of ideology is of central importance. Institutions like the media corporations are part of the dominant means of ideological production. As noted by Hall (1997), what these media industries produce is "representations of the social world, images, descriptions, explanations and frames for understanding how the world is and why it works as it is said and shown to work" (p. 20). Thus, dominant ideologies serve to reproduce social relations of domination and subordination.

Kellner (1995) illustrates the formation of worldview by describing how ideologies of class, for instance, celebrate upper-class life and denigrate the working class. Ideologies of gender promote sexist and biased representations of women, and ideologies of race use racist representations of people of color and various minority groups. "Ideologies make inequalities and subordination appear natural and just, and thus, induce consent to relations of domination" (Kellner, 1995, 95). Because we tend to be unaware of how ideologies naturalize human relations (relations between races, sexes, or with older people, etc.), we can unconsciously be lulled to believing that what we see or know is natural or simply the way things are, and it becomes difficult to detect bias or manipulations which may occur within the way statements about these relationships are framed or formulated. In such circumstances, "ideologies tend to disappear from view into the taken-for-granted "naturalized" world of common sense (Hall, 1997, p. 19).

Doug Kellner and Stuart Hall are among several scholars who have elaborated on the foundations of critical media literacy and contributed extensively to the emerging field of cultural studies, in particular, by laying out the dynamics of media culture, language, and systems of representation. Their seminal works have been applied to critical inquiry in various disciplines.

As a pedagogical approach, the theory and praxis of critical media literacy draws its practice from social theory studies of popular culture and from "constructivist" approaches to teaching and to learning. This practice of social inquiry grew out of a number of social philosophies influenced by critical theory such as Latin American theologies of liberation, the philosophy of liberation of Brazilian educator Paulo Freire, Marxist revolutionary theory, and neo-Marxist cultural criticism. In addition, the practice of social inquiry has been taken up in more recent years by educators influenced by new social theories such as deconstruction and poststructuralism (for which Jacques Derrida is best known). Examples of social inquiry include analyses of the media in its many forms, such as literature, the role of the state in the struggles over race, class, and gender relations, national and international economic structures, and the cultural politics of imperialism, postcolonialism, and poststructuralism.

Drawing largely from the social theory studies of popular culture, I have developed analytical frameworks of media literacy within the broad concept of critical literacy. The frameworks provide analytical schemes based on the theories and praxis of critical literacy. Such frameworks prompt students and teachers to carry out a critique of existing social systems and institutions "in the context of how they relate to structures of domination and forces of resistance. In addition, these frameworks also help to identify which ideological positions are advanced within the context of current debates and social struggles for a more democratic and egalitarian society" (Kellner, 1995, p. 95).

In classroom practice, therefore, critical media literacy aims to:

- initiate and develop in youngsters a process of questioning.
- teach an inquiry method with which children and adolescents can look for information to answer questions they have raised and use the framework developed in the course (e.g., the concept of life cycle) and apply it to new areas.
- help the youth develop the ability to use a variety of firsthand sources as evidence from which to develop questions and then investigating those questions to draw broader conclusions.
- conduct classroom discussions in which students learn to listen to others as well as express their own voices.
- legitimate the search: that is, to give sanction and support to open-ended discussions where definitive answers to many questions are not found.
- encourage students to reflect on their own experiences and take action following the newly found awareness.

By taking up a social critical theory as a pedagogical strategy for critical media literacy, my students and I analyze and evaluate texts using the conceptual and methodological work of people like Norman Fairclough (1989), Paulo Freire (1974), James Gee (1996), Gunther Kress (1988), Courtney Cazden and Judith Green (1992), among others, in conjunction with examples of classroom pedagogies provided by Catherine Wallace, and Chris Searle (1995), and Hillary Janks (1993).

Critical media literacy stands in contrast to works far removed from the students' experiences. The rationales for helping students study and understand racial bias, gender bias, class bias, and other types of bias found in the media texts they read and view are founded on theories and praxis of critical literacy. Gradually, as educators become familiar with the foundations of critical media literacy, they begin to recognize that media literacy has the potential to change the way we think, feel, and react to the world around us, and particularly in classrooms. Clearly, this is an important step toward becoming a responsible citizen. Kincheloe and Steinberg (1998) explain why this is important when they state that:

When a teacher who doesn't share the culture, language, race, or so-cioeconomic backgrounds of students enters the classroom, he or she becomes not an information provider but an explorer who works with students to create mutually understood texts. Based on their explo-rations, teachers and students create new learning materials full of mu-tually generated meanings and shared interpretations. At a time when educational dilemmas resulting from the rapid increase of diverse stu-dents in schools portend the future of North American education, such a pedagogical perspective becomes extremely important. If educators are unable to meet the challenges issued by this expanding diversity, disastrous consequences will result. (p. 19)

To meet the challenges outlined here by Kincheloe and Steinberg, a few years ago, the Pennsylvania legislature mandated educational goals related to communication. These standards define knowledge and skills required for students to learn before graduating from public schools in Pennsylvania. Two of the eight goals specifically target critical pedagogy of media literacy stating that: (1) all students will write for a variety of purposes, including to narrate, inform and persuade, in all subject areas; and (2) all students will analyze and make *critical judgments* about all forms of communication, as well as separating fact from opinion, distin-guishing propaganda from the truth, recognizing stereotypes and *state-ments of bias*, recognizing inconsistencies and judging the validity of evidence (*The Pennsylvania Education*, February 1993). [Emphasis added.] The goals were approved by the state board of education and have been in effect since fall 1995, and revised in 1998.

KEY CONCEPTS OF CRITICAL MEDIA LITERACY

As discussed in the previous section, critical media literacy has its ori-gins in critical theory and cultural studies, which first developed from the thinking of a group of German scholars in the 1920s, collectively called the Frankfurt School. However, variants of critical theory abound in all of the social science disciplines, but central themes that a media literacy educator might explore include the scientific media analysis of social in-stitutions, media culture industries, definition of difference, representa-tion of other cultures, and their transformations through interpreting the meanings of social life; the historical problems of domination, alien-ation, and social struggles; and a critique of society and the envisioning of new possibilities.

These themes have methodological implications, and they present an underlying common thread found in the existing array of media literacy curricula. On the one hand, one could detect in such curricula the following: (1) a study of media as texts, (2) an analysis of political economy or commercial media enterprises, (3) an understanding of how audiences relate to media messages, and (4) the art of producing media programs. Because of the omnipresence of television in the United States, a study of the key concepts of media literacy often focuses on television as a commercial media enterprise to the neglect of other less dominant mass media forms.

On the other hand, Luke (1997) sees this study of media as necessary to make students critical and selective viewers, individuals who are able to reflect critically on TV's messages, their own reasons for viewing, and to use those critical skills in the production of their own print and electronic texts. Since the curriculum of media literacy depends on frameworks of core analytic questions that are meant to interrupt students' unreflective acceptance of text and to develop new strategies for thinking about the meanings TV transmits, and how viewers construct meaning for themselves from those texts, a teacher cannot assume that such frameworks can be taught in a single subject area or in a workshop. Such frameworks of keys to interpreting television messages require a systematic and sustained effort to develop conscious habits of viewing and reading.

At this juncture, we can no longer deny the reality that children now for more than two generations have been growing up and developing their consciousness or identity in the form of pictorial images of movies and television. Rather than denying this reality, the challenge for educators lies in dealing with the very visual-oriented thinking process of their TV-reared students. They can do so by guiding them into a more active and critical exploration of the media and technology. Such effort can start by examining the basics of the ominous forces that the media put to play before our children, families, and the society as a whole. Coming to an understanding of these forces is what media literacy advocates have come to call the key concepts of interpreting media texts being communicated as information, entertainment, advertising, or political campaign messages. These concepts are a key to understanding why media institutions do what they do—peddle media messages—in such a manner that we have come to take for granted. Beginning the process of interpreting, evaluating, and analyzing these familiar languages of media is part of the curriculum of critical media literacy.

Over the years, several media literacy educators have made references to these key concepts and so far there is no agreement as to how many they are or can be (Considine & Haley, 1992; Garret, n.d.; Silverblatt, 1995; Semali, 1994; Thoman, 1998; Tyner, 1999). However, depending on one's social context, these key concepts provide the guide to interpreting media texts in a variety of formats. As such, they originate from critical theory perspectives and from constructivist and poststructuralist theories. (For a detailed discussion of the origins of these key concepts, see Kellner, 1995, Chapter 3.)

The key concepts I am talking about form the foundation of any serious analysis and an important analytic framework students can use to develop questions that engage a critical reflection of media texts in their everyday lives. The key concepts of this framework are:

- All media messages are constructions.
- Media messages are representations of social reality.
- Individuals construct meaning from messages.
- Media messages have economic, political, social, and aesthetic purposes.
- Each media form of communication has unique characteristics.

All Media Messages Are Constructions

Today, we are accustomed to seeing the news as it happens, whether it is a fire in a nearby community, a hurricane steaming up in the Gulf of Mexico, an announcement by the president, an actual battle between two foreign armies in Kosovo ten thousand miles away. It is important for students to realize that this experience has been made possible for us because of the technological advancement we have made over the past fifty years. Like the newspaper column, what we see in each TV program is scripted, edited, and tweaked many times before it is aired. Such tweaking or creation of programs and newspaper columns is known as production. Theorists equate media productions to "construction." Hence the label, "constructivists."

For example, such tweaking goes on in every newsroom. The content of news stories is gathered and created by reporters. Reporters go to the scenes of events, interview people, and research issues connected with events. They write their stories using conventional formats for news, sports, feature, or commentary styles. Photographers try to capture the content (see, for example, the movie, *The Paper*), the context, and the emotion of events in their photographs. Artists create graphics and captions to add information and interest to stories. Stories and photographs from wire service journalists are sent to newspapers over satellite feeds. All these activities are part of the construction of messages related to a media event. And this is not all.

Teachers and students will want to know that editors make choices about what to put in an issue of the newspaper from the news stories and photographs available from their staffs and from wire services. Editors look for stories that have an impact upon their readers' lives and stories they think will be of interest to readers. Editors use several criteria in selecting what to publish, such as importance, proximity, timeliness, emotion, conflict, suspense, and progress. Every step of the way to production is another level of construction with individuals making decisions about what to include and what to leave out.

Even the live report on television is a construction. The cameraperson makes choices of what to include in the picture and what to eliminate. This process is called editing. For the news program to be ready, often there will be an anchorperson to lead into the story, to frame the message, and help audiences to follow the unfolding of events. Sometimes, this production does not stop there. Footage from other sources, such as movies and past news reports, may be brought into the creation of the dramatic events unfolding before us as they happen thousands of miles away. Any media text—written or electronic—including, in large part, the school curriculum, is a construction. Also, the worldview, information, and perspectives created by both mass media messages and the school curriculum are primarily a construction of reality rather than reality itself.

Hall (1997) draws our attention to the seductiveness of documentary productions. He makes clear that its general form, evident in genres such as film and books, where the idea of documentary is objectively grounded but subjectively constructed, was widely used to fashion "real" experience. Despite the increasing awareness that depiction does not embody truth itself, photography remains a principal medium for our understanding of the world. We must therefore be aware every time we witness a live report or documentary photography that we can be easily seduced to accept the authenticity that derives from the sense of real experience (of being there), and thus giving a representational *legitimacy* (Hall, 1997, p. 84).

Critical theorists call to question this "legitimacy." Notably, Fulton (cited in Hall, 1997), explains that the "documentary" nature of photographic journalism, whether for a newspaper, magazine, or book, is essentially interpretative. The representations that the photographer produces are related to his or her personal interpretations of the events and subjects that he or she chooses to place in front of the camera lens. However, they are also assumed to have some "truth-value" in the sense that they allow the viewer a privileged insight into the events that the representations depict.

To understand this representational construction and how it occurs, let me outline the two steps. First, the photographer is involved in a process of construction in choosing and framing his or her images so as "to make known, to confirm, to give testimony to others" (p. 85). Through the photographer's construction, the subject—a football crowd, or a group of Haitian refugees crowded in a boat—is captured that seems to represent reality forever, not realizing that this dramatic picture(s) could be later interpreted in different ways by people positioned in other ways in society. The testimony that this picture carries to the world as it gets distributed over the wire services, as Fulton argues, makes "visible the unseen, the unknown and the forgotten" (p. 85). Through the selection of shots, the photographer aims the camera and frames the perspective of his or her choice and thus represents consciously and unconsciously decisions about what knowledge is valid and valued and relevant to his or her social context.

But the process of circulation and publication of the photograph does not end here. It enters a second process of construction where the photographs are selected out from their original ordering by the photographer and narrative context, to be placed alongside textual information and reports in a magazine or newspaper column. Such manipulation by editors provides ample evidence that the meanings available to the viewer/reader on the basis of a documentary photograph are a complex representational construction. It is important to remember therefore that in any textual construction, the representation of people and events incorporates the way the mass media use conventions, how audiences make meanings from them, and how these meanings are applied within a cultural context (Lusted, 1991, p. 123).

Often forgotten in this kind of analysis of representations in photographs is the motive of the photographer as well as the motive of the editor or producer who creates the media product to be distributed to audiences. The audience has no simple resource to rely on when it comes to examining the motive. That is why critical media literacy advocates questioning, particularly those ideologically-based motives. For students to engage actively in such analysis, they first have to begin to understand their own motives in learning, reading, writing, and so on. As noted by Dewey (1938) over a half-century ago, the proper interpretation of students' educational experiences rests on one's ability to understand thoughts, actions, and motives as they interact with others in social situations. Although he acknowledged the role of the teacher and the curriculum in shaping students' experiences, Dewey wrote, "[it is] the total *social* set up of the situations in which a person is engaged" that is most important in interpreting his or her experiences (p. 45).

Building on the ideas of Dewey, Rorty (1979) has given even more credence to the importance of the *social* context in interpreting one's experiences. Rorty deconstructed the metaphor of the human mind consisting of two mechanisms: one, the so-called mirror of nature that reflects external reality, and the other, an inner eye that comprehends the reflection. He did so on the grounds that this metaphor, which has influenced Western philosophy since the time of Descartes, leads to circular thinking about knowledge and to some extent accurately representing the nature and authority of knowledge. In place of the mirror and inner eye metaphor, Rorty would have us consider what can be learned from viewing knowledge as a social construct. His thesis is that all knowledge is socially constructed, such that the ways in which we come to describe or otherwise account for the world (including our experiences and ourselves) are derived from historically situated linguistic symbolic interactions with others.

Thus, one of the assumptions underlying social constructionism is that linguistic "entities we normally call reality, knowledge, thought, facts, texts, selves, and so on, are constructs generated by communities or life-minded peers" over time (Bruffee, 1986, p. 774; Gergen, 1985). This view of knowledge as socially justified belief constitutes and is constituted by a community's language. The inseparability of knowledge and language is a particularly useful construct for educators in their quest to understand how students say they experience classroom discussions of assigned readings. As construct, it provides the rationale for asking students to reflect and report on their subjective experiences as participants in small and large group discussions. A classroom teacher assumes that students' knowledge of such experiences (constructed as it was through the social interaction of group members) and the language they used to reflect that knowledge were inseparable.

However, a word of caution is in order. This assumption might address in part the limitations typically ascribed to self-report data. Although self-reports are open to criticism, they nonetheless "are useful for assessing how individuals make judgements about people and events, and they do register what people think they do or what they think is socially acceptable to do" (Goetz & LeCompte, 1984, p. 122). Ultimately, of course, we recognize "that what we call our data are really our own constructions" (Geertz, 1988, p. 42).

The student in the classroom working with his or her peers, the reporter in the newsroom, or the TV program producer in the studio—all are engaged in the collection of data/information and construction of messages. In their creations, the words or images they decide to use, or how they decide to organize them, or to present the completed message/information to readers and viewers, alter process meanings. Uncovering the many levels of construction that go on in developing media messages or texts is helpful to students to see that what is "constructed" by just a few people then becomes *the way it is* (or worldview) for the rest of us who buy into the message as news, textbook story, or TV sitcom.

Media Messages Are Representations of Social Reality

When media educators critique visual representations, they wish to distinguish social reality from the image of the reality. The central concept here is that media texts construct reality but they are not the reality itself. In other words, media texts, including spoken or written languages, objects, entities, and products, are representations of social reality (persons, groups, events, or experiences in the real world or reflections or abstractions thereof). Social reality refers to the perceptions about the contemporary world that are shared by individuals—their picture of the world around them. That reality is unique to specific historic time periods and different parts of the world. Newspapers, books, magazines, and films of earlier times provide a picture of the social reality of those times and places.

The picture of the world presented by media representations may or may not be completely accurate. Individuals need to be able to judge the accuracy of the messages. This is important because, as we saw earlier, media messages are constructions. In the process of being produced, they are manipulated for a variety of reasons by different people involved in the communication chain. As messages are massaged and manipulated, bias, stereotypes, and distortions are likely to be introduced into them and thus result in a less accurate representation of the event, group, or experience.

As noted by Richard Dyer (1992), "how we are seen determines in part how we are treated; how we treat others is based on how we see them. Such seeing comes from representation" (p. 32). Because representations of reality play such key roles in our understanding of our world and how we treat others, and because of the uncertainty of representations, it is important therefore to develop a level of skepticism to read/view media texts. This is an important consideration when evaluating texts, particularly those texts that represent the "Other."

In this regard, Hall (1997) draws our attention to examine even more carefully how "difference" is represented as "other" and the essentializing of "difference" that occurs through stereotyping. One way to raise our levels of skepticism is to ask questions such as these:

1. Who is speaking for whom in this text?
2. What sense do these representations make of the world we live in? What are the texts representing to us and how?
3. What are typical representations of groups in society?
4. What does this example represent to me?
5. What does it mean to others?

Audiences as Well as Individuals Negotiate Meaning

It is important to note that each individual interprets messages differently and consequently draws different meanings from the same message. In the process, individuals do not interpret the same message in the same way. Each individual's understanding is affected by prior knowledge of the subject, prior experience with the structure of the message, and consideration of the context in which the message is presented. Take, for example, the movie, *Forrest Gump*. I took a random selection of students in three English classes at an American university and asked them: "Tell me in a sentence, what is the film—*Forrest Gump*—about?" Some of the responses included the following:

1. The film is about feeling good in America.
2. It is about the Vietnam War.
3. It is about a new disease (AIDS) that has no cure.
4. It is about race in America.
5. It is about rewriting the history of the Vietnam War.

These responses kind of confirm this axiom: Audiences draw different meanings from the same message. Individuals with prior knowledge, experience, and familiarity with many media sources, say who read a newspaper review of the film, or watched TV commentaries, are more likely to interpret this film or any other media messages more accurately.

By this example, we realize, therefore, that readers bring their own knowledge, experience, and preconceptions to the television program or newspaper article or story in the textbook. Many times, stories about an emotional issue are interpreted completely differently by opposing groups. The same news story about a strike at a factory may be seen as "union bashing" by workers and "antimanagement" by owners. Readers' attitudes toward individual newspapers are often affected by whether or not the reader agrees or disagrees with the positions taken by the newspaper on its editorial pages. It is important, therefore, to pay attention to the fact that whereas media content and the producer's intent are significant, different audiences respond to these messages in different ways. Similarly, the message and the method of presentation in our schools is accepted or rejected by students on the basis of their culture and needs, including past experiences and racial, ethnic, and socioeconomic status. These are important considerations when analyzing all texts.

Media Messages Have Economic, Political, Social, and Aesthetic Purposes

I need to reiterate here that critical media literacy is concerned with examining the underlying ideological underpinnings to understand how economic, political, and aesthetic force influence the meaning of the messages distributed. One important task of media literacy is to remind students and teachers that the news we receive and the programming we enjoy every night and weekends come to us through commercial companies to whom the government has leased (licensed) the airwaves. Commercial companies like ABC, CBS, NBC, FOX, and CNN are presenting news under the constraint that they must be able to surround news broadcasts and other programming with commercials. Their primary income stems from the money they make by selling the audiences that watch them to advertisers. Every second counts. Indeed, sponsors pay for the time on the basis of the number of people the station predicts will be watching. The sponsors also target their advertising message to specific kinds of viewers—for example, children ages two to seven, who influence their parents' spending. Because of this prerogative, media companies must do everything to maximize their opportunity to make profit.

The *real* purpose of commercial TV, whether news or entertainment, is not just to entertain us but also to create an audience (and put them in a receptive mood) so that the network or local station can sell time to advertisers. They do so by rating their shows in terms of how big a draw of audiences they are able to deliver to the advertising agencies. Such ratings therefore drive the quality of programming, the type of program, the time of day it is aired, and sometimes, but not always, the content of the program. Likewise, newspaper editors lay out pages with advertisements first; the space remaining is devoted to news. Political messages try to persuade voters to support specific issues or candidates. Government officials and community leaders stage public events, hold press briefings, and grant interviews to get their ideas and positions in front of citizens. Political columnists and political ads try to build public support for specific positions on issues.

Social messages hope to convince individuals to behave in certain ways. Artists' messages elicit emotional responses from viewers. Skilled information consumers who are able to recognize the creator's purpose in constructing a message can better understand the context of the message, determine its validity, and judge its usefulness in their lives. In all these enterprises, we can easily detect ulterior motives, whether economic, ideological, or simply entertaining or for pleasure.

Each Media Text or Form of Communication Has Unique Characteristics Relative to the Medium That Produces It

In the 1960s, Marshall McLuhan wrote, "the medium is the message." Today, this phrase is echoed throughout the world and is cited in a variety of publications. One form of communication does not automatically displace another, however; each form carries particular aesthetics. As McLuhan (1962) noted, each literacy technology has unique aesthetic form that influences content, and these same elements are adapted by each medium in unique ways. For example, it has been argued that the book owes much to illustration, since the woodcut blocks used to create pictures inspired Gutenberg to experiment with type (Miguel, 1997). Generalization about codes, conventions, and aesthetics for each medium abound and are based as much on subjective personal tests as on objective observation. But comic books are iconic, and television is immediate and favors close-ups; in-depth information is more compatible with print, which allows reflection on content over time. Wide shots look better in cinema, digital media enable more user interaction (instant replay is commonly used in sports), and so on. The ability of digital tools to collapse sight, sound, and motion with relative ease accelerates experimentation with the convergence of aesthetic form and structure from different media.

Even though these forms coexist as they borrow and swap genre, style, codes, and conventions—with mixed aesthetics—each communication medium has its own identifiable characteristics, structure, and formats. They present cultural forms that reinforce hegemonic ideologies and practices dominant in society. A news story and a play may cover the same event, but the news story presents information in a concise, straightforward way while a play uses dialogue, scene changes, and other dramatic devices. New stories are written in an "objective" manner. Feature stories often have a more informal style. Editorials and commentaries use persuasive visual images and colorful language to attract readers' attention and interest.

The manner in which the story is told and the medium or media used influences how we interpret the meanings embedded in the story or message. For example, as commonly used in television and cinema, the choice of a character's age, gender, or race mixed in with the lifestyles, attitudes, and behaviors that are portrayed, the selection of a setting (urban? rural? affluent? poor?), and the actions and reactions in the plot are just some of the ways that the nature of the medium operates in telling stories. In this process, values become embedded in a TV show, a movie, or an advertisement. These are important factors to consider in the interpretation of texts. By recognizing the strengths, weaknesses, and constraints of various media forms, individuals can better interpret media messages and know texts more deeply. We must learn how to "read" the syntax and the different languages of particular media that are appropriate to each one. Only then can students and teachers judge whether to accept or reject these messages as we negotiate our way through our multimedia environment. I hope the critical media pedagogy that I advocate throughout this book gives students and teachers the framework they need as they struggle over the multimedia texts presented to them in today's media world and classrooms, to criticize dominant cultural forms, images, narratives, and genres.

DEVELOPING CRITICAL MEDIA LITERACY
IN MULTIMEDIA CLASSROOMS

In Chapter 2, I discussed how in a country as diverse as the United States and as well-equipped with multiple forms of media, meaning cannot assume a universal version, but rather multiform. What we know is very much a function of the company we keep (Wells, 1986). The company we keep informs us of who we are as we participate in a common language and the cultural conventions that are particular to each community. The production of meaning from media texts depends upon knowledge that is shared by a community. Such knowledge is constructed by the community's belief system, worldview, use of language, and by how members are positioned in their own culture. The community is instrumental in the ways in which we come to describe or otherwise account for the world. Such ways are derived from historically situated linguistic symbolic interactions with others.

One major aspect of teaching critical media literacy is to identify where that knowledge shared by a community comes from, and how it has been historically constructed. The assumption is that teachers can show students how the mass media use this knowledge to construct our understandings of the world and how media texts mean different things to different people. Developing skepticism about what we know about our world and how it has been mediated to us is the goal of media literacy. For example: How did we come to know what we know about certain events, or groups of people? Each event or what we know about other people, particularly people of different race, class, gender, or sexual orientation, is created, maintained, and legitimized by the discourses of the company we keep. I suppose, therefore, that the language of media is not innocent, natural, or neutral. For this reason, to be literate and educated, we must investigate the ways in which the language of media is socially and historically produced. We must examine its production, construction, and the meaning-making processes by which media imagery and popular representation of people help shape our personal, social, and political worlds. In order to achieve this, the relationship between media language and the realities it seeks to represent or construct needs, in various ways, to be "made strange" (Lusted, 1991). This means that the complex and contested ways in which media language embodies broader relationships of power, and the ways in which language users are themselves inevitably implicated in these relationships, need to be carefully examined and no longer taken for granted.

To explore this idea, it may be helpful to consider how our culture creates and sustains one of its most basic values, democracy, and then examine how it upholds meanings of race, class, and gender. It may also be necessary to examine the variety of narratives and media forms used to explain how the world works—that the institutions of school, family, church, and the mass media maintain and have maintained over the years. Such narratives may well be the stories our students cherish, or the myths we have known and used against people of color for years, or the grand narratives found in the great works of literature, the Bible, and the classics. To understand the variety of meanings embedded in a narrative or form of any media text is to know the codes and conventions that lie beneath its meaning.

The search for deeper meanings found in the grand narratives and classics can be rewarding but challenging. It is a challenge because understanding where meanings come from and how meanings are produced is a matter of complex inquiry that raises questions about the power to construct and maintain a certain pattern of meanings and to what effects. Courts (1997, p. 17) seems to suggest that "the word [in language] is one with that which it names." For him, naming presents an intellectual process that is as exclusionary as it is inclusive. In this process of naming, it is possible to find implicit goals of sanctioning some definitions over others, establishing universally accepted classification schemes, and then situating oneself within the boundaries of the definition and classification. Understanding this process, therefore, shows the power of words and how the pattern of meanings can lead to the bias that lies beneath the conventions of naming in cultures rooted in classical Western traditions. The hope is that once an entity (phenomenon) is named, it becomes manifest. It is also why definitions can cause such Sturm and Drang in academic circles. Nevertheless, the tension between the reality and what is named is always problematic. For me, it is important to underscore here the nature of representation—a concept too often mistaken for reality or life itself. "Naming" is a way of representing.

Media Texts and Meaning

When I talk about media text in this volume, I refer to conventions or simply a variety of meaning-making devices such as words in basic verbal communication, images, pictures, media messages, motion pictures, songs, and more recently the multimedia inventions including iconic texts found in computer operations and Internet communication. A media text can also be an illustration or symbolic presentation. For example, the way students dress and represent themselves, and the cultural specific symbolic and nonverbal communication of social and body gestures, constitutes complex sign systems that individuals produce and "read off" one another.

The constuctionist theory proposes a complex and mediated relationship between things in the world, our concepts in thought and language. The meanings prevalent in our culture that we almost take for granted form a set of interconnections between language and linguistic codes or conventions to produce meaning. According to Ferdinand de Saussure (1974), a Swiss semiotician, the interaction between forms of expression used by language (whether speech, writing, drawing, or other types of representation), which he called signifiers—and the mental concepts associated with them—the signifieds—both form the core explanation of how we come to know or understand the world we live in. The interaction between these two systems of signifier and signified produce signs, and when signs are organized into languages, they in turn produce meanings that can then be used to reference objects, people, and events in the real world. The general approach to the study of signs in culture and of culture as a sort of "language" is what has come to be known as *semiotics*. Semiotics has broadened our understanding of media texts and provides analytical tools for investigating texts, which is the foundation for critical media analysis. Since all media texts convey meaning, and all cultural practices depend on meaning, they must make use of signs; and insofar as they do, they must work like language works, and be amenable to an analysis that basically makes use of Saussure's linguistic concepts (e.g., signifier/signified).

To conclude this discussion about the implications of signifier and signified, Hall (1997) clarifies for us that the relationship between a signifier and signified is the result of a system of social conventions specific to each society and to specific historical moments. For this reason, then, all meanings are produced within history and culture. They can never be finally fixed but are always subject to change, both from one cultural context and from one period to another.

Therefore, there is thus no single, unchanging, universal "true meaning." Because the sign is arbitrary and is totally subject to history, the combination at the particular moment of a given signifier and signified is simply a contingent result of the historical process (Culler, 1976, p. 36). Hall concludes that this new realization opens representation to the constant production of new meanings and new interpretations. Therefore, if meaning changes, historically, and is never finally fixed, then it follows that "taking the meaning" must involve an active process of interpretation (p. 34). And I might add that this opens the door for those meanings to be contested or changed.

Critical education theorists have frequently used the word *resistance* to signify the actions of individuals and groups by which they assert their own desires, and contest the ideological and material forces that are imposed upon them by the prevailing culture. It is for this reason, then, that advocates of critical media literacy contend that meanings in and of themselves do not carry a universal and an all-time sense. Meaning has to be actively "read" or "interpreted." The meaning we take as viewers, readers, or audiences is never exactly the meaning that has been intended or given by the speaker or writer or by other viewers. Hall (1997) tells us why.

> We can't entirely prevent some of the negative connotations of the word BLACK from returning to mind when we read a headline, "WEDNESDAY—A BLACK DAY ON THE STOCK EXCHANGE," even if this was not intended. There is a constant sliding of meaning in all interpretation, a margin—something in excess of what we intend to say—in which other meanings overshadow the statement or the text, where other associations are awakened to life, giving what we say a different twist. Soon interpretation becomes an essential aspect of the process by which meaning is given and taken. The reader is as important as the writer in the production of meaning. Every signifier given or encoded with meaning has to be meaningfully interpreted or decoded by the receiver. Signs, which have not been intelligibly received and interpreted, are not, in any useful sense, "meaningful." (p. 33)

Because meaning must involve an active and systematic process of interpretation, Carmel Luke (1997) suggests that teachers take up a sociological analysis of the production and construction of media texts and an evaluation of the meaning-making processes that media imagery and popular representation of people help shape our personal, social, and political worlds. In such analysis, she suggests developing a framework for looking at representation of groups in society that commonly lead to studies of cultural stereotypes. Identification and description of stereotypes and bias, I might add, in the variety of media found in the United States today, are common projects of critical media literacy. An analysis might focus on how different gender, cultural, racial, national, and physical abilities are culturally constructed. Luke gives the example of analyses of how disability, gender, nationality, or racial/ethnic identity as "stereotyped," marginalized, or excluded in mainstream media texts can enable students' understanding of how "common sense" and public attitudes toward difference are inscribed in the media texts of everyday life. Texts known to do this tend to romanticize indigenous peoples and present their cultures as exotic, or blame urban poor for their poverty and misery.

Taking on this critical analysis encourages students to raise issues and questions in response to all media texts including those that are part of the textbook. Such critical evaluation of texts also helps students to penetrate the layers of meaning when they identify the symbols and understand their meaning and functions, when they analyze the structure and understand its power, when they articulate the meaning as (and whatever) it communicates to them within their culture's social context. We appreciate that we won't arrive at a definitive interpretation. Through such process of inquiry, we come to know the media text and visual statement with its multiple meanings much more intimately.

Clearly, media texts are not the only place where inquiry is legitimate. In fact, the context and subtext are important areas of inquiry to understand and detect meaning. However, context should not be confused with its correlates, namely, pretext, subtext, and intertext, even though they may also be areas of inquiry. Context is usually what is not explicitly stated, commonly referred to as social context. Also referred to as social background, social context, for example, tends to look outside of, as well as at the text or work being studied. By using social context as a method of interpreting texts, one might ask a variety of questions about the production of the text—from the text itself to the artist who produced it. Questions that seek out the race, class, gender, educational background, geographical location, nationality, ethnic descent, sexual orientation, age, and the like, are important variables that contribute not only to how the text was produced, interpreted, or understood but also how the text positions the reader. Some of the questions of interest might inquire about: Who is the artist? How was he or she historically placed in society? What were the cultural forces in society in which the artist was raised and/or is working? What is the message of the visual statement in terms of political cultural and social import? How can this message be evaluated using the prevailing values of the culture of the artist rather than the viewer?

Unfortunately, some authors who claim to promote a critical reading of popular texts ignore this dimension of inquiry. A critical media literacy approach does not stop with exploration of the text. Allowing students time to discuss and explain their rationale for their image formation and song lyrics when reading popular culture touches only the surface of what it means to be "critical." A critical pedagogy goes beyond the text and begins to engage action and problematize students' consumer habits, such as mindless spending on music products, and so on.

A critical pedagogy embraces the extra step to force a rupture from routine. Asking questions that begin to read the text against the grain may cause displeasure, discomfort, unsettlement, or loss of innocence. Every time a reader or audience is jolted from the comfortable position of what seems natural or commonsensical to our usual way of thinking about things, every time we are asked to give up taking for granted ideas so that we are open to new ways of seeing or thinking, is going to cause a feeling of loss, disorientation, and discomfort. This unsettling loss of innocence is the new dawn, the new realization, the acquisition of new knowledge.

Texts Share Common Codes

All texts share common elements, like codes, genres, structures, production elements, levels of meaning, and rhetorical and mythic devices. Authors, media producers, and filmmakers often use these elements to capture the attention of readers, viewers, and listeners. As discussed in Chapter 2, the use of media conventions and putting the power of these media languages into good use is known to leave readers and viewers mesmerized and for the most part invisible. This explains why some particular media texts draw and captivate our attention completely, such as a television show with a wide audience appeal, or a good book that once a reader starts reading, it is difficult to put it down.

A variety of techniques are employed by different media producers to convey particular meanings. For instance, in advertising, camera positions, lighting, music, glitzy digital effects, "magical" features, rapid pacing, or uses of color can reveal a kind of "semiotics" shorthand (Luke, 1997). In the dazzling array of programs in other scenarios, for example, in movies, one finds elaborate costuming, illustrious movie stars, outlandish scenes, breathtaking views, and so on, which are strategically used in cinema to manufacture believability and lend credence to the plot. Sometimes these elements make everything come alive.

Often enough, audiences are duped when they are told that a particular media product has been based on a "true story." Such a disclaimer is part of the techniques used to create a special appeal in audiences. These and many other devices have become commonplace in the history of mass media in the United States. Gradually, as we participate in the consumption of these media products, we become accustomed to the conventions used and quickly learn the new media languages that continue to hit the movie and television screens. For many audiences, such conventions are a source of pleasure that we have come to enjoy and participate in fully in popular culture.

Media conventions form part of our cultural knowledge. That is to say, we recognize with some familiarity when we hear certain music, see certain media images produced in a particular sequence or at a particular pace, relate to familiar actors and actresses, and anticipate with nostalgia the story they are about to tell. This kind of familiarity gives us ability to participate in the assumptions, widespread beliefs, and popular attitudes that form our cultural knowledge.

Power of Media Languages

A study of media conventions and the power of media languages cannot be complete or fully appreciated without examining the power of language marked by the social conditions of its use and its users—that is to say, its politicized power-bearing attributes. Hall (1997) reminds us that languages work through representation. That is to say, the different ways of producing and communicating meaning work like languages.

For example, spoken language uses sounds to express or communicate a thought, concept, idea, or feeling; written language uses words; musical language uses notes on a scale; the "language of the body" uses physical gesture; the fashion industry uses items of clothing; the language of facial expression uses ways of arranging one's features; television uses digitally or electronically produced dots on a screen; traffic lights use red, green, and yellow to "say something." Hall explains that through these elements, we are able to make sense of the world. These elements—sounds, words, notes, gestures, expressions, and clothes—are part of our natural and material world; but their importance for language is not what they are but what they do, their function. They construct meaning and transmit it. That is to say, they signify. According to Hall, these elements don't have any clear meaning in themselves; rather, they operate as symbols, which stand or represent metaphor, that is, they function as signs. Signs stand for or represent our concepts, ideas, and feelings in such a way as to enable others to "read," decode, or interpret their meaning in roughly the same way that we do (p. 5).

In a similar way, the mass media utilize these familiar signs and symbols to communicate their ideas. When educators talk about the mass media using media languages to represent concepts, ideas, feelings, and values of our culture, they are referring to the journalist, the TV anchorperson, the talk show host, and the advertiser, who use their cameras, special effects, and familiar images of our culture to send powerful messages to audiences through cultural signs and symbols. Cultural theorists like Stuart Hall, therefore, would have us pay attention to how our society is marked by a multiplicity of cultures, conventions, meanings, and values. By guiding students' attention to how powerful groups define their own particular meanings, values, experiences, and forms of writing and reading as the *valued* ones in society, students would better understand the inequalities and violations of social justice the mass media continue to peddle through its multiple forms of imagery, found in the entertainment programs and culture products.

Hall (1997) also points out that to understand the dominant discourses in the contemporary United States, for example, one needs to pay attention to its current multidiscursive and multicultural nature and therefore, "any analysis of its culture must be concerned with discursive practices." As defined by Hall (1997), discourse is simply a way of formulating a topic and a field of inquiry that answers specific "governing statements" (questions) and produces "strategic knowledge." For Foucault, however, discourse plays a strategic role in producing what we claim as "knowledge." Within the discourse of a community, knowledge operates as a historically situated social practice: All knowledge is power/knowledge. Thus, "strategic knowledge" is knowledge inseparable from relationships of power (Foucault, 1980, p. 145).

Discourses, according to this Foucaultian definition, do not simply reflect "reality" or innocently designate objects. Rather they constitute them in specific contexts according to particular relations of power. In other words, to understand a particular event or topic, one must uncover the knowledge/power axis and "the processes of discursive contestation by which powerful discourses (or dominant ideology) work to repress, marginalize, and invalidate others, by which less powerful ones struggle for audibility (voice) and for access to the technologies of social circulation and by which they fight to promote and defend the interests of their respective social formations" (p. 4).

To illustrate more closely how discourse operates in our culture, Hall (1997) gives the example of racial difference as part of the U.S. reality, which is a product of the discourse into which it is put. This, in particular, is a discourse of racism that advances the interests of whites and which has identifiable repertoire of words, images, and practices through which racial power is applied. It is important, therefore, to remember, as stated by Hall, that the repertoire or articulation of positions of what is valued and not valued is always a terrain of struggle, noting that the dominant discourses, those that occupy the mainstream, serve dominant social interests, for they are products of the history that has secured their domination.

This explains why it is important for any critical media literacy education program to examine race relations through a systematic inquiry of its dominant social interests and the institutions that support it. This inquiry must include the examination of the conventions and the meaning-making processes embedded in the ongoing discursive struggle students encounter about race in multimedia America. For example, one finds that controversies produced by media events like the sitcom *Murphy Brown*, or the television reporting of the Rodney King beating by the LAPD police and the subsequent riots in Los Angeles, carry specific codification that authenticates a particular explanation of why the events occurred the way they did.

This particular rendition of the story is not objective or innocent. It reflects particular relations of power. (See Fiske, 1996, Chapter 3). Similar authentication is found in the steady diet of literature consumed throughout the high school curriculum. Likewise, those books that occupy students' time of leisure and pleasure (e.g., romance novels, etc.) are equally implicated in this scrutiny because they peddle ways of looking at the world, including definitions of success, beauty, safety, and so on. In this vein, therefore, critical media literacy provides students with frameworks to read, view, and listen to a variety of texts they confront in their everyday lives. Such critical reading, viewing, and listening is not isolated or limited to any particular genre. But when these texts are taken together and critically analyzed, they provide a complete picture and a deeper meaning of what is going on in our society and in the circuitry of its popular culture.

The growing availability of multimedia forms of communication to society makes it possible for adolescents in America to spend tremendous amounts of time listening to the radio, watching television, going to see films, experiencing music, going shopping, reading magazines and newspapers, as well as participating in these and other forms of media culture.

For example, some teachers are surprised when they observe students who can surf the Internet all day without being bored, watch television while doing homework, and watch programs such as *Power Rangers*, *Sailor Moon*, and *ReBoot* in a manner that teachers have no patience for. This phenomenon is a clear sign of the new times. Thus, a new multimedia culture has emerged to dominate everyday life, serving as the ubiquitous background and often the highly seductive foreground of our attention, imagination, fantasies, and dreams, and to which some educators have expressed concern, is undermining human potentiality and creativity. Fiske (1987), Kellner (1995), Masterman (1985), Considine & Haley (1994), Worth and Gross (1981), and other media theorists advocate developing viewers' competencies into interpreting "codes and modes"—conventions of symbol-systems in various kinds of electronic media. These authors look to both aesthetic and social characteristics of the mass media and other multimedia as significant areas of educating readers and viewers. The frames and skills for constructing, interpreting, and questioning of the symbol-systems of multimedia are the essential frameworks of critical media literacy.

Questioning the Text

Using a critical pedagogy approach to question texts is complex. It requires a certain level of critical consciousness that the reader/viewer needs to develop. In Chapter 4, I call this critical consciousness "taking a critical stance." Such critical stance needs to permeate all inquiry. It is distinguished from other questioning of media texts that some media educators seem to advocate in the current literature. The critical consciousness and critical inquiry, which I advocate in this book, is an important resource for individuals and citizens in learning how to cope with the seductive cultural environment.

Learning how to read, criticize, question, and resist media manipulation can help students and teachers empower themselves in relation to dominant media and culture. It can enhance their sovereignty vis-à-vis media culture and give them more power over their cultural environment dominating schools and classrooms, and hence provide the necessary literacy curriculum to read and write new forms of culture. Such empowerment can help promote in the curriculum a more general questioning of the organization of society and can help induce students to join and participate in radical political movements struggling for social justice and cultural transformation.

Although the purpose of critical media literacy education is not to deny pleasure but to explore its causes, it is important to note that taking a critical look at the mass media should not be viewed as an opportunity of media bashing—that is, a senseless exercise of criticizing the shopping malls, television sitcoms, and music that students value. Rather, students should be encouraged to explore the values and the constructed nature of popular media. Media literacy is not about bashing or protecting students from popular culture. It is about empowering them and giving them the opportunity to develop a critical mindset in an age of expanding consumerism to learn to question how their identities are constructed by the various forms of popular culture that they choose to become part of their lives.

As facilitators, teachers need to help students take an exploratory stance to probe their relationship with media texts: What goes on in the text, between the reader and the text? What benefits could be drawn from questioning the relation of our position in the text? Will doing such an exercise deny students the pleasure in the media text? Barry Duncan (1993) warns that recognizing themes in literacy works is not the same as deconstructing media texts for their ideological messages. As will be explained further in Chapter 4, when analyzing media texts, teachers need to pay particular attention to the key concepts of media literacy, such as commercial considerations, technical codes and practices, and the audience's interpretation of meaning.

Suffice it to say, however, that for a novice teacher, questioning texts can be easily reduced to a mechanical enterprise. Some media educators seem to think that questioning must be controlled and carefully guided. Elsewhere, I have indicated that questioning of texts should not be turned into busy work but rather should be guided by a framework of inquiry. In this inquiry, students should be allowed to explore all questions, particularly those questions of race, gender, class, and all other issues that pertain to their everyday lives. Read the following example taken from an article published in the journal of the Association for Supervision and Curriculum Development, in which one media educator explains how to go about questioning media texts found in advertising. The *emphasis* is original.

> Analysis should go deeper than just trying to identify some "meaning" in an ad, a song, or an episode of a sitcom. Indeed, try to avoid "why" questions. They lead only to speculation, personal interpretation, and circular debate that can stop the inquiry process. Instead, ask "how" and "what": *How* does the camera angle make us feel about the product being advertised? *What* difference would it make if the car in the ad were blue instead of red? *What* do we know about a character from her dress, makeup, and jewelry? *How* does the music contribute to the mood of the story being told? The power of media literacy lies in figuring out how the construction of any media product contributes to the meaning we make of it.

Suggesting those students should try to avoid a "why" question is uncritical and misguided. One should rather focus of the quality of "why" questions, questions that lead to further questioning and research (see Chapter 7). Speculation is necessary, especially in trying to compare one's context with that described in the media text. Inquiry is speculation. It is part of the hypothesis generation and alternative thinking process that critical media literacy calls for. Perhaps taking a critical pedagogy perspective in this analysis would help students get at those questions of race, class, and gender that seem to have been overlooked here. Also, it will be important to stay focused on questions that aim at the critique of ideology in the text in question, particularly those hegemonic practices that tend to perpetuate routinely myth, bias, and stereotyping of people and events in the same old way.

In my view, asking questions that direct students' attention to the construction, interpretation, and critique of the symbol systems representing the product being advertised will necessarily lead to asking "why" questions. Questions such as: Who is in the ad and why? Which social class is represented? Is the social class represented different from that of the students'? Why did the producer choose to create the ad this way? Who (age group, race, class, gender) is he or she targeting and why? What roles do the actors of this ad play? What are they wearing? Why? How does their dress perpetuate particular attitudes in our society? For example, do the images of the ad show women scantily clad? In compromising situations? Does it denigrate, objectify women, young girls, and boys? Does it stereotype older people? People of color? So, rather than focusing on a "right" or "wrong" meaning, we need to ask questions that go beyond the preferred meaning—in other words, asking which of the images the ad means to privilege, objectify, stereotype, naturalize, select, or essentialize out of the many possible meanings from the image(s). Barthes (1974) reminds us that trying to understand texts like those found in ads is a recursive and ongoing process, not a linear or static one.

Unfortunately, the questions suggested by the educator quoted earlier seem to ignore questioning the social world in which students live. As presented, the questions in the quote do not interrogate or expose students' beliefs, myths, and cliches, nor do they confront students' misconceptions or stereotypes. Perhaps using the key concepts of critical media literacy that I outlined earlier in this chapter as a basis for inquiry would have eased the problem. Directing students' inquiry to the construction, commercial, aesthetic, and ideological/political nature of the media text might help them to see beneath the surface and get to the deeper meaning.

To conclude this discussion on how we arrive at meaning and how we understand and detect what we read/view as meaningful to us, and then critique it, it is important, therefore, to keep in mind that *questioning* means penetrating the layers of the text. Basically, this means that we consciously engage in a systematic inquiry in which we do a number of things: identify the symbols and understand their meaning and functions; analyze the structure and understand its power; articulate the meaning as (and whatever) it communicates to us within our social context; appreciate that we won't arrive at a definitive interpretation; and come to a deeper meaning that unpacks the contradictions and dilemmas furnished by the text. Such sustained questioning opens the gates for us to pursue the meaning and understanding through further inquiry.

PRACTICES OF CRITICAL MEDIA LITERACY

I have explained that critical media literacy teaches students and teachers to take a critical stance when they read, view, or think about textual or media representations. To illustrate this practice, I encourage students and teachers to (1) scrutinize their initial understandings of textual and media representations; (2) engage in a critique of their own ideologically mediated perceptions of the situation described or inscribed in the text in question; and (3) sort out "truths" from half-truths, accuracies from inaccuracies, facts from fiction, reality from myth, and objectivity from bias.

This practice aims to help demystify the dictates of media culture and its ideologies of biased representations of women, and the use of racist representations of people of color and various minority groups, to reproduce social relations of domination and subordination. Through critical media analysis, students learn to detect bias by examining its construction, production, and the meaning-making processes by which media imagery and popular representations of people help shape students' personal, social, and political worlds. Our goal is to increase awareness, question hegemonic cultural practices, and seek action toward social change, social justice, and social equality (Semali & Pailliotet, 1999).

However, accomplishing this goal in American classrooms is not an easy task. Learning to detect and understand media bias in U.S. classrooms today is one of the most difficult, but most important, tasks for media literacy education. While students find it easy to surf the Internet and TV channels, it is harder to convince them why and how bias in the media they access everyday can be a powerful determinant of how they view themselves, others, and the world around them. Most students, having been raised with *Sesame Street* and having seen 5,000 hours of TV programming before they ever came to school (Lutz, 1989), are reluctant to accept that the media contain biases of all kinds—racial, economic, gender, political, moral, and others. This challenge to recognize bias in our culture has been compared to fish by Hinchey (1998). Like the fish who has trouble understanding the very sea surrounding it, we and our children have trouble identifying the influence of our culture because we are immersed in it and are part of it, we have been since birth and we will be until death—or until an experience with a different culture shows us that things might be other than the way we've always known them to be.

Critical theorists like Stuart Hall (1997) and John Fiske (1996) argue that bias presented through the media does not merely reflect or reinforce culture but in fact shapes the thinking, attitudes, and values by promoting dominant ideology of a culture. This fact is daunting to some parents. A majority would wish to shield their children from such an onslaught of ideology embedded in the daily barrage of media messages, especially those laden with sex, violence and ideological lies. Others would like to know where to find the much-needed antidote to bias, false representation, emotional appeals, and the power of language in manipulating myths, stereotypes, and values.

Teachers are equally perplexed by the dawning of new media like the information superhighway and the new literacies these media have introduced to us in such a short period. These new literacies, which are rooted in the literacy traditions of oral/aural, visual, and alphabetic text modalities, have been called different names: print literacy, technology literacy, information literacy, visual literacy, media literacy, and so on. Teachers and parents are becoming increasingly aware of the impact of the new media on children's social, emotional, and cognitive functions. For parents who wish to become mediators or teachers of critical media literacy, how best to teach young children and adolescents about the messages relayed by television and the Internet and how to avoid biased viewpoints at odds with a family's ethics and moral concerns are difficult decisions.

Adding to this complexity, parents may not realize how they are implicated in the persistence of bias in our society, particularly in their involvement in the construction of a childhood now part of their children. Take, for example, what mothers wish for their girls—how they represent "femininity" to them—and that such representations may well coincide with (not necessarily conflict with) the image (modified or not) of Barbie. The emphasis of multiple outfits, makeup, and fashion and the values that such goods represent are replicated daily in the media. These highly valued commodities are frequently featured in teen magazines, television advertisements, and the movies. Think for a moment: What might a mother's advice to her daughter on her high school prom dress be like? How about makeup? With whom will she date: a white boy or a person of color? The son of middle-class parents or working class? These ways of doing are not removed from the way the media socialize us through its curriculum of the screen. Taken together this way of doing, of being a young girl, constructs a normative view of what it means to be a girl in today's society. Because many young girls are socialized in these gendered identities long before they enter school, teachers may find it quite a challenge to engage them in reflecting on how such Barbie-like images influence their thinking and acting.

More now than ever, social conditions and technologies require teachers to view literacy through broader, more critical lenses (Flood & Lapp, 1995). Such critical media literacy makes possible a more adequate and accurate reading of the world, on the basis of which, as Freire and others put it, "people can enter into 'rewriting' the world into a formation in which their interests, identities and legitimate aspirations are more fully present and are present more equally" (cited in Morgan, 1997, p. 6).

Perhaps the most crucial aspect of studying bias in the media is helping students understand that while many different kinds of people and situations are represented (fairly or unfairly) in the media, many people and their viewpoints are not. The selection process of who and what will be shown, or not shown, is a complicated one and most relevant to understanding how bias is created. Teaching students to understand this process and factors that affect selection decisions is critical to their knowledge of media influence in all areas of discourse. My goal is to enable students to understand how our emotions, positive and negative, are influenced by the content of the media programs and to be aware of what in the program causes such feelings.

Understanding how media bias confines and defines public discourse on diverse issues is a key concept of media literacy education and the primary goal of this book. Media literacy education teaches students to take a critical stance when they read, view, or think about textual or media representations (Semali & Pailliotet, 1999). The broader goal of such critical education is to enable students to understand and critique the insidious curriculum of media and to conceptualize social/economic justice more clearly. Such understanding leads to possibilities to celebrate diversity, develop a sense of fairness in the distribution of our society's cultural and economic resources, and challenge the exclusionary aspect of the Eurocentric one way of seeing the world (Dines & Humez, 1995, xviii). For these students, therefore, media literacy becomes a competency to read, interpret, and to understand how meaning is made and derived from print, photographs, and other electronic visuals. It is a pursuit for the understanding of connotative messages embedded in the text of the visual and media messages.

Clearly, teaching critical media literacy must aspire to teach the youth in our classrooms, particularly those impressionable groups or individuals in desperate search of an identity and a place in the adult world. Critical media literacy will bolster skills and knowledge they need to be able to consciously reflect on their interactions with media. It will enable them to address injustices; to become critical actors committed to combat problems of youth apathy, violence, substance abuse, rampant consumerism; and to generate a strong commitment to developing a world free of oppression and exploitation. Linking what students read/view with social concerns affirms what it means to be educated and to be media literate in a media saturated milieu, in which information gathering and distribution processes thrive on the manipulation of seductive media spectacles.

Because reading, writing, speaking, listening, thinking, acting, and viewing are synergistic, interdependent, and interactive processes (Barthes, 1971), it is important to note that when readers/writers/audiences read, produce, or receive media messages, they do not create meanings in isolation. Instead they draw from experiences of other texts, connecting past and present understandings. Strategies and understandings developed in one form of communication interact and support others. As heavy media consumers, students bring an enormous quantity of information to the media literacy classroom. In fact, their information about the media usually exceeds that of the teacher. Therefore, the role of the teacher will be that of co-learner and facilitator while discussing and contextualizing the media and clarifying value messages in media texts.

It is a rewarding enterprise for teachers to guide students to examine the ways in which the media and their producers create or tell stories in the English texts they read. After all, students are not always aware of the literary devices, codes, or conventions used in producing media messages as a technique to tell stories. Such devices are not always obvious as students read stories in literature or view films and television. The way the stories are told and the person doing the telling play important roles in formulating the motive of the telling as well as making the story entertaining and at the same time believable. Recent developments in digital imaging of videos and the use of computer graphics in the morphing of images (changing parts of an image using digitized editing) make deceptions and bias much easier and faster to accomplish and much harder to detect.

The ways of telling media stories explain the coded genres of situation comedy, soaps, action adventures, and so on, which define the system of commercial television and the movie industry in the United States. Therefore, we no longer can deny the fact that some of these conventions are continually used in telling mythic stories that allow bias, overt manipulation of the characterization or plot, stereotyping, ethnic jokes, and comedic entertainment to "creep in" to the story being told. By the same token, a particular worldview is portrayed as a value, a better way of being or doing, superior culture, morally good, a better person, race, gender, or simply put, the acceptable norm—the measure of success, beauty, sexual orientation, and so on. Such a normative worldview as represented in a story is often influenced by the attitude and background of its storyteller, and its interviewers, writers, photographers, and editors.

The danger presented by these mythic realities, such as those found in popular Disney movies and television situation comedy shows, is that audiences sometimes make decisions or judgments on the basis of these myths. The conventions used in advancing the plot or resolving the conflict seem so believable and yet are oversimplified. It is important, therefore, that teachers and students examine critically their worldviews and come to the realization that media representations of race, gender, class, age, or sexual orientation are creations of producers, writers, and artists. Furthermore, it is essential to recognize that the end result of this construction is to persuade, to render "natural" or "innocent" what is profoundly "constructed," motivated, and biased. Constructions offer positions for us, in terms of what we know, how we came to know it, and the attitudes or assumptions we can make of the reality being described or represented, through which we recognize images as similar or different from those around us and ourselves. A crucial step in any media literacy program according to Art Silverblatt (1995) is the awareness that one receives numerous messages daily through the media and that these messages can affect one's behavior, attitudes, and values. In the overview of media literacy, he examines the process of communication, which involves "receiving a message, selecting relevant information, forming appropriate responses, and responding to the message" (p. 14). In the next section, I will illustrate how my students apply these principles and practices in reading, viewing, and thinking about media texts.

CRITICAL LITERACY IN TEACHER EDUCATION

Pennsylvania State University faculty grapples with state mandates as they prepare elementary and secondary schoolteachers. The framework for secondary school teacher education, with which the faculty works, is built on a model of teaching as reflective inquiry. In reflective inquiry, teachers make collective and individual decisions about life in classrooms in order to help students develop into active, knowledgeable citizens of a multicultural world. These decisions are based on teachers' understanding of self and prior experiences; their students; human development and diversity; subject matter; educational theory; curricular design; instructional methods; federal, state, and institutional regulations; and political, social, and moral relationships between education and community and world affairs. Teachers develop their understanding through continual, systematic, intensive inquiry involving problem posing, data gathering through educational literature, product analysis, observations, discussion, probing the historical conditions that produced the present circumstances, and acting on this new knowledge (Zeichner & Liston, 1996). As reflective inquirers, secondary school teachers bring personal, social, and theoretical knowledge to bear, to promote curriculum change and school improvement. Clearly, reflecting critically and taking action on one's daily work is the hallmark of a profession engaged in self-improvement.

The new approaches to curriculum and instruction being implemented at the Pennsylvania State University are significantly different from traditional ones, in that they include the following assumptions: (1) all subjects are interconnected and interrelated with one another; (2) there is no "real" truth or no one correct method of doing or explaining things (i.e., it makes it possible to integrate critical analysis of social and cultural contexts and to analyze the multiple perspectives embedded in multiple truths and that what is learned is based on points of view and experiences of the dominant groups in society), (3) learning involves creating knowledge and learning through our own lived experiences (as opposed to rote memorization of facts) (see, e.g., Freire's [1974] notion of banking theory of knowledge), (4) curriculum is not fixed, rather it is seen as a "context specific" process changing with the evolving needs of society and individuals, and (5) finally, the new approach stresses the importance of focusing on the whole rather than the parts, for example, administrative and bureaucratic constraints, classroom setup, and so on (Kincheloe & Steinberg, 1998, pp. 4–5).

Within our teacher education classrooms, we aim to develop students' critical awareness of oppressive social forces, including school structures and knowledges. Grounded in critical pedagogy, our teaching practices systematically undermine the dominant ideologies, institutions, and material conditions of society, which maintain socioeconomic inequality. This is to say that we embrace a critical literacy approach in which our teaching practices strive to analyze all texts including printed and visual texts, by looking for class bias, gender bias, and racial bias. Even though this assignment has been difficult, we believe that this is an important task because all texts are constructions and contain a point of view of the writer or producer, which needs to be understood by the reader/viewer.

Masterman (1992) found good sense in such critical inquiry when he warned educators not to concentrate on or degenerate into laborious accumulation of facts or busy work but to motivate students to formulate their own opinions and ideas through examination of the evidence and through inquiry, reflection, and response. Hopefully, by applying the frameworks of inquiry, reflection and action, students will be transformed through this language of critique and through social action. Equally and rightly, as Lankshear and McLaren (1993) put it:

> In addressing *critical* literacy we are concerned with the extent to which, the ways in which, actual and possible social practices and conceptions of reading and writing enable human subjects to understand and engage the politics of daily life in the quest for more truly democratic social order. Among other things, critical literacy makes possible a more adequate and accurate "reading" of the world, on the basis of which, as Freire and others put it, people can enter into "rewriting" the world into a formation in which their interests, identities and legitimate aspirations are more fully present and are present more equally. (p. xviii)

The practice I describe in this book embraces much of Lankshear and McLaren's notions of critical literacy with special attention to social practices. By problematizing the texts students read every day in the classrooms, students embark on a path of social consciousness that examines texts beyond surface impressions, traditional myths, and clichés. My process involves: (1) inquiry (research); (2) reflection (examining and questioning prevalent contradictions, constructions, conventions, codes, practices, and minority—non-mainstream—culture, and applying the meaning to one's own social context); and (3) action (formulating a response based on the resolve to change social order, injustices, unequal access to resources, or existing worldview). Barbara Comber (1993) clarifies the objectives of reading media texts as social practice by insisting on (1) helping students to reposition themselves as researchers of language; (2) pushing students to understand and respect their resistance to mainstream interpretations of text and exploring minority culture constructions of literacy and language use; and (3) problematizing classroom and public texts. This viewpoint echoes much of what we try to do in our language and literacy program for preservice teachers.

HOW TO USE CRITICAL MEDIA LITERACY TO STUDY BIAS

To illustrate how bias affects the content of media and confines public discourse, every semester I encourage my undergraduate preservice teachers who enroll in my media literacy class to learn to detect bias in all texts they read, view, or produce. My assumption is that by modeling this process for them, they will in turn expand and replicate the model in their own classrooms as future teachers. Activities that help students to come to terms or start to understand what I am talking about follow in this section to demonstrate how one might go about investigating the insidious cultural pedagogy of the media, particularly in the daily press. I encourage students to explore a text from the daily press in order to find questions that are significant to the learner, and then systematically investigate and critically analyze the values embedded in those questions. As an introduction into this process of studying bias, I ask them to begin watching a movie such as *The Paper*. After they watch this movie on their own, they come to class prepared to design their own newspaper for their school. Students must make decisions about who and what pictures will be shown or written about, what information or message they are trying to communicate, how to fit it into the allotted space or time, and how to get this all done on a deadline. They must take notes on the ethical dilemmas they encounter, the viewpoint(s) they take, and the moral stand they choose to uphold in the stories or opinions they select to publish.

As each group presents its version of a newspaper, peers are encouraged to note what has been included, what excluded, what message is being put forth, how people and events are portrayed, and what the overall effect might be on viewers and readers. The outcome of this exercise is that students gain firsthand experience with the way bias in the media system affects the content of media. We accomplish this by assisting students to identify their mental, sensory, and emotional positions, to develop new methods and stances, and then to choose appropriate courses of action when engaging with texts.

In the next step, students examine literature texts they are reading in their English classes. They quickly realize how bias permeates the pages of these books: gender bias, racial bias, and how the characters in the stories they read have been manipulated by the authors to suit a certain moral stand or to perpetuate a myth or value system. Such discoveries are an important realization for these future English teachers, because they soon will be standing in front of impressionable minds looking up to them for firsthand interpretations of texts from literature and the media, from Shakespeare and Chaucer to popular educational movies like *Stand and Deliver*, *Dead Poets Society*, and so on. Their opinions, values, or biases, which might reinforce myths, stereotypes, or clichés, will become primary examples students will take away as valid ways of seeing the world. If we want our students to function and thrive in modern communicational environments, we must help them develop the means to critically read, write, and connect aspects of their lives. By introducing students to critical media literacy enterprises such as these, they are able to bridge existing learning contexts and build new ones.

In taking up media literacy in a classroom, it is not enough to simply decode or understand existing biases in texts. Students and teachers must transform their newly found critical understandings into agency: positive acts and effects in themselves and others. This might transpire through generation of new texts and knowledge, developing ways of thinking and acting, or working toward alterations of unjust social conditions. Such activities might well include writing to the radio/TV station, writing letters to the editor, or encouraging students to voice their opinions or comment on detected media bias in the school newspaper. In the past, students have visited local newspaper publishing houses and a radio station, and met with community radio anchorpersons. These encounters

generated lots of questions and follow-up community actions produced
by students on their own.

LEARNING TO DETECT BIAS FROM THE NEWS

Helping students understand and detect bias in media representations is
not easy. This is so partly because bias is difficult to detect when embedded in everyday information using commonsense practices. When I encourage my students to understand and detect bias, I ask them to apply a
familiar framework. For example, I prompt them to examine the motives
of media producers and the techniques used to construct the messages
conveyed. I ask them to consider what role they, as media consumers,
may be able to play in changing the media messages and representations
they find offensive or oppressive. They also need to be aware that not all
bias is deliberate but nonetheless insidious in spite of the journalistic
ideal of "objectivity." The attitudes and background of its interviewers,
writers, photographers, and editors influence every news story. However,
students can develop awareness in reading or viewing the news by
watching for specific journalistic techniques that allow bias to "creep"
into news stories. As summarized by Newskit (1994), some of the techniques are: (1) bias through selection and omission; (2) bias through
placement; (3) bias by headline; (4) bias by photos, captions and camera
angles; (5) bias through use of names and titles; (6) bias through statistics and crowd counts; (7) bias by source control; (8) and bias in word
choice and tone. This consumer guide is a useful tool to examine both literal and surface meanings produced by journalistic styles and techniques
designed to attract readers' or viewers' attention. (See also the example
of detecting bias in newspaper articles in Chapter 6.)

WAYS TO COMBAT BIAS

To help students critique bias and their own cultural stances, I ask students to read oppositional texts and employ the language of criticism.
Reading oppositional texts allows students and teachers to move beyond
"commonsense" readings of daily life narratives. Oppositional texts are
those texts whose message runs against the grain of preferred-dominant
texts. This practice is a sure way to stop recycling myths and bias. Thus,
if teachers continue to ask the same questions on social issues, they will
simply recycle prevailing views or biases. But through *questioning*, *reflection*, and *action*, students get to know their social context, evaluate it,

and plan action to take to make changes. McMahon and Quin (1993) list "alternative questions" that lead to oppositional texts, which I employ in my classroom. I ask these questions to help students identify social issues raised by the text (literature or visuals related to them): (1) Through whose eyes or perspective do we get the information? (2) What assumptions are being made in the view presented? (3) What representations are there of the group concerned? (4) Whose voices are not being heard? (5) If a key piece of information were changed, how would the meaning change? (6) Why has this group been singled out for depiction in this manner? Who gains from this representation? (7) What would be the effect if the various depictions were reversed? (p. 18).

I also advocate and teach the language of criticism to detect biases. This process coincides with what John Dewey (1933) called the creation of an articulate public and its attendant concerns with these issues, institutions, and public spheres that are attentive to human suffering, pain, and oppression. Taking such a critical stance on media representations will effectively take reading and viewing of texts a step beyond surface impressions, traditional myths, and clichés. As far as taking action is concerned, I encourage students to engage in an interdisciplinary unit about the local environment, examining varied media to understand and detect bias. They create public service announcements, research reports, Web sites, newsletters and action plans to address issues. In secondary social studies or English/language arts classrooms, they apply critical analysis of content and points of view represented in their content area. After identifying missing information, students employ community interview, oral histories, original documents, and mass media or artistic resources to build broader pictures of events or texts. As part of social action, students make plans to apply what they learned into their social context. Silverblatt (1995, p. 304) outlines several action plans that my students take up. For example:

- Cancel subscriptions or turn off objectionable/biased programming.
- If your students have concerns about a newspaper article, or biased viewpoint, write a letter to the editor.
- If students have objection to a biased television or radio program, write to the general manager of the station.
- Register a complaint of bias with the Federal Communications Commission (FCC).

- Attempt to meet in person with the staff of the newspaper or the TV or radio station.
- Organize a petition drive.
- Organize a grassroots letter-writing campaign.
- Picket the media organization.
- Organize a boycott against the advertisers of the program or newspaper. Taking out an ad in the paper explaining your concerns and listing the program's advertisers can be an effective action step.
- Promote the instruction of critical media literacy throughout the school system (K–12) by contacting members of the school board in your school district, board of education, PTA, and principals.
- Encourage teachers and students to join a media literacy organization so that they will have access to information about media content not commonly available to the public.

As a culminating activity, these students choose to write their own books, create a newspaper, a Web site, a mural, or a dramatic presentation to convey their new understandings that are then displayed. They invite the public (usually peers, students from other disciplines, or high school students from a nearby school) for comment and critique. By using readings, observations, personal interviews, artifacts in their own lives, videos, and list server discussions, these students access, articulate, examine, and adapt their beliefs about teaching, make professional changes, and formulate plans for their own future growth, as well as that of their respective communities.

CONCLUDING COMMENTS

The potential outcomes for a critical media literacy program include:

- Become well informed in matters of media coverage.
- Be aware of your everyday contact with the media and its influence on lifestyle, attitudes, and values.
- Apply the key concepts to interpreting/analyzing media messages to derive insight into media messages.
- Develop sensitivity to programming trends as a way of learning about the culture.
- Keep abreast of patterns in ownership and government regulations that affect the media industry.

- Consider the role of the media in individual decision making. Think carefully about the possible role of media messages on specific decisions or behavior. In what ways have the media affected the purchase of consumer items, the selection of political candidates, the choice of activities or standards of conduct?

These outcomes confirm one of the key concepts of critical media literacy—that all media are constructions. Because all texts are creations with potential bias, we need to bring a critical stance to all texts that inform our worldview, a competency gained through critical media literacy education. Within this perspective, the mass media are no longer viewed as windows of the world nor objective representations of our world, but rather as subjective and sometimes loaded with social biases regarding race, class, sexual orientation, gender, and ethnic differences. In critical media literacy, teachers must ask students to take a hard look at what the media tell them about the world—as media continue to be a major source of information, culture, and entertainment. The media are not neutral conduits of messages, but rather, they actively create notions of what constitutes truth, values, racial relations, bias, stereotypes, and representations of people. In sum, critical viewing, critical reading, and critical authoring are pivotal components by which to integrate media literacy across the school curriculum.

VIGNETTE 3

Reflections on a Newspaper Picture

One day in October 1994, after the U.S. invasion of Haiti, the *Philadelphia Inquirer* published a front-page picture shot by Carol Guzy, a photographer of the *Washington Post*. This picture captured the looting of a school warehouse in Port au Prince while the U.S. troops looked on. The caption read: "A Haitian woman, clutching a sack of rice that is caked on her face, lies injured during a food riot at the Catholic school warehouse in Port au Prince. Groups of men fought over the food yesterday, attacking even women and children. Passing U.S. troops did not intervene" (*Inquirer*, 1994, p. 1).

Troubled and perplexed by this graphic picture, I wondered what it would mean to my American students. What images might this picture evoke in their minds? What do images of the poor and hungry mean for my students? So I took the picture to my preservice student teachers. My concern was how much did they know about the U.S. intervention in Haiti? Did they know anything of the history of U.S. intervention in the Caribbean—Grenada, Panama, and now once again Haiti? What preexisting understandings about America and the developing world did they hold that allowed for their reaction to the picture? What role in forming those understandings was played by the mass media on this day, as on most others, was uncritical—even celebratory—of American military intervention?

I felt the need, more than ever, to understand the models of the developing world and of cultural difference, broadly shared by white, middle-class Americans, that many of our undergraduate students brought to the classrooms and that I myself struggle with and against. After much consideration, I turned to the examination of network news, particularly the visual pictures presented as one of the most culturally valued and potent media vehicle shaping American understanding of, and responses to, the world outside the United States.

My interest was, and is, in the making and consuming of images of the non-Western world, a topic raising volatile issues of power, race, and history. What does popular education tell Americans about who non-Westerners are, what they want, and what our relationship is to them? As any other popular media in America, the network news exists in a complex system of artifacts and communication devices: newspapers and magazines, television news and special reports, museums and exhibitions, geography and world history textbooks, student exchange programs, travelogues and films from *Rambo* and *Raiders of the Lost Ark* to *El Norte*.

Yet these diverse contexts are in communication with one another, purveying and contesting a limited universe of ideas about cultural difference and how it can or should be interpreted. To use television network news or newspaper photographs as pedagogical sights is to study not a single cultural artifact but a powerful voice in an ongoing cultural discussion of these issues. The history, culture, and social reality of North-South relations is primarily written, of course, in corporation boardrooms, government agency offices, and encounters between tourists, bankers, military personnel, and State Department employees, on the one hand, and the people of the developing nations on the other. The role of a cultural institution like the network evening news or the *Philadelphia Inquirer* and its viewers and readers, respectively, might seem small by comparison. But its role is not simply to form an "educated public," nor is it simply to mislead or err in describing those relations; it can also provide support for American state policies and for voting and consumer behavior.

While a front-page picture of the *Philadelphia Inquirer* is seen as a straightforward kind of evidence about the world—a simple and objective mirror of reality—it is, in fact, evidence of a much more complex, interesting, and consequential world of reality. It reflects as much on who is behind the lens, from photographers to newspaper editors, and graphic designers to the readers who look—with sometimes different eyes—through the *Philadelphia Inquirer*'s institutional lens. A photograph can be seen as a cultural artifact because its makers and readers look at the world with an eye that is not universal or natural but taught to look for certain cues. It can also be seen as a commodity, because a newspaper concerned with revenues sells it.

The visual structures represented in the photograph, and the reading rendered by audiences, can tell us about the cultural, social, and historical contexts that produced them. An attempt to study visual structures leads us to the way in which meanings are offered to us and *our part* in actively making sense of them. It is important to keep in mind that the assumptions we make, what we consider as common knowledge or common sense, or "*general*" knowledge, or widespread beliefs and popular attitudes, are conventions we form as part of our cultural knowledge.

The fundamentally critical perspective I take on media and its social context as illustrated in this brief vignette is thus linked in a range of ways to deeply personal concerns. I am concerned with how to imagine and value difference, how to foster both empathetic forms of understanding and historically grounded perceptions. These perceptions emerge out of childhood and adolescent experiences and the choice one makes of adult work. My goal here is to bring a critical perspective into the ways media, such as newspaper photographs are constructed, to point out some of the prevailing cultural ideas about others through which any photograph of the non-Western world has often been filtered, and to raise questions about what could be done in the classroom and in the curriculum to develop such critical perspectives. We need to know how to make knowledge and knowing meaningful to the students we teach, so that the knowing they acquire affects their lives as adults.

REFERENCES

Allen, R. L. (1993). Conceptual models of an African-American belief system: A program of research. In G. L. Berry, & J. K. Asamen (Eds.), *Children & television: Images in a changing social cultural world.* Newbury Park, CA: Sage.

Alvermann, D. E. (1996). Middle and high school students' perceptions of how they experience text-based discussions: A multicase study. *Reading Research Quarterly, 31*(3) July/Aug/Sept: 244–267.

Alvermann, D. E., Hinchman, K. A., Moore, D. W., Phelps, S. F., & Waff, D. R. (Eds.). (1998). *Reconceptualizing the literacies in adolescents' lives.* Mahwah, NJ: Erlbaum.

Anderson, J. & Ploghoft, M. (1993). Children and media in media education. In G. L. Berry, & J. K. Asamen (Eds.), *Children and television: Images in a changing sociocultural world.* Newbury Park, CA: Sage.

Barthes, R. (1974). *S/Z* (R. Miller, Trans.). New York: Hill and Wang/The Noonday Press.

———. (1971). *Image, music, text* (S. Heath, Trans.). New York: Hill and Wang.

Bourdieu, P., & Passeron, J. C. (1985). Reproduction. In Aronowitz & Giroux, *Education and siege.* Westport, CT: Bergin and Garvey.

Bradley, D. F. & West, J. F., (1994). Staff training for the inclusion of students with disabilities: Visions from school-based education. *Teachers Education and Special Education, 17*(2): 117–128.

Bruffee, K. (1986). *A short course in writing practical rhetoric for teaching composition through collaborative learning* (3rd ed.). Boston: Little, Brown.

Cazden, C., Green J., & Wallace, C. (1992). Critical language awareness in the EFL classroom. In N. Fairclough (Ed.), *Critical language awareness.* (52–92) Harlow: Longman.

Center Daily Times, October 28, 1994.

Comber, B. (1993). Classroom explorations in critical literacy. *The Australian Journal of Language and Literacy, 16*(1).

Considine, D. M., & Haley, G. E. (1992). *Visual messages. Integrating imagery into instruction.* Englewood, Co: Teachers Ideas Press.

Courts, P. (1997). *Multicultural literacies: Dialect, discourse, and diversity.* New York: Peter Lang.

Culler, J. (1976). *Ferdinand de Saussure.* New York: Penguin Books.

Cyer, R. (1992). *Only entertainment.* London: Routledge.

De Saussure, F. (1974). *Course in general linguistics.* London: Fontana Press.

Derrida, J. (1986). Structure, sign, and play in the discourse of the human sciences; of grammatology; difference. In H. Adams, & L. Searle (Eds.), *Criti-

cal Theory Since 1965 (pp. 83–137). Tallahassee: Florida State University Press.

Dewey, J. (1938). *Experience in education.* New York: Macmillan.

―――. (1933). *How we think.* Chicago: Henry Regnery.

Dines, G., & Humez, J. M. (1995). *Gender, race, and class in media.* Thousand Oaks, CA: Sage.

Duncan, B. (1993). Surviving education's desert storms: Adventures in media literacy—A retrospective and a guide for tomorrow. *Telemedium, 39*(1–2), 13–17.

Fairclough, N. (1989). *Language and power.* London: Longman.

Fiske, J. (1996). *Media matters: Everyday culture and political change.* Minneapolis, NM: University of Minnesota Press.

―――. (1987). *Television culture.* New York: Methuen.

Flood, J., & Lapp, D. (1995). Broadening the lens: Toward an expanded conceptualization of literacy. In K. A. Hinchman, D. J. Leu, & C. K. Kinzer (Eds.), *Perspectives on literacy research and practice: Forty-fourth yearbook of the National Reading Conference* (pp. 1–16). Chicago: National Reading Conference.

Foucault, M. (1980). *Power/knowledge: Selected interviews and other writings.* C. Gordon (Ed.). New York: Pantheon.

Freire, P. (1974). *Education for critical consciousness.* London: Sheed and Ward.

Garret, S. (n.d). *Messages and meaning: A guide to understanding media.* Lancaster, PA: Newspapers in Education.

Gee, J. (1996). Social linguistics and literacies: Ideology in discourses (2nd ed.) London: Taylor & Francis.

Geertz, C. (1988). *Works and lives: The anthropologist as author.* Palo Alto, CA: Stanford University Press.

Gergen, K. (Ed.). (1985). *The social construction of the person.* New York: Springer-Verlag.

Goetz, J. P., & LeCompte, M. D. (1984). *Ethnography and qualitative design in educational research.* Orlando, FL: Academic Press.

Hall, S. (1997). *Representation. Cultural representations and sgnifying practices.* London: The Open University.

Hammer, R. (1995). Rethinking the dialectic: A critical semiotic meta-theoretical approach for the pedagogy of media literacy. In P. McLaren, R. Hammer, D. Sholle, & S. Reilly, (Eds.), *Rethinking media literacy: A critical pedagogy of representation* (pp. 33–85). New York: Peter Lang.

Hardt, L. (1993). *Giles Deleuze: An apprenticeship in philosophy.* Minneapolis, MN: University of Minnesota Press.

Hinchey, P. (1998). *Finding freedom in the classroom: A practical introduction to critical theory.* New York: Peter Lang.

Hirsch, E. (1987). *Cultural literacy: What every American needs to know.* Boston: Houghton Mifflin.

Hobbs, R. (1994). Teaching media literacy—are you hip to this? *Media Studies Journal* (Winter).

Janks, H. (1993). *Language, identity and power.* Johannesburg and Rundburg: Witwatersrand University Press and Hodder and Stoughton Educational.

Kellner D. (1995). *Media culture: Cultural studies, identity, and politics between the modern and the postmodern.* New York: Routledge.

Kincheloe, J., & Steinberg, S. (1998). *Unauthorized methods. Strategies for critical teaching.* New York: Routledge.

Kress, G. (1988). *Communication and culture.* Kensington, NSW: University of New South Wales Press.

Krueger, R. A. (1994). *Focus groups. A practical guide for applied research.* Thousand Oaks, CA: Sage.

Lankshear, C., & McLaren, P. (Eds.). (1993). *Critical literacy: Politics, praxis, and the postmodern.* Albany: State University of New York Press.

Levarance, D., & Tyner, K. (1966). What is media literacy? Two leading proponents offer an overview. *Media Spectrum, 23*(1): 10.

Luke, C. (1999). Media and cultural studies in Australia. *International Reading Association* (pp. 622–626).

———. (1997). Media literacy and cultural studies. In S. Muspratt, A. Luke, & P. Freebody (Eds.), *Constructing critical literacies: Teaching and learning textual practice* (pp. 19–49). Cresskill, NJ: Hampton Press.

Lusted, David (Ed.). (1991). *The media studies book: A guide for teachers.* London: Routledge.

Lutz, W. (1989). *Doublespeak.* New York: Harper Perennial.

McLuhan, M. (1962). *The Gutenberg galaxy: The making of typographic man.* Toronto: University of Toronto Press.

McMahon, B. & Quin, R. (1993). Knowledge, power, and pleasure: Direction in media education. *Telemedium, 39*(1–2): 18–22.

Masterman, L. (1992) *Teaching the media.* New York: Routledge.

———. (1985). *Teaching the media.* London: Routledge.

Miguel, A. R. (Ed.). (1997). *Powerless fictions? Ethics, cultural critique, and American fiction in the age of postmodernism.* Atlanta, GA: Rudopi.

Morgan, W. (1997). *Critical literacy in the classroom.* New York: Routledge.

Newskit. (1994). *How to detect bias in the news. A consumers' guide to news media.* Lake Zurich, IL: The Learning Seed Company, p. 2.

Pennsylvania Education, 24, (5), February 1993: pp. 3–5.

Philadelphia Inquirer, October 27, 1994, p. 1.

Rorty, R. (1979). *Philosophy and the mirror of nature.* Princeton: Princeton University Press.

Searle, C. (Ed.). (1995). *Heart of Sheffield.* Sheffield: Earl Marshal School.

———. (Ed.). (1994). *Lives of love and hope: A Sheffield herstory.* Sheffield: Earl Marshal School.

Semali, L. (1994). Critical viewing as a response to intermediality: Implications for media literacy. In L. Semali, & Pailliotet, A. (Eds.), *Intermediality: The teachers' handbook of critical media literacy.* Boulder, CO: Westview.

Semali, L., & Pailliotet, A. (1999). Introduction. What is intermediality and why study it in U.S. classrooms? In Semali, L. & Pailliotet, A. (Eds.), *Intermediality: The teachers' handbook of critical media literacy.* Boulder, CO: Westview.

Silverblatt, A. (1995). *Media literacy. Keys to interpreting media messages.* Westport, CT: Praeger.

Stewart, D. (1990). *Focus groups: Theory and practice.* Thousand Oaks, CA: Sage.

Thoman, E. (1999). Skills and strategies for media education. *Educational Leadership.* (February):50–54.

Tyner, K. (1998). *Literacy in a digital world: Teaching and learning in the age of information.* Mahwah, NJ: Erlbaum.

Ukadike, N. F. (1990). Western images of Africa: Genealogy of an ideological formulation. *Black Scholar, 21*(2): 30–48.

Wallace, C. (1992). Critical language awareness in the EFL classroom. In N. Fairclough (Ed.), *Critical language awareness* (pp. 49–92). Harlow: Longman.

Walmsley, S. A., & Walp, T. P. (1990). Integrating literature and composing into the language arts curriculum: Philosophy and practice. *Elementary School Journal, 90:* 251–274.

Wells, G. (1986). *The meaning makers: Children learning language and using language to learn.* Portsmouth, NH: Heinemann.

Worth, S., & Gross, L. (Eds.). (1981). *Studying visual communications.* Philadelphia, PA: University of Pennsylvania University Press.

Zeichner, K. & Liston, D. (1996). *Reflective teaching.* Mahwah, NJ: Erlbaum.

CHAPTER 4

Critical Viewing, Reading, Authoring, and Thinking
The Practice of Media Literacy

Critical viewing is a concept built around what has become known as the discourse (or simply the language) of "criticism." A discourse of criticism is a critical analysis of social practice (or what is going on, how things are, the dominant view). Stuart Hall (1997) describes the term *discourse* as ways of referring to or constructing knowledge about a particular topic of practice, namely, a cluster of ideas, images, and practices that provide ways of talking about forms of knowledge. This may also include conduct associated with a particular topic, social activity, or institutional site in society. Many of the ideas of critical viewing are drawn from the fields of media theory, critical pedagogy, discourse analysis, postmodernist thought, and cultural studies, to which Stuart Hall has made a monumental contribution, particularly with his ideas on representation.

Critical viewing provides teachers and students ways of thinking about the production of knowledge and about negotiating through praxis the relationship among classroom teaching and the larger institutional structures of the school, and nation-state. By teaching critical viewing in public schools, media educators aim to develop new strategies and frameworks for thinking about the meaning texts transmit and the meaning viewers and readers construct themselves. Critical viewing directs our attention toward the practices of what Hall (1997) calls "signifying." When he talks about signifying practices, he implies reading and interpreting cultural texts. These cultural texts require analysis of the actual signs, symbols, figures, images, narratives, words, and sounds—the material forms in which symbolic meaning is circulated.

Luke (1999) adds to the clarity of what I mean by language of criticism when she focuses on specific analytic questions that lead to a critical understanding of how texts position readers or viewers including the cultural and social contexts of viewers and texts. Such analytic framework would include schemes that target:

- How society, culture, and persons are portrayed.
- What attitudes and values images promote.
- What technical, symbolic, and semiotic features are used to generate meanings.
- How what we see and read influences our opinions of others, our worldviews, our social relations, and behaviors.
- How others, reading from different social cultural positions, view a certain text, and what it might mean to them.

By using these analytical schemes of the language of criticism, innovative teachers struggle to find analytical strategies and frameworks that illuminate their understanding and interpretation of textual references and social contexts found in school structures, literature, and the modern mass media, which tend to perpetuate inequalities on the basis of social class, race, gender, and sexual orientation. These teachers ask: What does this image mean? What is this ad saying? Since there is no social order which can guarantee that things will have "one, true meaning" or that meanings won't change over time, viewing and reading of media texts are bound to be interpretative—a debate between, not what is "right" and who is "wrong," but between equally plausible, though sometimes competing and contested meanings and interpretations (Hall, 1997).

When these teachers talk about critical viewing as a form of social critique in their classrooms, they are talking about actively extending and transforming students' understanding of the ways meanings are constructed by developing strategies to analyze, evaluate, critique, and interpret systems of beliefs and communicative practices embedded in printed texts, television programs, and other popular media. Such strategies are important since reality exists outside language. Hall (1980) emphasizes this point when he states:

> Since the visual discourse translates a three-dimensional world into
> two-dimensional planes, it cannot, of course be the referent or concept
> it signifies. . . . Reality exists outside language, but it is constantly me-

diated by and through language: and what we can know and say has to
be produced in and through transparent representation of the "real"
language but of the articulation of language on real relations and conditions. Thus, there is no intelligible discourse without the operation of
a code. (p. 131)

By this statement, Hall informs us that language use, particularly media
language, which operates a code system and conventions that are historically derived, plays a crucial role in mediating meanings, or what we call
knowledge. Because of the uncertainty of its representational code, readers and viewers must be vigilant and must take the time to analyze the
referent the visual or text signifies. Hall further explains that language is
constantly changing and shifting with context, usage, and historical cir-
cumstance. By paying attention to language, soon educated and media
literate viewers and readers will discover that meaning is not straightforward or transparent, and does not survive intact the passage through representation.

POSSIBILITIES OF THE VISION OF CRITICISM

In the past, discourse analysis and reader/viewer response have dominated classrooms as analytical schemes (Karolides, 1992). These response-centered transactional approaches, which insist on the reader's
role in conjunction with the text, the reader's individuality affecting and
being affected by the text, have influenced many teachers in how they
teach the interpretation of meaning in literature. In spite of considerable
disagreement among theorists as to what these analytical approaches can
do for students as they learn how language works and struggle with interpreting meaning in literature, for many teachers discourse analysis has
become a significant and viable tool for (1) deciphering and clarifying
the reading process, (2) determining the role of the reader in relation to
the text, (3) exploring how meaning is made, (4) defining the nature of
the interpretative act, and (5) assessing the influence of reading communities and literature conventions (Karolides, 1992, p. xi).

    In more recent years, this preoccupation with meaning has taken a
different turn, being more concerned not with detail of how language
works but with the broader role of discourse in culture. Proponents of
cultural studies contend that culture is a terrain on which there takes
place a continual struggle over meaning, in which subordinate groups
attempt to resist the imposition of meanings that bear the interests of

dominant groups or cultural practice. It is this struggle over cultural practice that makes culture ideological. Stuart Hall (1997), in particular, draws our attention to the term *discourse* as a cultural practice as Michel Foucault used it. As such, Hall insists that "discourse" suggests "a group of statements which provide a language for talking about—a way of representing the knowledge about—a particular topic at a particular historical moment" (p. 44). It is important to note that the concept of *discourse* in this usage is not purely a "linguistic" concept. It is about language and practice. Considering discourse as language and practice attempts to overcome the traditional distinction between what one *says* (language) and what one *does* (practice). Thus, discourse, Foucault argues, constructs the topic. It defines and produces the objects of our knowledge. It governs the way that a topic can be meaningfully talked about and reasoned about. It also influences how ideas are put into practice and used to *regulate* the conduct of others. Just as discourse rules in certain ways of talking about a topic, defining an acceptable and intelligible way to talk, write, or conduct oneself, so also, by definition, it rules out, limits and restricts other ways of talking, of conducting ourselves in relation to the topic or constructing knowledge about it (Hall, 1997, p. 44).

When theorists use this concept "discourse" to talk about a "discourse of criticism," they are making reference to ideas that go beyond language in its current use to include its practice within a culture. Therefore, it will be difficult for educators to develop strategies to analyze, evaluate, critique, and interpret a system of beliefs and communicative practices without understanding how meaning is constructed within the [tele]visual discourse. So when I talk about a discourse of criticism, I aim at the domains of knowledge construction and power that comes with possession of the knowledge to define the "talk" and to regulate the conduct of others. It is important for teachers and students to understand these theoretical underpinnings surrounding cultural texts as socially constructed and as forms of knowledge guarded or controlled by those in control of the discourse. As educators examine such texts, they can recognize oppression and inequality. As an educator, I would hope that students would be able to reconstruct in their own productions and writings more inclusive, less denigrating cultural texts for mass or classroom consumption. It is within such reconstructions that a discourse of criticism opens up those spaces locked up by dominant groups in society. A discourse of criticism enables students to come to their own realizations that some texts they read or view are racist, sexist, ageist, or that homophobic language and images oppress and subordinate others. A discourse of criticism urges students and teachers to develop analytical schemes to get at, not only the language, but also its practice and what we need to know about the visuals, signs, and symbols it carries in the present text as well as historically. Thus, analyzing the discourse of culture is in part a process of social critique envisaged in the vision of criticism.

Carmen Luke (1999) understands these analytical schemes, which have been used in classrooms in Australia, to include four levels of practice:

1. Coding practice—what analytic skills can I apply to crack the codes of this text? How does this text work?
2. Text-meaning practice—what different cultural meanings and readings does this text enable? How does the combination of language, ideas, and images hold together to produce meanings?
3. Pragmatic practice—How does this text work in different contexts? How does context shape its uses? What does this text mean to me and what might it mean for others in different situations and cultural contexts?
4. How does this text attempt to position me? Who is the ideal person this text addresses? Whose interests are served in this text? Who is present or absent in this text?

While critics of this language of criticism often decry this educational approach for its idealist multiculturalism, its advocates, including Freire, Aronowitz, Giroux, Kincheloe, McLaren, and others, have complained that such a critical pedagogy has often been domesticated and reduced to student-directed learning approaches devoid of social critique. By this, critical theorists insist for students unawares, a language of criticism that is rooted in practice pedagogy can easily become irrelevant or even dogmatic or prescriptive in certain circumstances. For example, when the notion of critical reading/viewing is used in English/language arts classrooms, analysis of texts tends to remain at the reader-response level and does not always take a "critical stance" or include the language of criticism. At this level, often the questioning of texts does not challenge students to create their own knowledge or go beyond the prepackaged knowledge that is in a text that needs to be actively deconstructed.

This chapter challenges teachers to reevaluate these analytical schemes to gain a more contextual understanding of the mutually constitutive nature of theory and practice. With this objective, I propose critical viewing as a vision of criticism—a vision of enabling students and teachers to become "co-creators" of knowledge. By creating their own knowledge, students no longer accept the preferred meanings that some educators would wish them to memorize. Instead, as they consume media texts, students become aware of the multiple ways in which texts position them or represent other people, events, and desires. By resisting the preferred or dominant meaning, students are moved to resist routine hegemonic practices and explore other alternative texts that open the spaces for imagining other possible worldviews.

The underlying assumption that runs throughout this chapter is that taking a critical stance calls for analytical strategies to sift through the multiple layers of texts presented in such multimedia environments of Web sites, videos, and electronic bulletin boards. As a reflective approach to teaching and learning, critical viewing bridges theory and teaching practice. Advocates of this language of criticism would have us pay attention to how our society is marked by a multiplicity of cultures, meanings, and values. If students' attention were guided to how powerful groups define their own particular meanings, values, experiences, and forms of writing and reading as the *valued* ones in society, students would better understand the inequalities and violations of social justice the mass media continue to peddle through its production of culture products. Furthermore, through this reflective approach, we hope to illustrate the theory and practice of a critical pedagogy that helps students to engage in the social struggle over meaning and to navigate today's classrooms, which have become inundated by diverse and multiple layers of printed and electronic texts.

To implement the vision of criticism illustrated in this chapter, students will be able to (1) analyze the hierarchical positioning of individuals within the social order on the basis of race, class, gender, and sexuality, and (2) acknowledge the multiple and insidious ways in which power operates in the larger society "to reproduce the interests of the dominant culture" (Hammer, 1995, p. 79).

EXTENDING CRITICAL MEDIA LITERACY PRACTICES

In the past, textual analysis was confined to the literary scrutiny of printed words. Students analyzed stories, plays, poems, essays, and novels. Today, even though this literary analysis in classrooms has been expanded to include visual images and electronic messages, analysis has remained limited to response-centered transactional approaches. Teachers using these approaches are often content to seek to see in literature what has previously been invisible and to hear what has previously been inaudible.

Furthermore, by adhering to a traditional reader/viewer-response model, teachers in the English classrooms maintain that their approach fosters critical thinking and critical viewing skills. Typical response-centered teaching practices include exercises such as: making students write a review of a film, testing for a good cinematic scene, or asking students to indicate or imagine what they would miss if they only heard the dialogue of a film (Teasley & Wilder, 1997, p. 47). Such activities strive to ensure that content is mastered by encouraging students to take copious notes, pause to ask questions, and keep track of time elapsed, main events, and notable literary, dramatic, or cinematic aspects (Teasley & Wilder, 1997, pp. 114–145).

Within this pragmatic approach, critical reading/viewing is confined to literary or artistic analysis notably appropriate for film criticism, which, for the most part, provides key analysis of media for entertainment and to enhance enjoyment of the arts. A similar superficial transfer of analytical strategies from a reader-response approach of printed works to visual images has recently been adopted by some educators in their classrooms as well as some Newspaper in Education (NIE) organizations throughout the country (Garret, n.d.). Teachers take up such transfer to legitimize viewing of films and television in the classroom in order to respond to the longtime criticism about these mass media of entertainment. By carrying out this acclaimed active viewer model with their students (which has been for the large part adopted from Eddie Dick of the Scottish Film Council), these educators claim that they are in fact teaching critical media literacy (Dick, 1987).

Even though the reader/viewer-response approach calls for students to be active viewers—paying close attention to details, writing down immediate responses, discussing interpretations with their fellow students, and supporting opinions with evidence from the film—such analysis rarely moves beyond the content of the visual imagery or beyond the ability to simply remember and understand visual information. Unfortunately, this approach and other student-centered teaching strategies like it demand a teaching paradigm markedly different from that practiced in most U.S. classrooms today. The typical U.S. model is pragmatic and skill-based, relying on rote learning and lecture (Tyner, 1993). Most often, media texts are treated like pieces of literature; students typically spot themes, do a chart, fill out a log, complete worksheets, make a list, write a response, neglecting a critical analysis of media (see examples provided by Davies, 1996, pp. 207–208). As explained earlier, perhaps what Davies and others have overlooked and is probably needed, as surmised by Barry Duncan, president and founder of the Association of Media Literacy (founded in 1978), are "more cultural approaches to literature and not more literary approaches to popular culture" (Duncan, 1993, p. 14).

Therefore, teaching critical viewing must aspire to teach the youth in our classrooms, particularly those impressionable groups of youth in desperate search of an identity and a place in the adult world. For these groups, critical viewing will bolster skills and knowledge they need to be able to consciously reflect on their interactions with media. It will enable them to address injustices; become critical actors committed to combat problems of youth apathy, violence, substance abuse, rampant consumerism; and generate a strong commitment to developing a world free of oppression and exploitation. Linking this vision of criticism with social concerns affirms what it means to be educated and to be media literate in a media-saturated milieu in which information gathering and distribution processes thrive on the manipulation of seductive media spectacles.

LANGUAGE OF CRITICISM AND PERSISTENT MYTHS

Although the language of criticism on education has, for the past twenty years, proliferated within academic circles, it has received practically no attention in public schools or society at large. Critical theorists in academic institutions, particularly theorists who engage the debates in the emerging field of cultural studies (Aronowitz & Giroux, 1991; Freire, 1970; Giroux & McLaren, 1989; Hall, 1997; Simon, 1987), used this language of criticism to provide educators with numerous insights. As a cross-disciplinary study, cultural studies are concerned with institutions, representations, systems of beliefs, and communicative practices. This language of "criticism" and the insights gained from cultural studies have uncovered several myths persistent with media knowledge. For example: the myth that schools in our society serve as the "great equalizer," allowing children from all social and economic backgrounds to compete fairly in our marketplace economy (Bowles & Gintis, 1976, p. 26). It has also exposed the way in which conventional schools in society transmit a "hidden curriculum," which undermines most of our children's sense of self-esteem, efficacy, and compassion, and which also profoundly narrows whose "voices" (e.g., men over women, whites over people of color, industrialists over laborers, militarists over peace activists) and what epistemological and social values are expressed in classrooms (Goodman, 1992, p. 271).

Since the mid-1980s, however, conservatives have set the agenda and tone for public mood regarding education in our society with issues like school choice, vouchers, tightening standards, emphasis on phonics, back-to-basics, and so on. Clearly, the vision of criticism illustrated in Goodman's (1992) comments represents an alternative to this conservative, dominant agenda, as well as to the common view of teachers in U.S. society as educational and classroom managers. Myths are without doubt more pervasive in the media than we are willing to admit. It is important to realize that improvements in communication technology have given the media, particularly television, the power to present an electronic world that appears so realistic that it is easily mistaken for the real world, which lies beyond the one created by the media. As media consumers, people use the media to fill in gaps as they view drama unfolding on television. Most people know that media programs are a construction, and that make-up and stylists work for hours to create an image of beauty on the screen. In his televisual communication model, Hall (1973) warns that the circulation of meaning in televisual discourse is manipulated by media professionals (perhaps for no ill intent) to suit their worldview. He states:

> [The media event] is framed throughout by meanings and ideas; knowledge-in-use-concerning the routines of production, historically defined technical skills, professional ideologies, institutional knowledge, definitions and assumptions, assumptions about the audience and so on frame the construction of the program through this production structure. Further, though the production structures of television originate the television discourse, they do not constitute a closed system. They draw topics, treatments, agendas, events, personnel, images of the audience, "definitions of the situation" from other sources and other discursive formations within the wider socio-cultural and political structure of which they are a differentiated part. (p. 129)

Clearly, the manipulation of texts is not limited to televisual events but also takes place in all texts. For this reason, therefore, when impressionable minds are confronted with myths in the texts they read or view every day, teachers need to help them scrutinize its content on two levels: realism and ideology. A responsible attitude toward a myth demands critical questioning of whether its contents stand up to reality, and of whose interests it legitimizes. This is important, because stories about the world never originate in a void; they always represent a preselected point of view and acquire a normative dimension as affirmed by Hall in the quote above. Myths also tell us how the world ought to be and that some kinds of acts are objectionable.

Besides, the media also are able to create in front of our eyes a world that is composed of dichotomies, that there are only the good and the bad, the rich and the poor, the right and the wrong, the fat and the thin. McNeil (1983) (cited in Davies, 1996) argues that this simplicity derives from the fact that media, in this case television, must appeal to the broadest audience possible. He notes the irony that, as our society becomes increasingly more complex, "television, with its dominant communication instruments, and its principal form of national linkage, becomes an instrument that sells simplicity and tidiness; neat solutions of human problems that usually have no neat solutions" (p. 5). No wonder young female adolescents who watch soaps or sitcoms end up with feelings of angst, wondering why it feels as if they are the only ones who feel so low and so unworthy. When they turn to television for answers, they find that the characters' lives, especially the ones lived by girls on the television show *Melrose Place*, are wonderful—gorgeous bodies, happy smiles, and great boyfriends. They feel that their own lives don't measure up to this world of perfection.

Perhaps the most important myth to recognize is the means by which media and our culture drive ideologies. We have been socialized to believe that the function of today's mass media is to entertain. As a measure, however, media success is not based upon how well they entertain, as much as how well they are consumed. We are consuming culture in terms of media products (movies, sports, sitcoms), material goods (fashion, electronic gadgetry, cars, etc.), and food (more than two hundred brands of cereal, beverages, etc.). The advertising media convince us that we absolutely need certain products, and unfortunately, that we need to look and act a certain way as well.

In her essay "Beauty and the Beast of Advertising," Jean Kilbourne (1995) writes:

> Advertising is an over $130 billion a year industry and affects all of us throughout our lives. We are each exposed to over 1,500 commercials a day, constituting perhaps one of the most powerful educational force in society. But the commercials sell other things too. They sell values, images of people, and concepts of success and worth, love and sexuality, popularity and normalcy. They tell us who we are and who we should be. Sometimes they sell addictions. Advertising is the foundation and economic lifeblood of the mass media. The primary purpose of the mass media is to deliver an audience to advertisers. (p. 121).

Adolescents are particularly vulnerable to these messages because they are still in the process of forming their own identity. But unfortunately, the identities that young women find in the mass media are all too often either the housewife ideal or the sex object. Kilbourne insists: "Women are constantly exhorted to emulate this ideal, to feel ashamed and guilty if they fail, and to feel that their desirability and lovability are contingent upon physical perfection" (p. 122). What can schools do to help these young women and other youth to detect the commercial persuasive appeals, myths, media bias, distortion, and lies? What strategies must they use? In an increasingly global tapestry of mass media and mass culture, vigilance and scrutiny of the politics of consumerism and instant gratification are crucial as ever.

In Pennsylvania, for example, teachers in many school districts have until now paid little or no attention to the language of criticism, particularly with specific reference to the unexplored resources of media texts. Perhaps this situation is more so because teachers accept media information as entertainment and therefore see mass media as having little to do with literacy, learning, or schools (Watkin, 1994). This is by no means an attack on Pennsylvania teachers for benign neglect of their teaching profession. Far from it. For many educators, critical viewing and the concept of interpreting and "reading" television are foreign concepts. Perhaps, this stems from social attitudes about the entertainment media and the scant attention given to media and television during teacher education. In studies of visual communication and media education, critical viewing is not used widely in U.S. classrooms as a tool for deconstructing media images, particularly those images that represent people's culture, identity, or ethnicity (Semali, 1997). This may be because the media literacy movement is fairly new to many schools.

While addressing the National Leadership Conference on Media Literacy, Francis Davis (1992) outlined the long history in the United States—a history of the electronic media—regarding the influence of mass media and how the far-reaching expansion of the media has led to strategies of protecting or empowering the public: regulation, pressure on advertisers and those responsible for the creation of mass media, and media education. As Davis rightly concludes from his presentation, these three current strategies are unified by their common assumption that something about the mass media environment is problematic. The public must either be protected against media or empowered so that the negative effects of the mass media are lessened and the positive enhanced.

These protectionist and civic defense arguments have driven the movement of media literacy in the United States (Buckingham, 1991, p. 13). Not so long ago, the movement to teach media literacy in public schools, which began in Britain and spread to Canada and Australia (also known in these countries as media education), was sparked by a 1972 report by the Surgeon General's Advisory Committee on television and violence. This comprehensive research study indicated that heavy viewing is related to a decrease in creativity and violence is linked to criminal or aggressive behavior (U.S. Department of Health, 1982). This study resulted in government funding to teach critical viewing skills in the public schools including those strategies developed by WNET–New York (WNET, 1979, p. ii). Twenty-two years later, President Bill Clinton signed into law the Goals 2000: Educate America Act, which describes what students should be taught and tested in core subjects. Later, after months of national debate, and capitalizing on the successes of passing the Children's Television Act of 1990, the arts were added to the list of core subjects, which included teaching media literacy in all primary and secondary schools (Semali, 1994). As a result of teachers steadily joining the national movement of media literacy, the importance of critical pedagogy has increased. Overall, most teachers seem positive about its validity and its social relevance to students, particularly in the efforts to enable students to resist media manipulation and rampant consumerism (National Council of Teachers of English [NCTE], 1994, 1996).

So far, efforts, research, and debates have taken place to develop a rationale for teaching media literacy in schools to enable everyone to resist media manipulation. To develop such a rationale, at least a rationale and an empowering classroom model, media literacy must be promoted widely beyond earlier protectionist strategies. Debates and lectures by the British media educators Len Masterman (1985) and David Buckingham (1991) have suggested that television prepares viewers to be consumers through its constant repetition of commercials and fancy bedroom suites. In addition, the mass media promote male dominant gender roles and racist attitudes (Buckingham, 1991). These views sum up the widespread idea that the media are powerful and have negative influences. Viewed this way, the mass media are seen as contributing to the perpetuation of a number of objectionable ideologies. Over time, these arguments focusing on negative effects have been used to a great advantage by media education advocates in establishing the need for media literacy. But Buckingham (1991) has warned that a distinction needs to be made between "simpler, more rhetorical arguments which may be of use in promoting media literacy, and more complex understanding that should inform classroom practice" (p. 8). In other words, Buckingham (1991) warns against pushing the "negative" media effects card to sell the idea of media literacy, because in practice, it results in an activist stance in which certain ideologies about media literacy are pushed, rather than a critical stance in which participants probe the relationship with media, and raise issues and questions in response to media texts. Buckingham argues against the protectionist stance held by conservatives who view the media as corruptive, responsible for illiteracy and the reason for moral decadence looming large in society.

THEORIES OF CRITICAL MEDIA ANALYSIS

Media experts have relied on the study of language, the study of signs (semiotic/textual analysis), and constructivist and postmodern critical theories to develop methods of analysis of media texts. Some of these analytical approaches include (1) content analysis (Gerbner et. al., 1969), (2) uses and gratification analysis (Blumler & Katz, 1974, 1975), (3) semiotic/textual analysis (Hurley & Fiske, 1977; Metz, 1974; Heath, 1977; Wollen, 1969), (4) cultural analysis (Bigsby, 1976; Hartley & Hawkes, 1977; Berger, 1972; and more recently, Rushkoff, 1996; Giroux, 1997), (5) critical analysis (Bigsby, 1975; Schiller, 1970), and (6) representation (Hall, 1997). Unfortunately, there is no one method that is capable of analyzing adequately all texts in all circumstances. That is why I have enlisted in the chapters of this book a variety of theories, concepts, and frameworks to help unlock the secrets of visual representations.

Current literature offers examples of single methods or a combination of these analytical frameworks. For example, in their book *Visual Messages*, Considine and Haley (1992) summarize the growing research on critical viewing of media programs. Their methods as outlined do not originate from any one theory. Viewed as a process of reading television rather than analytical tools, Considine and Haley list five constituent elements: (1) interpreting the internal content of the program (e.g., focusing on the narrative analysis of what happened and why, with reference to genre codes and conventions), (2) interpreting the internal construction of the frame (e.g., media form and style), (3) recognizing the external forces and factors shaping the program (e.g., media ownership and control), (4) comparing and contrasting media representations with reality (e.g., detecting stereotyping, bias, distortion of facts, and what happens in real life), and (5) recognizing and responding to the potential impact of television form and content (e.g., taking action on the information, such as expressing opinions or outrage to producers or newspaper editors).

Apparently, the main preoccupation of the authors of *Visual Messages* is the form and content of the media artifact(s) rather than the process of analysis to get at the *manipulation, distortion, overt bias,* and *stereotyping*. Such content-based framework overlooks issues of power relations, economic inequalities, and hegemonic ideologies that tend to preserve practices of dominant groups in the existing society. The making sense or reflection and action to be taken as a response of the exposure to the media are left to the individual. Considine and Haley equate critical reading with content analysis, where students in an English classroom are urged to recognize themes and lessons that are embedded in a media program (e.g., see Considine & Haley, 1992, Chapter 2, p. 14). Unfortunately, this approach tends to focus on the parts rather than the whole picture. Considine and Haley assume that being able to recognize the advertising tricks is sufficient to guard students against unconscious and unwise consumption, let alone persuasive seductive appeals and lies.

Clearly, there is considerable tension between content (what teachers teach), form (how teachers teach), and practice within the context of culture. So far, there does not seem to be an easy resolution of such tension in the horizon. Media educators (e.g., Barry Duncan, 1993) have complained about teaching critical viewing in terms of content. They suspect this because media education is often defined and directed by media critics and theorists, not media educators. As explained earlier, many critical viewing practices have been prescribed by teachers of literature, borrowing much of the analytical approaches from literary analysis.

As lamented by Kellner (1995, p. xiv), the analytical steps summed up by Considine and Haley (1992), as well as other media literacy advocates including the Frankfurt School, do not go far enough in the reading of media and cultural products. The majority of studies in reading television have neglected the language of criticism to the extent that it touches on social, political, and ideological domains. For instance, Kellner insists that these theorists, particularly the Frankfurt School, developed a powerful critique of the culture industries and the ways that they manipulate individuals into conforming to the beliefs, values, and practices of the existing society, but the critical theorists "lack theories of how one can resist media manipulation, how one can come to see through the ruses and seductions, how one can read against the grain to derive critical insights into self and society through the media, and how one can produce alternative forms of media and culture" (Kellner, 1995, p. xiv). Perhaps critical viewing, when conceptualized as "a vision of criticism," of popular media and culture industries can provide teachers and students with a framework necessary for the critical analysis of media texts and culture as practiced in society. Teachers can benefit from utilizing this framework to recognize the alternative sources of information available to students in school and out of the school environment.

CRITICAL VIEWING VERSUS MEDIA CRITICISM

The concept of critical viewing is distinguished from the kind of viewing for pleasure or entertainment so often limited to television and film criticism. As a form of social critique, critical viewing goes beyond the art of critique of the arts. It refers to the gaining of skills necessary to analyze and critically dissect all forms of culture, whether print, visual, or performance, with which individuals interact, ranging from books to the artifacts of film, television, radio, and the other products of the culture industries. A critical viewing of these forms of culture extends the process of *critical literacy,* which gives individuals power over their culture and thus empowers them, "enabling people to create their own meanings, identities, and to shape and transform the material and social conditions of their culture and society" (Kellner, 1995, p. xv).

While reviewing recent works of Peter McLaren, Henry Giroux, Ira Shor, Alan Luke, and Norman Fairclough, Colin Lankshear (1994) elaborates critical literacy as a form of alternative pedagogy that examines the politics and sociolinguistic stances. Lankshear (1994) delineates what it means to be critical. He stresses that critical literacy represents a vision of criticism. His vision does not only aim at the "text" but also aims squarely to critique the traditions and institutions that produce it. But Giroux's critical vision reflects the analysis of individual contexts in as far as such context is part of their everyday life. Combining Gramsci's (1971) notion of the engaged intellectual with Foucault's (1977) notion of the specific intellectual, Giroux advances the idea of teachers as "transformative intellectuals" to replace the dominant notion of teachers as educational "technicians," "managers," or "professionals." Giroux sees teachers as individuals who connect their work to broader social concerns that deeply affect how people live, work, and survive (Giroux, 1991, p. 57).

As "transformative intellectuals," Giroux (1988) believes that teachers can potentially play a significant role in creating schools as "democratic public spheres" that produce this vision of criticism, grounded in social transformation. He writes:

> Teachers need to develop a discourse and set of assumptions that allow them to function more specifically as transformative intellectuals. As intellectuals, they will combine reflection and action in the interest of empowering students with the skills and knowledge needed to address injustice and to be critical actors committed to developing a world free of oppression and exploitation. Such intellectuals are not merely concerned with promoting individual achievement or advancing students along career ladders, they are concerned with empowering students so that the students can read the world critically and change it when necessary. (p. xxxiv)

Put in different terms, this vision of criticism attempts to merge theory and practice and seeks to identify interrelationships and interconnections between everyday life and knowledge learned in books. Through this vision, Giroux perceives a critical pedagogy of representation doing two things: first, providing the basis for "education to be attentive to a politics of location, one which recognizes and interrogates the strengths and limitations of those places one inherits, engages, and occupies"; and second, articulating "a pedagogy that frame[s] the discourses through which we speak" (Giroux, 1992, p. 126).

IMPLEMENTING A VISION OF CRITICISM

In an attempt to bring about this vision of "criticism," described by Giroux and Lankshear in my own teaching, I teach a literacy block of courses at the Pennsylvania State University for preservice teachers. Drawing on a range of concepts and frameworks elaborated by theorists and teachers working in various critical language studies, I have developed activities around a simple media text I believe has interesting possibilities for an interdisciplinary practice of critical pedagogy. I bring into the course the possibilities of working with media texts in conjunction with a set of rather different but relevant texts to address questions adapted from linguists and literacy educators such as Allan Luke, Paulo Freire, Donaldo Macedo, Castell, and Egan. This block of courses calls for a context where preservice teachers across several subjects—English, social studies, early childhood education, and science—work together in an integrated way to explore texts critically through their disciplines. The assumption is made that teachers will immerse themselves in a media text or topic and take the time to explore the text in order to find questions that are significant to the learner and then systematically investigate those questions.

One competency that students acquire in this course is the ability to apply the narrative analysis method to study visual and other media representations. Preservice teachers are encouraged to use the narrative analysis method because this method shifts attention from the content of stories to the structure and process of their telling; students learn to avoid rushing hastily to the judgment of moral tales without examining the evidence or analyzing the multiplicity of forms (fictional, nonfictional, print, oral, visual, or pictorial, etc.). Throughout this course, students practice to question the text, the context, and the subtext. They learn how to analyze what is in the text as well as what is omitted from the text, namely the context.

Preservice teachers learn that media literacy consists of competencies in reading, interpreting, and understanding how meaning is made and derived from print, photographs, and electronic visuals. They learn how to generate their own frameworks—lessons of analysis—to be applied to the subjects or themes they develop in subjects they teach. Critical viewing consists of understanding connotative messages embedded in the text of the visual messages as well as interaction of pictures to words, the context of the viewer, and relayed messages obtained from the maker of the image. For example, in the analysis of visuals used for advertising in various print media or textbook illustrations, students strive to uncover some of the narrative meaning by questioning: (1) the order of events depicted, (2) the actual history of visual production, circulation, and consumption, and (3) who produced the visual, under what circumstances, and for what possible reasons. Therefore, media literacy expands the notion of critical literacy, which includes taking a critical stance to all media texts. For teachers and students, the classroom becomes a media literacy learning environment, where the learning process is not disconnected from the institutions that create knowledge and information, nor from the legal, cultural, political, and economic contexts that surround the texts students read, whether from books, films, or the Internet.

My experience in working with preservice teachers has been insightful but challenging. It is particularly striking to observe them at the end of each semester and noticing the extent to which their critical awareness has been raised. The level of awareness is especially visible in the rate of adoption of critical viewing, critical reading, and critical

thinking skills they tend to bring into their work, that is, the broad definition of "literacy" these students eventually apply to a variety of projects
they embark on long after completing the education courses.

At the core of the critical pedagogy movement that I advocate in my
teaching is the need (1) to develop an awareness of the constructed nature of representation in both print and visual media, (2) to provide
knowledge about the social, cultural, economic, and political contexts in
which media messages are produced by a variety of different institutions
with specific objectives, and (3) to encourage renewed interest in learning about the ways in which individuals construct meaning from messages—that is, about the processes of selecting, interpreting, and acting
upon messages in various contexts. Taken together, the process described
here provides a critical stance, a method students and teachers can
choose to take up to resist the overt race, class, and gender biases and
manipulation in the media texts students read/view.

EXPLORATIONS OF MEDIA TEXTS

Elsewhere, I have explored how the notion of intermediality serves to extend critical literacy and the vision of criticism. (see Semali & Pailliotet,
1999). In this context, I emphasized the need of theory and practice to
guide teachers and students' reflection and action as suggested by Freire,
Giroux, Kellner, and others. I also insist that educators keep in mind that
practice and theory are complementary and interrelated. For instance, all
classroom practice must be informed by specific theoretical concepts.
Furthermore, theory can only fully be understood in relation to specific
media practices and through practical application.

But some questions persist: How can teachers' reflective and teaching practices develop a critical stance to generate a critical authoring,
reading, and viewing of texts that enable students to navigate the seas of
multiple texts, especially those represented in multimedia formats currently flooding students' learning environments through the Internet,
video, CD-ROM, and so on, at a time when literacy education is no
longer confined to paper-and-pencil technologies or "reading" and "writing"? How does the current climate of cultural conservatism present specific challenges to critical education? How can reader/viewer response
analysis stimulate and help students develop critical reading, critical
viewing, critical listening, and critical thinking for lifelong learning?
How will teachers integrate these ideas on Monday morning in a lan-

guage arts or social studies class? How do they fit with the requirements of academic standards and assessment prerogatives?

To illustrate the vision of criticism I am talking about, let me make a quick reference to Pailliotet's "Deep Viewing" method outlined in intermediality (Pailliotet, 1999, pp. 31–51). *Deep viewing* is a method of critical construction and analysis of textual understanding of children's writing that was borrowed from Himley's (1991) notions of criticism to all visual texts to include the electronic media. As an analytical framework, it is drawn from varied theories that explain ideas such as:

- Participants "read' or deconstruct textual meanings and "write" or construct new ones (Barthes, 1974), through discourse analysis and personal responses, within a heuristic framework (Lusted, 1991).
- Understandings are guided by semiotic codes of print and visual information (Barthes, 1974; Saint-Martin, 1993; Kervin, 1985).
- The use of varied texts fosters active meaning construction of multiple signs, symbols, and signification (de Saussure, 1986; Silverman, 1983), and promotes literacy learning in multiple modalities (Flood & Lapp, 1995; Pike, Compain & Mumper, 1997; Sinatra, 1986; Watts Pailliotet, 1997).

According to Pailliotet, deep viewing is a structured process through which participants first identify elements and discourse forms such as language, sound, images, and structures, then interpret and respond to them through varied transactions. In practice, this critical reader/active-viewer approach to media texts employs a three-level analysis to critically analyze, understand, and interact with information. This approach's design combines a heuristic framework and semiotic codes for understanding text.

One outstanding feature that the deep viewing method brings into the language of criticism is the insistence of reflection and action in the classroom. Pailliotet underscores that for deep viewing to work, participants must pose questions and develop ways they might act in the future, based on their own assessments and those of their code group and those within the classroom. Participants are encouraged to relate text to their own experiences, expectations, feelings, and knowledge. In essence, deep viewing makes explicit the language of criticism discussed in this chapter. It provides a practical way of making critical inquiry, personal reflection, active learning, ethical decision-making, ongoing research, and analytical observation to become a daily activity for teachers and students. Through constant questioning of texts and modeling to students, Pailliotet successfully pilots the vision of criticism in her classroom. The results confirm that students were able to analyze, respond, think complexly, critically evaluate, and teach with many texts.

TAKING A CRITICAL STANCE

Taking a critical stance to critical viewing sounds like tautology. However, it is important to caution that not all instances or projects involving critical viewing are "critical." Put simply: Critical viewing means different things to different people. Some conservative and liberal educators continue to neutralize the term *critical* by repeated and imprecise usage, removing its political and cultural dimensions and reducing its analytic framework to mere thinking skills. Such imprecise usage, especially when supported by powerful school administrators, fuels the debate and adds to the confusion in some teachers' minds as to what the value of engaging in such controversy might be in a public school classroom. Furthermore, traditional educators have ignored the critique of schooling, social conditions, and ideological contexts for so long that it is not natural for teachers to incorporate such contexts in readings or classroom discussions.

The kind of critical inquiry advocated in the chapters I describe in this book stands apart from the positivistic, ahistorical, and depoliticized analysis employed by both liberal and conservative educators who have adopted the viewer-response and active-viewer approaches without taking a critical stance. As shown in the examples described in this book, the vision of criticism implied in critical media literacy attempts to merge theory and practice to coincide with Giroux's critical democratic vision of schools and society. It further seeks to identify interrelationships and interconnections between everyday life with knowledge learned in books. In practice, these analytical strategies provide teachers with concrete and viable forms of critical inquiry.

To take a critical stance one must ask: Do we want our schools to create a passive, risk-free citizenry, or a politicized citizenry, capable of fighting for various forms of public life and informed concern for equality and social justice? When Peter McLaren raises these kinds questions in his writings, he intends to infuse a vision of criticism (McLaren, 1988, p. 3). In this vision, he hopes to encourage teachers to take a critical stance in their teaching practice. In taking such a critical stance, teachers would no longer define curriculum in terms of the abstract categories of various isolated disciplines (such as history, English literature, social studies, etc.), but rather would incorporate themes and issues that address the concrete conditions and problems of adult life. In this new role, teachers are guides and facilitators rather than managers and dispensers of knowledge.

As a method of curriculum and instruction, therefore, critical viewing challenges teachers and students to examine visual media as an object of study by exploring its languages, codes, and conceptual frameworks and asks what sense students in classrooms today make of visual media as an object of study (Manzi & Rowe, 1991, p. 42). Through the questioning of media texts, students engage in a process of learning the "deeper" meaning, and thus become empowered to form identities and worldviews that are their own, resisting the media spectacles that persuade and manipulate them to accept the interests of supposedly neutral formulations of science and politics of illusion.

CRITICAL VIEWING, READING, AUTHORING, AND THINKING OF MULTIMEDIA TEXTS

Critical viewing, reading, authoring, and thinking are interconnected processes. In this chapter, I have assumed that to critically engage students with multimedia texts that they read every day, they must not only take a critical stand on what they read, but also must question the visual images they see. They must think analytically as well. In this vision of criticism, we are talking about these activities not as separate or disjoined skills. As suggested by Hall (1973), speaker and hearer or writer and reader are active participants in a process that is always interactive. As students read, view, and think critically they are faced with three positions in the process of evaluating multimedia texts and like a pendulum swing and shift their positions as meaning becomes clearer. According to Hall, the interaction with texts take (1) the "dominant-hegemonic" position (accepting the preferred meaning), (2) the negotiated reading (accepting aspects of the preferred meaning but rejecting others), and (3) the oppositional reading (rejecting the preferred meaning).

Some media educators have often ignored these three reading/viewing positions. Often, the dominant-hegemonic position is articulated through the professional code. This occurs when the viewer/reader takes the "connoted" meaning from, say, a magazine, television newscast, or current affairs program full and straight, and decodes the message in terms of the reference code in which it has been encoded. In this case, we might say that the viewer is operating inside the dominant code. Like so often, for example, we see in photographs displayed in billboards or scantily clad women in advertising magazines: Which of the many meanings does the magazine mean to privilege? Which is the preferred or dominant meaning? Taking the intended meaning or view as presented is to comply with the preferred or dominant meaning. To decode a photograph or television discourse in this way is to be in harmony with the professional code (interpretation) of advertisers and broadcasters. Hall (1973) explains further:

> The professional code is "relatively independent" of the dominant code, it applies criteria and transformational operations of its own, especially those of a techno-practical nature. The professional code, however, operates *within* the "hegemony" of the dominant code. Indeed, it serves to reproduce the dominant definitions precisely by bracketing their hegemonic quality and operating instead with displaced professional codings which foreground such apparently neutral-technical questions as visual quality, news, and presentational values, televisual quality, "professionalism" and so on. (p. 136)

When the audience focuses on the physical attributes and ignores the ideological premises, they let the dominant code prevail over them. In the preferred-dominant position the audience displays less skepticism about the information being circulated.

There is another position possible. The second possibility is "the negotiated code" or position. Hall suggests that this position is probably the majority position:

> Decoding within the negotiated version contains a mixture of adaptive and oppositional elements: it acknowledges the legitimacy of the hegemonic definitions to make the grand significations (abstract), while, at a more restricted, situational (situated) level, it makes its own ground rules—it operates with exceptions to the rule. It accords the privileged position to the dominant definitions of events while reserving the right to make a more negotiated application to "local conditions," to its own *corporate* positions. The negotiated version of the dominant ideology is thus shot through with contradictions, though these are only on certain occasions brought to full visibility. (p. 137)

In a negotiated reading, the audience accepts some aspects of the program while comparing to one's contexts or experience as the yardstick for the veracity, practicality, or accuracy of the messages being conveyed. For example, a negotiated code might be a worker who agrees in general terms with the news report's claim that increased wages cause inflation, while insisting on his or her right to strike for better pay and conditions. In this position, the audience displays a certain amount of skepticism. He or she does not subscribe wholesale to everything the program or ad is saying.

Hall identifies "oppositional" reading as a third position possible in the interaction process with text. The "oppositional" reading/viewing is taken by the viewer who recognizes the preferred code of the televisual discourse but nonetheless chooses to decode within an alternative frame of reference. This is the case, for example, of the viewer who listens to a debate on the need to limit wages but "reads" every mention of the "national interest" as "class interest" (p. 138). This third position is possible with an individual who displays a skeptical mindset. When one seeks more than one explanation of an event, when one searches for reasons by asking "why" things are in a certain way, then such inquiry is oppositional, since it leads to a critique of the original proposition.

CONCLUDING COMMENTS

In this chapter, I proposed the language of criticism as a reflective teaching approach to theory and classroom practice. I used the language of critical pedagogy to situate critical viewing as a method of analysis of media texts. I also examined the ways in which the language of media is socially and historically produced. Throughout this chapter, critical viewing was described as a process rather than an analytical tool with which to engage students to question the clarity and strength for reasoning, identify assumptions and values, recognize points of view and attitudes, and evaluate conclusions and actions provided by all narratives across the curriculum whether they be short stories, poems, plays, picture books, film, or pieces of nonfiction. The framework of analysis described here moves away from the limited approach of presenting course materials in the flat monotone of objectivity, and thus conveying the false impression that knowledge is static, monolithic, and universal. The assumption here is that when students are introduced to critical viewing they implement a vision of criticism grounded in multiple ways of knowing and their experiences will become part of the multiple texts that form part of the instruction. Such approaches provide a solid foundation for students' critical consciousness in the construction of knowledge.

REFERENCES

Aronowitz, S. & Giroux, H. (1991). *Postmodern education: Politics, culture, and social criticism.* Minneapolis: University of Minnesota Press.

Barthes, R. (1974). *S/Z* (R. Miller, Trans.). New York: Hill and Wang/The Noonday Press.

Berger, J. (1972). *Ways of seeing.* London/BBC: Penguin.

Bigsby, C. (1976). *Approaches to popular culture.* London: Edward Arnold.

——. (1975). *Superculture: American popular culture and Europe.* London: Paul Elek.

Blumler, J., & Katz, E. (Eds.). (1975). *The uses and gratification approach to communication research.* Beverly Hills, CA: Sage.

——. (Eds.). (1974). *Use of mass communications.* Beverly Hills, CA: Sage.

Bowles, S., & Gintis, H. (1976). *Schooling in capitalist America.* New York: Basic Books.

Buckingham, D. (1991). Teaching about the media. In D. Lusted (Ed.), *The media studies book: A guide for teachers.* London: Routledge, pp. 12–35.

Considine, D. M., & Haley, G. E. (1992). *Visual messages: Integrating imagery into instruction.* Englewood, CO: Teachers Ideas Press.

Davies, J. (1996). *Educating students in a media saturated culture.* Lancaster, PA: Technomic.

Davis, F. (1992). Media literacy: From activism to exploration. Background paper for the National Leadership Conference on Media Literacy, Wye Woods, *The Aspen Institute, Communications and Society Program,* December 7–9.

De Saussure, F. (1986). Course in general linguistics. In H. Adams, & L. Searle (Eds.), *Critical theory since 1965* (pp. 646–663). Tallahassee, FL: Florida State University Press.

Dick, E. (1987). *Signs of success: Report of the media education: Development program.* Glasgow: Scottish Film Council.

Duncan, B. (1993). *Telemedium, 39*(1–2): 13–17.

Foucault, M. (1977). *Discipline and punish: Birth of the prison.* London: Allen Lane.

Flood, J., & Lapp, D. (1995). Broadening the lens: Toward an expanded conceptualization of literacy. In K. A. Hinchman, D. J. Leu, & C. K. Kinzer (Eds.), *Perspectives on literacy research and practice: Forty-fourth yearbook of the*

National Reading Conference (pp. 1–16). Chicago, IL: National Reading Conference.

Freire, P. (1970). *Pedagogy of the oppressed.* New York: Continuum.

Garret, S. (n.d.). *Messages and meaning: A guide to understanding media.* Lancaster, PA: Newspapers in Education.

Gerbner, G., Holsti, O., Krippendorf, K., Paisley, W., & Stone, P. (Eds.) (1969). *The analysis of communication content.* New York: John Wiley.

Giroux, H. (1997). *Channel surfing: Race talk and the destruction of today's youth.* New York: St. Martin Press.

———. (1992). Introduction. In F. Schwoch, M. White, & S. Reilly (Eds.), *Media knowledge: Readings in popular culture, pedagogy and citizenship* (pp. ix–xxxiv). Albany, NY: State University of New York Press.

———. (1988). *Teachers as intellectuals: Toward a critical pedagogy of learning.* Westport, CT: Bergin & Garvey, p. 126.

———, & McLaren, P. (Eds.). (1989). *Critical pedagogy, the state, and cultural struggle.* Albany: State University of New York Press.

Goodman, J. (1992). Towards a discourse of imagery: Critical curriculum of theorizing. *The Educational Forum, 56*(3): 269–289.

Gramsci, A. (1971). *Selections from the prison notebooks of Antonio Gramsci.* New York: Inernational Publishers.

Hall, S. (1997). *Representation. Cultural representations and signifying practices.* London: The Open University.

———. (1980). Encoding and decoding. In S. Hall, et al. (Eds.), *Culture, media language.* London: Hutchinson.

———. (1973). *The popular arts.* Boston, MA: Beacon Press.

Hall, S., et al. (Eds.). (1980). *Culture, media, language.* London: Hutchinson.

Hammer, R. (1995). Rethinking the dialectic: A critical semiotic meta-theoretical approach for the pedagogy of media literacy. In P. McLaren, R. Hammer, D. Sholle, & S. Reilly. *Rethinking media literacy: A critical pedagogy of representation.* New York: Peter Lang, pp. 33–85.

Hartley, J. & Hawkes, T. (1977). *Popular culture and high culture.* London: The Open University.

Heath, S. (1977). *Image-music text.* London: Fontana.

Hurley, J., & Fiske, J. (1977). Myth-representation: A cultural reading of News at Ten. *Communication Studies Bulletin, 4,* 12–33.

Karolides, N. (Ed.) (1992). *Reader response in the classroom. Evoking and interpreting meaning in literature.* White Plains, NJ: Longman.

Kellner, D. (1995). Preface. In P. McLaren, R. Hammer, E. Sholle, & S. Reilly (Eds.), *Rethinking media literacy: A critical pedagogy of representation* (pp. xxiii–xvii).

Kervin, D. (1985). Reading images: Levels of meaning in television commercials. In Thayer, & S. Clayton-Randolph (Eds.), *Readings from the 16th annual conference of the International Visual Literacy Association* (pp. 36–43). Bloomington, IN: Western Sun.

Kilbourne, J. (1995). Beauty and the beast in advertising. *Media and Values, 49,* 8–10.

Lankshear, C. (1994, May). Critical literacy (Occasional Paper No. 3, pp. 4–26). *Australian Studies Association.*

Luke, C. (1999). *Media and cultural studies in Australia.* International Reading Association, pp. 622–626.

Lusted, D. (Ed.). (1991). *The media studies book: A guide for teachers.* London: Routledge.

McLaren, P. (1988). Language, social structure, and the production of subjectivity. *Critical Pedagogy Networker 1*(2–3): 1–10.

Manzi, K., & Rowe, A. (1991). Language. In D. Lusted (Ed.), *The media studies book: A guide for teachers.* London: Routledge, pp. 40–52.

Masterman, L. (1985). *Teaching the media.* London: Routledge.

Metz, C. (1974). *Film language.* London: Oxford University Press.

National Council of Teachers of English (NCTE). (1994). *Standards for the assessment of reading and writing.* Urbana, IL: Author.

NCTE. (1996). *English/language arts: Reading, writing, speaking, listening, viewing, and visual representation.* Washington, DC: Author.

Pailliotet, A. (1999). Deep viewing: Intermediality in preservice teacher education. In L. Semali, & A. Pailliotet (Eds.), *Intermediality: The teachers' handbook of critical media literacy* (pp. 31–52). Boulder, CO: Westview.

Pike, K., Compain, R., & Mumper, J. (1997). *New connections: An integrated approach to literacy* (2nd Ed.). New York: Longman.

Rushkoff, D. (1996). *Playing the future: How kids' culture can teach us to thrive in an age of chaos.* New York: HarperCollins.

Saint-Martin, F. (1993). *Semiotics of visual language.* Bloomington, IN: Indiana University Press.

Schiller, H. (1970). *Mass communication and American empire.* Fairfield, NJ: Kelly.

Semali, L. (1997). Still crazy after all these years: Teaching critical media literacy. In J. Kincheloe, &. S. Steinberg (Eds.), *Unauthorized methods: Strategies for critical teaching* (pp. 137–151). New York: Routledge.

———, & Pailliotet, A. (1999). *Intermediality: The teachers' handbook of critical media literacy.* Boulder, CO: Westview.

Silverman, K. (1983). *The subject of semiotics.* New York: Oxford University Press.

Simon, R. (1987). Empowerment as pedagogy of possibility. *Language Arts,* *64*(4):, 370–81.

Sinatra, R. (1986). *Visual literacy connections to thinking, reading, and writing.* Springfield, IL: Charles C. Thomas.

Swanson, G. (1991). Representation. In D. Lusted (Ed.), *The media studies book: A guide for teachers.* London: Routledge, pp. 123–145.

Teasley, A., & Wilder, A. (1997). *Reel conversations: Reading films with young adults.* Portsmouth, NH: Heinemann, Boynton/Cook Publishers.

Tyner, K. (1993). Treading water: Media education in the United States. In R. Aparici, (Ed.), *Projecto sidactico queria Madrid.* Madrid, Spain: Ediciones de la Torre. (Extracted from Media Strategies Newsletter, San Francisco, CA.)

U.S. Department of Health, 1982. *Television and behavior: Ten years of scientific progress and implications for the eighties.* Washington, D.C.: Author.

Watkin, M. (1984). A defense of using pop media in the middle school classroom. *English Journal, 83*(1), 30–33.

Watts Pailliotet, A. (1997). Questing toward cohesion: Connecting advertisements and classroom reading through visual literacy. In R. E. Griffin, J. M. Hunter, C. B. Schiffman, & W. J. Gibbs (Eds.), *Visionquest: Journeys toward visual literacy* (pp. 33–41). State College, PA: International Visual Literacy Association.

WNET/Thirteen Education Department. (1979). *The television criti-kit: Teachers' guide.* New York: Author.

Wollen, P. (1969). *Signs and meaning in the cinema.* London: Socker & Warburg.

CHAPTER 5

Analytical Frameworks of Interpreting Media Representations

To uncover the deeper meaning embedded in media texts that represent people and events is a complex enterprise. It involves the complicated process to disassemble and dismiss ideologically biased representations, to identify stereotyping and how it works, to detect classist, sexist, or racist content, and to decide what to do about it. Seeking this kind of deeper meaning means analyzing, comparing, interpreting, and finding meaning that is different from the usual, routine, and preferred meaning. It means going beyond the preferred-dominant position of interpreting media texts to find (or adopt) an oppositional or alternative frame of reference/explanation. Such process is a complex matter because representation of people and events form part of a complicated process by which meaning is produced and exchanged between members of a culture. Since this process is not straightforward, it becomes difficult to disentangle.

Representations of people and events are so difficult to unpack (let alone to teach others how to do it), because they are historically centered on values, interests, and desires. For example, teachers may ask students to "see through" media texts with critical analytical lenses, but what students write in the essay or what they tell us in classroom discussion is no measure of what goes on in their heads. Boys can easily show outrage at sexist portrayal of women in advertising as much as white kids can feign to be appalled at racist portrayals of Haitian "boat" people.

To get at the values, interests, and desires in media representations, one has to examine the use of language, or signs and images that stand for or represent things. I suppose to do this is complex simply because the meaning so produced or constructed by representation is not a universal truth or neutral fact and cannot be read in a straightforward manner. As explained in previous chapters, meaning is entangled in social, cultural, economic, and political settings, which preside over the context through which both the reader/viewer and the communicator engage in an exchange and interpretation of messages. Hall (1997) reminds us that when we decide to examine the representation of an event or people, we are in fact entering into the very constitution of things; this is a constitutive process, as important as the economic or material "base" in shaping social subjects and historical events—not merely "a reflection of the world after the event" (p. 5).

For Hall, therefore, media representation is a way of giving things meaning by how we represent them—the words we use about them, the images of them we produce, the emotions we associate with them, the ways we classify and conceptualize them, the values we place on them (p. 3). In other words, media representation refers to the way images and language actively construct meanings according to sets of conventions shared by and familiar to makers (producers) and audiences (viewers). In this sense, it is a continuous struggle over meaning.

CRITICAL LITERACY AND MEDIA LITERACY CURRICULUM

Critical literacy is a contested educational ideal. Even though "critical" pedagogy has been *en vogue* for the past fifteen years, scholars continue to question what it means to be critical and how such a concept can be implemented across the curriculum. As I explained in Chapter 3, critical literacy and media literacy overlap. Critical media literacy is an extension of the practice of critical literacy. As explained earlier, critical media literacy is grounded in the Freirian notions of emancipatory education. As part of an alternative pedagogy in schools, critical literacy has emerged as the most talked about educational paradigm (see, for example, Muspratt, Luke & Freebody, 1997). In the education field, the project of teaching, learning, and constructing critical literacies stands in contrast to the practice of teaching the classics and a canon of acceptable literary works far removed from the students' experiences for dry memorization of exams.

Following a constructivist approach to teaching and to learning, critical media literacy is a particularly useful resource of the many forms of critical inquiry, the driving engine behind any critical literacy. This practice reasserts the stance that discursive critical consciousness is necessary to critical education and to democratic public life (Fensham, Gustone, and White, 1994; McLaren et al., 1995).

At the core of the critical pedagogy movement is the need (1) to develop an awareness of the constructed nature of representation in both print and visual media; (2) to provide knowledge about the social, cultural, economic, and political contexts in which media messages are produced by a variety of different institutions with specific objectives; and (3) to encourage renewed interest in learning about the ways in which individuals construct meaning from messages—that is, about the process of selecting, interpreting, and acting upon messages in various contexts.

This chapter introduces a framework of critical media literacy that teachers and students might pursue in classroom practice to understand representation of people and events. In this framework, I use five concepts as a guide to critique and to examine film images of indigenous people in order to expose the oppressive spaces in the daily dose of media and visual messages designed to provide information and entertainment to credulous audiences. The framework I am proposing here exposes students and teachers to an alternative method of inquiry that allows them to go beyond the traditional, basal, or whole language approach to literacy to resist, oppose, and challenge the authority/knowledge of a text.

This project crosses classroom borders and opens up the learning space to become an action research laboratory where questioning is the objective. Such inquiry seeks to search for deeper meaning and not right or wrong answers.

Thus, this chapter aims to be a model for teachers contemplating the use of such analytical elements in their own classrooms to teach critical viewing, critical thinking, and critical reading skills. In the study of visual communication and media literacy, critical viewing is not used widely in American classrooms as a tool for deconstructing media images, particularly those images that represent people's culture, identity, or ethnicity. While this practice has begun to occur in schools in other countries, it is not yet happening in all U.S. schools. With critical literacy, students learn to become critical consumers of texts and other media products, as well as aware of visual manipulation of stereotyping as an important project of education.

They also learn that literacy education is not limited to reading and writing but rather it is a political and ideological project. They must know that neither does critical literacy provide a canonical version of, what it means to be literate nor resolve the problems of students' reading and writing. Rather than subscribing to a particular version or practice of literacy, it is important to realize that there are multiple approaches of literacy, a diversity of definitions of literacy—depending on the ideological position of the person who is doing the defining—that have often been in theoretical, practical, and political contest with one another. That is why I tend to concur with Luke (1997) that critical literacy is not a panacea and that it does not stand for a unitary approach. However, it marks out a coalition of educational interests committed to "engaging with the possibilities that the technologies of writing and other modes of inscription offer for social change, cultural diversity, economic equity, and political enfranchisement" (p. 1). By the same token, I must caution my readers that because teachers ask students to be "critical" to see through media texts with politically correct, critical analytical lenses, teachers should not assume that students cannot do so on their own, and that they see what they watch to be necessarily real.

Let us now take one such definition of critical literacy. For example, Ira Shor (1993) defines critical literacy as:

> [a]nalytic habits of thinking, reading, speaking, or discussing which go beneath surface impressions, traditional myths, mere opinions, and routine clichés; understanding the social contexts and consequences of any subject matter; discovering the deep meaning of any event, text, technique, process, object, statements, image, or situations; applying meaning to your own context. (p. 32)

This definition is a useful guide to defining what is "critical" as well as delineating the parameters of critical inquiry. Students will see that this definition pushes them to critically examine all texts, particularly those texts they encounter outside of the classroom and that it is a project that is continuous and ongoing, which implies lifelong learning. Critical media literacy thus expands the notion of school literacy, principally the ability to read the printed text, to include a critical reading of all media texts. For teachers and for students, the classroom becomes a media literacy learning environment, where the learning process is not disconnected from the institutions that create knowledge and information, nor from the legal, cultural, political, and economic contexts of texts whether they are books, films, or Internet resources.

STILL CRAZY AFTER ALL THESE YEARS: FIVE CONCEPTS FOR CRITICAL PEDAGOGY

As a media representation of storytelling, films, for example, share much in common with the historical or fictional narrative, including plot, theme, character, setting, conflict, and resolution. Through the maneuvering of camera angles, cutting, and lighting, the manipulation of time and space is effectively accomplished to give the viewer a sense of realism. In addition to these techniques, film producers use old stereotypes, beliefs, myths, and history to engage the feelings, attitudes, and emotions of the audience. These techniques, broadly known as film language, are specific to each genre of filmmaking. Filmmakers have used these techniques for years to mobilize fears and anxieties in the viewer (fear of the unknown and the unlike) at deeper levels than we can explain in a simple, commonsense way. For this reason, media representations of people demand a careful analysis to discover:

- What is at issue?
- How is the issue/event defined?
- Who is involved?
- What are the arguments?
- What is taken for granted, including cultural assumptions?

These questions set the theme of the practice of critical literacy that is the central focus of this chapter. Adapted from Werner and Nixon's guide for teaching critical mindedness, and from Fairclough's framework for teaching critical language awareness, these five concepts provide an important starting point for critical pedagogy (Fairclough, 1989; Werner & Nixon, 1990).

In this analysis, I introduce a discussion about the Sani. The Sani are the indigenous people of the Kalahari Desert in southern Africa. These people have for many years been called the "bushmen," a derogatory name coined by early European settlers in the early 1900s. This name has been used until 1990 when Namibia got its independence. The culture, language, and social life of the Sani have been represented in the film *The Gods Must Be Crazy* (1984), now available on videotapes (*Gods I* and a sequel, *Gods II* [1990] and distributed all over the world. As the name "bushman" suggests, the Sani have been portrayed as creatures of the Stone Age that are obstacles to progress, civilization, and modernization.

In an analytical examination of the visual representation of the Sani in this film, the complex issues surrounding culture, identity, and ethnicity are brought to bear. The representation of this group of Africans coincides with old prejudices about Africans that have been prevalent in films, museum displays, and novels read by students in schools. Hall (1997) explains this typification of Africans as a system of representation that uses the concepts of "naturalization" as a device to drive a wedge of difference between the object of the film—the Sani and the Subject—the filmmaker. As defined by Hall, the concept of "natural" is a representational strategy used "to fix difference." "Natural" distinguishes the Sani from the white South Africans who are "cultural." If the differences between the Sani and the whites are "cultural," then they are open to modification and change. But if they are "natural," then they are beyond history, permanent and fixed. This is a good strategy to stop the inevitable "slide" of meaning to secure discursive or ideological "closure." To understand what Hall is saying here, it is important to reflect on the binary implied in the culture/nature dichotomy. Racial theory applied culture/nature distinction differently to two racialized groups. Among whites, "culture" was opposed to "nature." Whites developed "culture" to subdue and overcome "nature"; for Africans, "culture" and "nature" were interchangeable.

By engaging critical viewing skills, and by taking into account the insights provided by Hall, viewers can recognize the social location of their interpretations, rather than believing those interpretations are somehow natural or idiosyncratic to the individual. The myth that the accepted conventions of film, video, and photographic representation are mere neutral carriers devoid of content implications no longer hold ground. By posing questions that seek a deeper meaning and understanding, critical viewers avoid the inclination to oversimplify their social identities into a collection of unified, discrete, and mutually exclusive territories that can be related only through dichotomous opposition: good versus bad, hero versus villain, right versus wrong, moral versus immoral. This approach to critical pedagogy provides students as audiences and viewers alternative ways of knowing, and gives room for multiple voices to be heard in the interpretation of meaning(s). How might one apply such a critical pedagogy to visual representations of *The Gods Must Be Crazy*?

WHAT IS THE ISSUE?

We must ask what context motivated the production of *The Gods Must Be Crazy*. By questioning the production and construction of the meaning-making process in media representations, we will examine closely the visual imagery and popular representation of people that help shape their personal, social, and political worlds. In thinking about "what is the issue," I direct attention toward the broader issues:

1. What sense do representations make of the world?
2. What are the visuals represented to us? How is it done? In other words, how do the individuals represented in the film become seen and how does the way we see them influence how we treat them or talk about them?
3. What are typical representations of groups in society—particularly those groups who are different from us?
4. What does this example of visual represent to me?
5. What do the visuals mean to other people who see them?

To decipher the meaning of *The Gods Must Be Crazy* as a visual representation of culture, identity, and ethnicity, it is necessary first, to know something about South Africa's past history, its present domestic and foreign policies, and the single-mindedness with which South Africa, before majority rule elections in 1994, used the system of apartheid to shape its future. Within its borders, South Africa had for almost four decades been creating a new territorial and demographic entity. Although we tend to hear only the pretty aspects of apartheid, its greatest manifestation was the manipulation of people within a finite space. As several reviewers of the film have acknowledged, *The Gods* is an expression of this aspect of apartheid (Brown, 1982, p. 42; Denby, 1984, p. 47; Davis, 1985, p. 51; Keneas, 1984, p. 22). Accordingly, the film delves into this aspect of racist apartheid by inversion.

In the comical, visual, and humorous images of *The Gods*, a South African writer-director, Jamie Uys, makes jokes about the absurdities and discontinuities of African life. While the landscape of *The Gods* looks very much like South Africa, it is set in what some film critics have identified as a mythical country of Botswana. Uys's Botswana does not exist, except in his imagination; features of the landscape, dress, and costumes are not to be found in real Botswana. Uys's Botswana is instead a dream of a happy-go-lucky bantüstan, those equally fictitious homelands that the South African government tried to create all over South Africa, literally out of dust, for the dumping of African people. Clearly, the central issue is the value questions defined by the filmmaker's goals, ideals, and hopes. As always, the contention or challenge, therefore, is to recognize that many of the things of value to us are not necessarily valued to the same degree by other people.

Second, to understand what the film producer is doing to Africa and to Africans, one must look at other works, particularly Edward Said's account outlined in his book *Orientalism* (1978). Said argues that "Orientalism" was a discourse by which European culture was able to manage—and even produce—the Orient politically, sociologically, militarily, ideologically, scientifically, and imaginatively during the post-Enlightenment period.

Within the framework of Western hegemony over the Orient, he says, there emerged a new object of knowledge—"a complex Orient suitable for display in the museum, for reconstruction of the colonial office, for theoretical illustration in anthropological, biological, linguistic, racial, and historical themes about mankind and the universe, for instance, of economic and sociological theories of development, revolution, cultural personalities, national or religious character (pp. 7–8). Said's rich and elaborate discussion of Orientalism breaks the code of racialized representation of the Mideastern people that closely parallels Foucault's power/knowledge argument: A discourse produces through different practices of representation (scholarship, exhibition, literature, painting, etc.) a form of racialized knowledge of the Other (Orientalism, Africanism) deeply implicated in the operations of power. These thoughts in turn enlighten us to begin to realize that the construction of a film like *The Gods Must Be Crazy* is along the lines of maintaining the distance from the racialized Other underlined with a racialized representation of Africans.

HOW IS THE ISSUE/EVENT DEFINED?

As we consider how the event is defined, several questions come to mind: (1) What is the source of the information? (2) What form does the event take? (3) How does the form shape my understanding of the event? (4) How does the form serve or not serve my purposes? (5) What information is left out?

The first ten minutes of the film address the relationship between illusion and reality. The imposing voice of the narrator intones: "It looks like a paradise, but it is in fact the most treacherous desert in the world, the Kalahari." After a series of cutaways and short narrative bits that set the stage for a childlike character, we see footage of the placid Kalahari "bushmen" looking for water. In this desert, we meet the "dainty, small and graceful Sani (bushmen)." Suspecting satire, we're unsure of the filmmaker's intent, but the sequence turns out to be a fairly predictable documentary with dry, straight-faced narration about a peaceful, "primitive" tribe of tiny "bushmen" who live in a gracious, simple world digging for roots and foraging for berries, without any knowledge of crime or violence. A Coke bottle drops from a great silver bird in the heavens and into the orderly lives of the nomadic "Bushman" Xi and his family. The bottle, as it soon turns out, is a gift from the gods. You can blow on it and make a windy music; you can roll it and crush millet. Pretty soon comes arguing over the bottle's possession followed by acrimony, anger, and fights. When one of the "bushmen" decides to return the bottle to the gods by throwing it off the end of the earth, his search for the earth's edge forces him to enter urban society for the first time, so the story goes. An outsider who does not include the point of view of those whose story is being told narrates the story about the Sani. In this narration, the culture of the Sani and that of other African societies is presumed to be a quaint relic of the past rather than a vibrant contemporary culture.

One might ask: Who are these "gods" who are crazy? They are the technologically advanced whites whose very garbage is a source of wonder to most of the developing world! In their indigenous wisdom, the Sani come to reject what white society has to offer, symbolized in the discarded bottle. This very rejection is a sop of white angst, because it means that the Sani do not covet the white standard of living, and so cannot be considered rivals—for South Africans, the ideal state of affairs. However admirable, the kind of decision this rejection represents is completely absent for the everyday lives of the indigenous peoples of South Africa. If there is one overwhelming fact of the dispossessed Tswans, Zulus, Xhosas, and Sani, as it is for many Africans, it is that they have no control whatsoever over what they can accept or reject. For most Africans, the decision continues to be made by outsiders, and that decision has never concerned itself in the least with what the Africans want.

It would be curious to know how much Xi was paid for acting in the movie. Did he ever see the movie? What did he think of it? Has he read some of the rave reviews about his movie? Will he read this article? These rhetorical questions illustrate the predicament in which the continent of Africa lies in relation to the rest of the world. Unfortunately, a set of ethics that binds those who exploit indigenous knowledge systems for our own advantage does not seem to exist. For many Africans, the media are still out of reach and will be so for many years to come. Poverty is rampant; amenities of the modern world like telephones, electricity, plumbing, or permanent housing is a dream of many indigenous people who live in remote areas and out of the urban circle. Why is it this way? The context within which *The Gods Must Be Crazy* was made is not explained anywhere in the production of this film. It is egregiously missing.

WHO IS INVOLVED?

As we explore "what groups are involved," our attention is drawn to two important questions: (1) What point of view is present? (2) Who is the target audience? The idea of whose interest or point of view prevails helps us to be critical of how a particular representation, issue, or event may be biased. Less obvious than identifying the filmmaker may be realizing that his reasons or arguments could be self-serving, designed largely to protect or to enhance the invested interest or dominant perspective in some way. A vested interest includes any privilege that a group enjoys and considers their "right." Arguments may be designed to protect or to enhance this interest—whether position, benefit, status, or credibility—perhaps at the expense of an opponent who is made to look foolish, selfish, stupid, immoral, uninformed, or downright perverse.

The film *The Gods Must Be Crazy* employs a narrator to guide the viewers and to intone who and what is important. Some people are cast as victims, others as heroes. An ethnocultural bias runs throughout the plot. This bias portrays Africans as childlike, incompetent, and unscientific. This bias reinforces a long-standing myth about Africa—the Dark Continent. Even though the theme of this film may pretend to portray simplistic tale of the search for the tranquil life and to satirize white urban living, beneath that tranquil life lies a parable about white South Africa with its basic values—those values of the privileged, for it is only those content with the world's goods who can afford to poke fun at them!

Who is in the film? The film's story involves Xi, the so-called "Bushman." As Uys show it, the life of the "bushmen" is idyllic, completely in harmony with their environment, living communally, until a careless aviator throws a Coke bottle into their midst. In another subplot, set in a neighboring African-governed country, a revolutionary Sam Boga attempts a coup. He is unsuccessful, and together with his followers flees into Botswana. A third subplot involves a white teacher who suddenly gets bored with her meaningless job in a city office and takes a job as a teacher in an African school in Botswana. There she meets with Andrew Steyn, a shy, awkward biologist who eventually wins her. These three plots fuse at the resolution, when the African revolutionaries seize the white schoolteacher and her African pupils as hostages, and the biologist and Xi work as a team to rescue them.

For many people, Africa is not a place but a state of mind, the heart of darkness. Africa has never been dark, however, to those who live there. It is ignorance on the part of outsiders that was, and continues to be, dark. The great tradition that *The Gods Must Be Crazy* draws upon is the journey through Africa—not the sort of expedition where you hunt for animals, but the missionary journey where you hunt for the souls of human beings. When applied to white South Africa before independence, the notion of "missionary," someone with a mission, derives a new meaning! This "mission" is essential to the white man's view of Africa. Europe sent its missionaries, including its fanatics, to Africa. The Afrikaner, the white man in that part of Africa we now call South Africa, decided early on that his mission was to bring the Word of God to the wilderness. Unlike Dr. Livingstone's ambition to bring the Word of God to the people of central Africa, the Afrikaner had no desire to share that world with the kaffir, the unbelievers, for Afrikaners were God's Chosen People, and the Chosen do not share with the unchosen, for then how would He tell the difference (Davis, 1985, p. 51). In the middle of this country, the Afrikaners' mission came to mean the protection of white Christian civilization (against the Africans and communism). In Uys's film, these two—the Africans and communism—are personified by Sam Boga and his guerillas.

A figurative interpretation of the plot, then, reveals that Africans are like children who are easily led astray by outside agitators (i.e., African liberationists). When this happens, the threat is not only to Africans but also to the white race personified by the heroine. To save Africans and Europeans alike, white organizational skills must mobilize all indigenous people and even African nature itself (in the shape of a poisonous bush). As the film illustrates, Andrew Steyn, the pacific, unworldly scientist—the personification of a technologically advanced but nonaggressive South African—beats all the odds.

WHAT ARE THE ARGUMENTS?

This question drives the inquiry. Besides looking at what groups are involved in the film, an examination of the arguments postulated in the film reveals that *The Gods* has a strong point of view! What arguments enhance the interests of its dominant side and what arguments detract from the credibility of the other side? More specifically, students and teachers must ask the following critical questions:

1. Why was a particular visual image selected?
2. What information presented in the visual image is factual?
3. What portion of content is inaccurate?
4. Why are shots/camera work arranged that way?
5. Do visual images match narration?
6. How does sound affect visual images?
7. How is repetition of visual images and text used?
8. How do graphics affect the message?
9. How does stillness or motion aid the message?
10. What is left out?
11. How is the message affected by what is left out?

Readers may be troubled in two contrasting ways: On the one hand, some who are shocked by the obvious racism of the film may wonder why I worry about basic principles of media representation; on the other hand, many may wish that the questions I pose could just be ignored, simply because, in their opinion, the film was only a piece of art and entertainment—why not just follow one's pleasures and savor the riches that the world of narrative provides? Unfortunately, there are many sides to any piece of art! Because all media and visual productions are produced from a variety of social locations and motivations, such underlying positions and motives need to be questioned. Perhaps if we can find a responsible way of defending the ethical criticism of narrative, we will encourage similar probing in the other arts or texts that I must neglect here.

It is important to look at how the visuals are manipulated in this film. For example, after about six minutes the film cuts to a big city, where we are introduced to "civilized man." Civilized humans, we are told, managed to make their lives more complicated by trying to make them easier. By contrast, the "bushmen" have a very simple life—until the Western world intrudes upon it. The mission of Andrew Steyn, the biologist, is scientific discovery, in the innocuous form of examination of elephant droppings. Xi's mission, however, is the preservation of the way of life of the "bushman."

The arguments are made through anecdotal stories of the way the people in the film go about their everyday work. As it is shown, the white scientist comes to the aid of the kidnapped children. Here, the underlying platitude by which most South Africans rationalize their relationship with Africans comes to the surface: "Africans are like children." In the film, they *are* children. By introducing the guerilla fighters, the film shows that their own government, being African, cannot be relied upon to protect them. They must be rescued by the ingenuity of a white man *in collaboration with Xi the "Bushman."*

All these people scurrying around the landscape of southern Africa, colliding in pratfalls, constitute a distorted microcosm of the class of people and ideologies that is in reality deeply tragic. What Uys has done in the film, in fact (albeit a fact disguised by humor), is to create the never-never land that the architects of apartheid would have us believe in, in which South Africa's intentions are good for everyone. In this land of make-believe, entire villages drop their work and turn out to sing a hymn of welcome to a white teacher. This gesture depicts the relationship of Africans toward white people as gratitude for the help being given, of whites toward Africans, as protective paternalism. This peaceful, dependent relationship would continue forever were it not for the advance of the guerillas.

WHAT IS TAKEN FOR GRANTED?

To examine the assumptions or what is taken for granted, several questions come to mind: What attitudes are assumed? Whose points of view are assumed? Implied in these questions are the cultural assumptions. The ways in which media constructions are read or received by their audiences are often not questioned enough. For example, different disciplines of science measure Africa in different ways. Geographers point to a climate that ranges from the burning Sahara, to the steamy rainforests of Zaire (now the Republic of Congo), to the dry savannas of Kenya. Cartographers note the enormous size of Africa compared to the other continents. For example, Africa occupies 11,668,545 square miles— China, Europe, and the United States could fit within this area, with room to spare. Biologists note the astonishing abundance and variety of the continent's wildlife, with a particular mention of Tanzania's Serengeti and the Ngorongoro Crater. Epidemiologists speak with horror of the deadly viruses like HIV and Ebola that are presumed to have come out of the jungle, and countless undiscovered microbes waiting to emerge.

For anthropologists, Africa's most impressive statistics are the ones that measure the enormous diversity of its indigenous people. The diversity of the different African societies, from the Ashanti to the Zulu, and their elaborate attires with their elaborate customs and rituals provide a rich heritage rather than a deficit culture. With varying histories, cultures, and lifestyles, these indigenous peoples have lived on the continent for centuries and are spread over fifty independent countries. A majority of the indigenous people includes pastoralists, agro-pastoralists, hunters, and gatherers. Some thirteen hundred languages are spoken on the continent, about a third of the world's total. Each language represents a distinct indigenous group with its own beliefs and its own rituals and ceremonies—some of which have been performed for hundreds of years.

Africa is often misunderstood, however, because of the Western media's dismissal of the continent as backward and therefore unworthy of coverage, until disaster strikes, like in the case of the recent famine in Ethiopia, Somalia, and Rwanda. The Western media does not portray Africa as a diverse continent, of reemerging democracies, and of troubled areas with leftover vestiges of colonialism, made up of many countries, climates, geographies, histories, and peoples.

By now it is common knowledge that Africa overflows with indigenous forms of communication: theater, drumming, dancing, music, traditional storytelling, and village meetings that have informed and entertained for centuries. And yet, in the past thirty years, the continent has been inundated with radios, televisions, VCRs, and other Western products at the expense of dislodging these indigenous artforms, practices, and knowledge systems. This persistent state of affairs makes African communities "knowledge colonies" of outside powers. Most economies, apart from South Africa, are too poor to compete with European and American economies in terms of media production and dissemination. The reliance on the West for all but local news results in reduced and distorted coverage of Africa, consistent with the legacy of colonialism as portrayed in *The Gods Must Be Crazy*.

Tanzanians, for instance, get news about their neighbors, the Kenyans, from the Western media. Nigerians learn about Tanzanian events from the British Broadcasting Corporation (BBC). All over Africa the pattern is the same. The image we see in the United States, the corrupt, incompetent, starving, dependent, and hopeless Africa, is the image manufactured in the West and transmitted to Africa (although there are pockets of resistance to this inundation). Raised on a diet of Westernized history, Tarzan books and films, and sensationalized news media, many students in the United States believe Africa to be a primitive land of hot, steamy jungles inhabited by wild animals and savages. This myth is normalized and reinforced by *The Gods Must Be Crazy*.

Even though present-day technological changes have brought far-reaching structural changes in industrialized countries, particularly in the area of production and distribution of information and literacy materials, the situation in Africa and in much of the developing world remains a challenge. Communities in metropolitan cities like Dar es Salaam, Johannesburg, Lagos, and Nairobi look to the communities of Los Angeles and New York with awe and wonder, imitating their music and fashion, and craving the instant gratification and escape that movie entertainment has to offer.

Non-Africans have distorted the reality about Africa. For centuries, starting with perceptions of the remote "Dark Continent," the worldview of many non-Africans, particularly Europeans, was clouded over with myths and stereotypes. Some of the simplest myths are most common: lions in the jungles, the isolated "Dark Continent," inferior savages, a race of Negroes (heathens developed only by the grace of God and the white man), and a land of turmoil, incapable of self-government. Because these myths and stereotypes are alive today in schools' curricula (however unintentional the distortions and omissions may be), in the hands of unaware and unskilled teachers, the curriculum continues to feed the racist doctrines and practices of white superiority and privilege.

CONCLUDING COMMENTS

In this analysis, I have employed critical inquiry as an alternative pedagogy to unravel a discourse of ethnic bias and denigration of indigenous peoples disguised in humor as clear-cut realism. I encourage teachers to unmask such disguises embedded in media representations of everyday life. The five concepts for critical pedagogy about media representation outlined in this chapter cannot claim to substitute for or to uproot the century-old myths, fears, and stereotypes about Africa and the African people. These five concepts, however, provide a framework to question such myths and stereotypes, which have, to a large extent, been created in storybooks, literature, media, and cinema. By posing these questions, we investigate and critically evaluate the various assumptions underlying the production values of dominant news, pictures, and entertainment media. In fact, by using these concepts in critical pedagogy, we also examine the ways in which the language of media is socially and historically produced. We need to encourage students as well to question the clarity and strength or reasoning, to identify assumptions and values, to recognize points of view and attitudes, and to evaluate conclusions and actions provided by all narratives across the curriculum whether they be short stories, poems, plays, picture books, films, or pieces of nonfiction.

REFERENCES

Bordwell, D., Staiger J., & Thompson, K. (1985). *The classical Hollywood cinema: Film style and mode of production to 1960.* New York: Columbia University Press.

Brown, R. (1982). *Monthly Film Bulletin,3*: 42.

Canby, V. (1990). "Sequel to South Africa's 'Gods Must Be Crazy.' " *New York Times*, Section C, p. 14.

Davis, P. (1985). *Cineaste, XIV* (1): 51.

Denby, D. (1984). *New York 7*: 7.

Dyer, R. (1985). "Taking popular television seriously." In D. Lusted, & P. Drummond, (Eds.), *TV and schooling*. London: BFI.

Fairclough, N. (1989). *Language and power.* London: Longman.

Fensham, P., Gunstone, R., & White, R. (Eds.). (1994). *The content of science: A constructivist approach to teaching and learning.* London: Falmer Press.

Freire, P., & Giroux, H. (1989). Pedagogy, popular culture and public life. An Introduction. In H. Giroux, & R. Simon (Eds.), *Popular culture: Schooling and everyday life* (pp. 199–212). Westport, CT: Bergin & Garvey.

Giroux, H., & Simon, R. (1989). Popular culture as pedagogy of pleasure and meaning. In H. Giroux, & R. Simon (Eds.) *Popular culture: Schooling and everyday life* (pp. 1–29). Westport, CT: Bergin & Garvey.

———. (1987). "Critical literacy and student experience: Donald Graves' approach to literacy." *Language Arts, 64*: 175–181.

Hall, S. (1997). *Representation. Cultural representations and signifying practices.* London: The Open University.

———. (1982). *The rediscovery of 'ideology': Return of the repressed in media studies.* New York: Routledge.

———. (1981). "Notes on deconstructing 'the popular'." In R. Samuel, (Ed.), *People's history and socialist theory.* London: Routledge.

Kellner, D. (1995). *Media culture: Cultural studies, identity and politics between the modern and the postmodern.* New York: Routledge.

Keneas, A. (1984). *Newsday 9,* Part 11, p. 22.

Luke, A. (1997). Introduction. In S. Muspratt, A. Luke, & P. Freebody (Eds.), *Constructing critical literacies: Teaching and learning textual practice* (pp. 1–18). Cresskill, NJ: Hampton Press.

Lusted, D. (Ed.). (1991). *The media studies book: A guide for teachers.* London: Routledge.

McLaren, P., Hammer, R., Sholle, D., & Reilly, S. (1995). *Rethinking media literacy: A critical pedagogy of representation.* New York: Peter Lang.

Muspratt, S., Luke, A., & Freebody P. (Eds). *Constructing critical literacies: Teaching and learning textual practice.* Cresskill, NJ: Hampton Press.

Shor, I. (1993). *Education Is politics: Paulo Freire's critical pedagogy.* In P. McLaren, & P. Leonard (Eds.), *Paulo Freire: A critical encounter* (pp. 25–35). London: Routledge.

Werner W., & Nixon, K. (1990). *The media and public issues: A guide for teaching critical mindedness.* London, Ontario: The Althouse Press.

CHAPTER 6

Values in Media Representations

There are many things that we do, see, or talk about in our culture that we never ask questions about. We do things without thinking about them because we have always done them in the same way. When we are in another culture or with people from a different culture, we see that people do things in many different ways. One of the first differences we notice is the form of greetings that are used in the culture. The language that people use to address each other tells us many things about a culture. For example, the language of address gives cultural information about cultures, values, relationships, and communication style, both verbal and nonverbal. The focus of this chapter is on how language communicates values—the way in which values are constructed in media representations and conveyed through the language of media.

VALUES VERSUS MORAL CODES
IN MEDIA REPRESENTATIONS

Values and moral education are used interchangeably in education in the United States today. Since Dan Quayle's speech on values, "Restoring Basic Values: Strengthening the Family," theorists have used this as a landmark of the debate on values. Quayle's speech promotes three values: God, family, and adoption. He stated:

> Marilyn and I have tried to teach our children these values, like faith in
> God, love of family, and appreciation of freedom. We have also taught

them about family issues like adoption. My parents adopted twins
when I was ten years old. We've taught our children to respect single
parents and their challenges—challenges that faced my grandmother
many years ago and my own sister today.

Quayle's comments provided the foreground of the debate of family
values in America. Popularly known as the Dan-Murphy debate, the family values campaign was sparked by references by Quayle to TV's Murphy Brown, who was to have her child while unmarried. This episode has
become the most talked about when the topic of values comes up. Much
of what is not considered in schools, however, is the underlying question:
What are values? With this ambiguity, is the more disturbing question:
Which values must students be taught in school?

This chapter explores notions of education and power in the media
curriculum of global values. As for most values included in moral education, global values are inscribed in the fairy tales, myths, and stories students read, listen to, or view, narrated by peers, teachers, parents, and
church personnel. Community-inspired stories pass on community values. Global values underscore global interests. However, many stories
today no longer come from parents, schools, churches, community, or
native countries. They come from the mass media. And the media retell
these mythic stories on a daily basis as they perform the primary functions of mass communication: to entertain, inform, transmit, or reflect
culture, and to persuade.

Global values such as democracy, patriotism, consumerism, justice,
honesty, liberty, the pursuit of happiness, family, security, and good
overcoming evil have dominated U.S. mass media presentations for
decades. The mass media are in the business of producing a media curriculum in the stories distributed through programs such as network
news, soaps, films, MTV, and situation comedies. Through these genres,
the mass media create global values out of a mythical world by establishing a social hierarchy of *who* and *what* are important within the
worldview of the program. This social hierarchy constitutes what Gramsci called hegemony. Hegemonic or global values are the imposition of
an ideology within a culture. Critical theorists like John Fiske (1996)
and Stuart Hall (1997) argue that the worldviews presented through the
media do not merely reflect or reinforce culture but in fact shape the
thinking, attitudes, and values by promoting the dominant ideology of a
culture.

By addressing the way power emanates through the "global values" of the school, the workplace, and the courthouse, and how these social conversations are retold through coded genres of situation comedy, soaps, action adventures, news, movies, and so on, one can begin to analyze the way the dominant social order reproduces itself in personal identities, cultural practices, school curriculum, disciplinary structures, and attitudes toward authority. This seems like a tall order to address in the limited space of this chapter. However, we know that to have power, myths must be retold.

Myths demand critical questioning to see if they stand up to reality and whose interest they legitimize. It is my task, therefore, to concentrate on how the mass media peddle this insidious cultural pedagogy and examine the exclusionary one-way flow of media information, through which the news media promote a Eurocentric idea of popularized values that shapes the perceptions of European and European-descended people and marginalizes others. The frameworks of critical media literacy I propose in this book lay the foundation for investigating the role beliefs and values play in our "knowing" and "doing" as teachers. I direct our attention particularly to those beliefs, actions, and values shaped by media culture.

When I suggest exploring the media curriculum of global values, this suggestion is not meant to be an attack on television or the media in general, but an assault on its mythic realities, against the realism and the system of coded genres that define values, normalcy, and ideology in society. The rationale for exploring the media curriculum of global values is based on postmodern, multidimensional, and multiperspectival connections between the economic, social, and cultural views of the world. The goal of such critical education is to enable students to understand and critique the insidious cultural pedagogy of media and to conceptualize social justice more clearly and consequently develop a sense of fairness in the distribution of our society's cultural and economic resources (Semali & Pailliotet, 1999). Taking such a critical stance empowers students to systematically challenge the exclusionary aspect of the Eurocentric way of seeing the world (Dines & Humez, 1995, p. xviii). The underlying assumption of this view is that popular culture as represented in the media of films and television is a site of struggle over popular meanings and global values. At times, popular culture produces meaning and regulates pleasure. At other times, it subordinates the groups' use of popular culture as means of focusing on a particular ideological reading of the world (Kellner, 1995).

HOW MEDIA CREATE GLOBAL VALUES

To engage students and teachers in critical examination of the media curriculum of global values requires an ardent effort both in school-based curriculum development and instruction. An understanding of global values must begin with an examination of how such values are constructed, legitimized in a democratic society, and distributed through mass media presentations. According to Silverblatt (1995, p. 318), a media presentation is defined as the specific programming that is produced within mass media. For example: particular films (e.g., *Ordinary People* [1980], based on the novel by Judith Geist), newspapers (e.g., the December 3, 1996, edition of the *Washington Post*), or television programs (e.g., the October 12, 1996, episode of *Rosanne*).

The way films have represented families, for example, poses a curious observation about values—from traditional, tight-knit "nuclear" families of mother, father, child, and a dog, to families torn apart by divorce and death, to groups of people united by choice and love rather than kinship. The stories told and the images portrayed in these media examples have three things in common. They move us emotionally, they embody values, and cumulatively they construct a particular worldview.

However, there is a great deal more in such media products than information, emotion, and good feeling. We must also consider the way in which these messages can contribute to social attitudes. These media presentations peddle images, and concepts of love, sexuality, romance, success, popularity, and perhaps of most importance, *normalcy*. For example, the idea of having a two-gendered, two-parent household is defined as the normal family. Quite often in media presentations, this idea of family is defined, reinforced, and perpetuated in contrast to other representations of family that might point to dysfunctional families, or divorced or gay parents. By defining normalcy, these media presentations also define the "abnormal." They tell us who we should be regardless of what the reality might be. They give us a myth, a story through which the world is explained to us.

In this general sense, the mass media reflect a mythological world—a world in which men outnumber women by almost two to one. In addition, it is a world in which absolutely everyone is heterosexual and furthermore still living in a nuclear family in which the man goes to work and the woman stays at home with the children. This is to say in sum, the mass media legitimate not only what is considered more or less acceptable but also confirm ideas about what people are like and how they are meant to be understood even if in a stereotypical way.

Today, this mythological world describes only about one-fifth of the world's population. And even more importantly, it is a world in which no one is disabled, either physically or mentally. We are surrounded by these media presentations every day—we know such presentations are illusions (not real) and yet it is difficult not to compare our own lives with these "universal" messages and images, or worse, let these images define for us what we should believe as "truth." Within this framework, this mythological world shapes the kinds of global values that insist on a *values hierarchy* dominant within the worldview of the media presentation.

To understand this mythological world and how it garners support for unchallenged, universal values, let's recall Toni Morrison's writing in *The Bluest Eye* (1970), where she makes this apparent. She writes:

> Adults, older girls, shops, magazines, newspapers, window signs—all the world had agreed that a blue-eyed, pink-skinned doll was what every girl treasured. "Here," they said, "this is beautiful, and if you are on this day 'worthy' you may have it."

This quote attributed by Morrison is only one among many examples that go undetected. As I explained in the opening paragraph of this chapter, like culture, values get inscribed in what we believe without thinking about them because we have always believed them in the same way. Only when we are in another culture or with people from a different culture do we see the contradictions—that people do things in many different ways or believe in different values. Morrison understands how the values of one group, with the help of media, were judged to be the "norm" in their worldview against which all other dolls were evaluated. The fact that there might be little girls in the world for whom blue eyes and pink skin (or any other color) are not considered "beautiful" (or at least not the only combination of eye and skin color possible) is overlooked, consciously or unconsciously, as the case may be. Norms tend to create a "blind spot" in our vision of appreciating other values, or simply other worldviews.

When critical theorists talk about a "worldview" they mean the *values hierarchy* created by media presentations to form a mythic reality that people buy into over a period of time. For example, the construction of such worldview may be a result of news reports about a country, an ethnic or racial group of people, or an idea. In the United States, for instance, media presentations have often been influenced by world events as well as domestic social and political agendas such as the Vietnam War, the Gulf War, the wave of church burning in the South, the Oklahoma City bombing, and the O.J. Simpson criminal and civil trials in Los Angeles. In sum, such a worldview is based on fictional or nonfictional stories with certain fundamental assumptions about how the world operates. Even though these events may seem pure news on the surface, they may not be free of bias. Instead, they may be value-laden or present a one-way flow of information that paints a worldview such as news media do when they portray a certain country or neighborhood as "a dangerous place."

Many students believe to a large extent what is reported in the newspapers as objective, and therefore the "truth." However, objectivity in reporting is upheld by popular opinion only as a standard of performance toward which journalists strive. This code assumes that an absolute truth exists and that journalists are in a position to present an accurate depiction of this ideal, without distortion or personalized bias. But, as we now know, we live in a complex, subjective world in which the truth may be difficult to identify. My students as well as many newspaper readers confuse the statement of fact with truth. Since there is no universal agreement on truth, faithfulness to this ideal becomes an illusion or an impossibility. Such illusion is based on the traditional belief in the functions of the press: to inform, entertain, persuade, and transmit or reflect culture. Some scholars find this notion of objectivity in the press to be not only unrealistic but also undesirable. Ben Bagdikian (1992) maintains that the basis of solid journalism is values: "Objectivity contradicts the essentially subjective nature of journalism. Every basic step in the journalistic process involves a value-laden decision."

Oftentimes, audiences are not aware of the devices or conventions used in the reporting of news and of telling these fictional stories. As explained in Chapter 3, the way these stories are told and the person who is doing the telling play an important role in formulating the motive of the telling as well as making the story entertaining and at the same time believable. These ways of telling explain the coded genres of news reports, situation comedy, soaps, action adventures, and so on, that define the system of commercial television in the United States. It is therefore these conventions that are used in telling mythic stories that allow bias, overt manipulation of the characterization or plot, stereotyping, jokes, and comedic entertainment to "creep into" the story being told.

By the same token, a particular worldview is portrayed as a value, a better way of being or doing, superior culture, morally good, or simply put, the norm. Such a worldview represented in the story is often influenced by the attitude and background of its storyteller, its interviewers, writers, photographers, and editors. The danger presented by mythic realities such as those found in popular films and television shows is that audiences sometimes make decisions or judgments on the basis of these myths. The conventions used in advancing the plot or resolving the conflict seem so believable, and yet they are oversimplified. Complex problems are trivialized or made to look ridiculously easy. Lifetime enemies are shown to resolve their differences with a handshake, and romantic encounters end up in sexual intercourse without courtship, love, or even considering consequences of the sexual act.

In the past students read these cultural stories in fairy tales, plays, novels, and poems. In these genres, authors took time to develop the plot, the characters, and also put lots of thought into the resolution of conflict. Today, television and movies have in fact replaced years of storytelling familiar to children. Television in particular has replaced fairy tales and myths as the primary producer of children's stories. Unlike authors in literature, producers of television shows and movies have limited time to accomplish what authors of novels claim to do. Producers of television shows have twenty-three minutes in a half-hour show, and movies take ninety minutes to introduce the characters, the plot, the conflict, and the resolution. These time constraints infringe upon how the story is told in all commercial media, including advertising. The typical conventions of showing characters as heroes or villains, good guys versus bad guys, winners and losers, black or white, have become commonplace in storytelling in commercial media. This binary way of telling the moral of the story excludes other variations, versions, or possibilities, and thus, such exclusions introduce bias into a popular story. Within this framework, producers of mythic stories are caught up in a race of trying to satisfy audiences who want more programs. As this race accelerates in a cycle of "the more the better," producers fall into the trap of sensationalizing, bias, stereotyping, and manipulating the story to reach a quick fix or resolution of the conflict.

The desires of American audiences constantly fuel the number of stories that get told. These desires are collectively evaluated by what happens at the box office and the ratings derived from television programs unleashed every year. It is a known fact that American audiences consume lots of media. They spend tremendous amounts of time listening to the radio, watching television, going to see films, experiencing music, going shopping, reading magazines and newspapers, and participating in other forms of cultural pedagogy. Thus, an insidious cultural pedagogy has come to dominate everyday life, serving as the ubiquitous background and often the highly seductive foreground of people's attention and activity. This cultural pedagogy, many experts argue, is undermining human potentiality and creativity.

As suggested by Kellner (1982), television has become a powerful socializing machine. (Consider, for example, the TV series *Dallas* or the television movie *Roots*, adapted from the novel by Alex Haley, which captured the minds and hearts of many people all over the world.) "Both television entertainment and information may well gain in power precisely because individuals are not aware that their thoughts, attitudes, and behaviors are being shaped by the ubiquitous idea and image machines of their homes" (Kellner, 1990, p. 126). This means that television provides continuous education throughout life, offering a popular day and night school for the nation.

The media, particularly television, have become the nation's teacher of choice, and many young people who are exposed to these media find themselves in a quagmire of myths about everyday life. Unfortunately, little help is available in their school curriculum to assist them in understanding the forces at work that exploit them or at least to assist them to develop strategies to counteract this exploitation. For example, advertisers prey on the insecurities of young people, convincing them that they should look a certain way, dress a certain way, and act a certain way to be acceptable—and that the purchase of the advertiser's product will help bring this about. The advertising industry uses a similar approach with other age groups, but "the practice seems especially insidious and exploitative given the vulnerability of youth" (Arnold, 1993, p. 6).

Perhaps one way for students and teachers to explore global values and the attendant exploitation is to begin to question the role global media play in the arenas of domestic and world affairs. The claim is made that the purposes of global media are to foster a sense of global community, to disseminate information, to serve political interests in order to isolate political enemies, to preserve and maintain friendship with allies, and to demoralize actual and potential enemies of national interests (Silverblatt, 1995, pp. 294–298). In any global media campaign, what is often ignored and generally not examined critically, especially in American classrooms, is how the proliferation of these global values in turn impacts students' behavior toward other cultures and individuals from other ethnic groups or countries. Rarely are students helped to raise questions such as:

- What culture or cultures populate the world?
- What do students know about the people who populate this world?
- Does this world present an optimistic or pessimistic view of life?
- What does it mean to be successful in this world?
- What is the hierarchy of values that appears in this constructed worldview?

Questions such as these present an important pedagogical venue for curriculum inquiry of global values. When students and teachers explore global values within the context of critical media literacy, such inquiry takes the power away from the media industry and allows students to tell their own stories.

POWER RELATIONS: VALUES IN "KNOWING" AND "DOING"

In this section, I shall examine more specifically the role that beliefs and values play in our "knowing" and "doing" as teachers, particularly those beliefs, actions, and values shaped by the media curriculum. I will analyze how economic and other resources, advantages, and privileges are distributed inequitably, in part because of power dynamics involving beliefs in racial, gender, and class divisions. By no means is such analysis to be limited to TV and films only, but must be extended to other multimedia forms of representation including those found in textbooks, book covers, paintings, and other school-related texts. As explained in previous chapters, critical media literacy is not just a *technique* to be learned or memorized, but rather a *process*, central to the entire notion of communication and the construction of meaning.

The production of meaning from media presentations depends upon knowledge that is shared by a community. Such knowledge is shaped by the community's belief system, its worldview, its use of language, and by how one is positioned in her or his own culture in relation to other people. One major aspect of teaching critical media literacy is to identify where that knowledge comes from and how it is constructed. One may ask: How did we come to know what we know about a certain event or group? The common belief is that an individual's sense of self is organized according to various *categories*, such as gender, race, class, age, sexual orientation, and so on, as well as those categories encompassing different "interest groups," which include political affiliation. The characteristics and values associated with these categories include the way we look, how we behave, the lifestyle we adopt, even the way we buy goods and services.

As individuals or groups, we come to recognize how certain characteristics are considered more or less socially appropriate or acceptable. Ideas about what people are like and how they are meant to be understood already prevail in our culture. These ideas are embedded in mass media presentations and are part of the agenda of media executives, who are in the business of reproducing a social hierarchy through the stories distributed by programs from news and sitcoms to MTV and rap music. These stories allow a certain gender, race, or class to dominate or be dominated by another that claims superiority. These ideas give meaning to our sense of self and allow us to position ourselves in relation to others. Such *context of meanings* and attitudes can be recognized in the media. But the way representations of race, gender, class, or age are constructed is as important as the ideas and meaning they project, since they offer *positions* for us, through which we recognize images as similar or different from ourselves and those around us. While images and meanings change over time, we continually define ourselves in changing relations to these images and meanings.

The important lesson to be derived from this thinking is that assumptions, "common knowledge," common sense, "general" knowledge, widespread beliefs, and popular attitudes are all part of the *context of meanings* within which cultural norms or values are enhanced and circulated. Often overlooked in this perspective, however, is the fact that people construct the context of meanings out of their experiences within specific social contexts of race, gender, and class. As explained in Chapter 3, rather than one abstract psychological process, contexts of meanings are historically defined social practices that are subject to political, academic, and cultural hierarchies. This context and our individual ranges of knowledge, values, and attitudes are governed in turn by a system of power that offers varied "legitimacy" to these meanings, ideas, and conventions. It is in this hierarchy, therefore, that some values or meanings come to be dominant and others marginalized.

From this perspective, therefore, there are no absolute values or "how things are" but only many competing versions, some of which are more highly regarded than others in society and hence are circulated more widely. Ultimately, the relationship between media institutions and media audiences is an unequal and yet a contested one. However, this inequality is not merely a question of access (Who is allowed to speak?) but, more crucially, one of language (How are they allowed to speak?). Insofar as the ability to control language, and thereby to define the terms in which the world may be talked about and represented, can be seen to reside with certain powerful groups in society, language may itself inevitably function to maintain existing inequalities. Therefore, in looking at the media as representations of people, teachers may examine global values as versions of values that have currency, the elements that are repeated across them, and the relation to commonsense definitions individuals acquire as participants of a global culture.

UNRAVELING THE MEDIA CURRICULUM
OF GLOBAL VALUES

Traditionally, "values education" has not been taken up in schools systematically. Little has been written about global values and how they get constructed, legitimized, and distributed worldwide, especially through the mass media, to manufacture consent of people within the country and outside. On the one hand, educators assume that values education rests within the domain of parents. On the other hand, parents hope that schools will educate and socialize their children with the values of discipline, sense of justice, morals, and ethical values of "knowing good from evil." However, many students leave high school after reading novels, plays, poetry, and other narratives, thinking that they know how the world operates. Their definition of values gained from reading these classic works is often told through the familiar and sometimes predictable refrain: "The moral of the story is . . ." Encoded in such a refrain is a particular values system that encourages students to learn from stories written in the school canon about honesty, patriotism, individualism, decency, respect, and so forth, in order to abide by a cultural norm and accept a national culture without questioning it. A cultural norm is defined as the social practices that affirm the central values of the social class in the material and symbolic wealth of society (Swanson, 1991, pp. 123–129). Such norms form part of students' cultural knowledge—they know "what to do" with media products they come across even if they don't do it—and the media presentations used are as familiar to these students as participants of a particular culture as the meanings they make.

How might students begin to unravel this insidious cultural pedagogy of the media? Unraveling media curriculum of global values involves immersing oneself in a media presentation to explore the text in order to find questions that are significant to the learner and then systematically investigating and analyzing critically the values embedded in those questions. For example, one may ask: What kind of global values are depicted in the lead character of *Forrest Gump* (Robert Zemeckis, 1994)? Whose worldview is presented in movies like *ET* (Steven Spielberg, 1980), *Boyz N the Hood* (John Singleton, 1991), *Star Wars* (George Lucas, 1977)? By questioning the assumptions that underlie these media presentations, we also critique the embedded values and beliefs about how the world operates.

For example, teachers must investigate the ways in which the language of media is socially and historically produced. They must examine its production, construction, and the meaning-making processes by which media imagery and popular representation of people help shape our personal, social, and political worlds. Furthermore, the complex and contested ways in which the language of media embodies broader relationships of power, and the ways in which language users are themselves inevitably implicated in these relationships, need to be carefully addressed.

By engaging a critical examination of global values, teachers and students begin to read American cultural pedagogy critically from the way values have been encoded in the daily narratives of media texts, such as television programs, newspapers, film, and consumer advertising. This critical way of reading American cultural pedagogy goes counter to the monoculture of objectivity often found in textbooks in today's classrooms. Intellectual growth demands questions, not answers. Students won't learn to think critically if they approach their education as a matter of imitation or the mechanical application of rules.

Quite frankly, if teachers hope to create learning environments that will help students change oppressive literacy practices, these teachers must think critically about what kinds of values they want to go into the pedagogical spaces in which learning occurs for most students, that is, how these values are articulated in other social, political, and ideological forces. Teachers engaged in the process of critical literacy recognize that dominant social arrangements are dominant not because they are the only possible arrangements but because those arrangements exist for the advantage of certain privileged groups. Critical literacy is not satisfied that students know 4,700 items that all Americans need to know according to E. D. Hirsch, Jr., or that they can reflect the cultural capital of Roger Kimball. Critical literacy does not seek a universal truth, or a truth whose ideological effects permit some groups to survive at the expense of others.

Intellectual growth demands questions not answers. Students won't learn to think critically if they approach their education as a matter of imitation or the mechanical application of rules or prescriptions. Critical media literacy rather seeks to produce partial, contingent, but necessary historical truths that will enable students from diverse backgrounds to be free—truths that reflect the multiplicity of experiences these students bring into the classroom and that acknowledge the social constructedness, historicity, institutions, and social arrangements and practices they legitimate (Shor, 1993).

Within this critical framework, teachers will also realize that students do not develop easily the habits of mind necessary for inquiry. These intellectual habits include the ability to imagine and value points of view different from their own—then to strengthen, refine, enlarge, or reshape their ideas in light of those other perspectives. These habits also include openness to new ideas combined with a skepticism that demands testing those ideas against previous experience, reading, and belief. They include a desire to see things as a whole and to integrate specific knowledge into larger frameworks. This critical approach to media in particular, and to all texts in general, forms what has now come to be known as critical media literacy. In sum, as a form of inquiry, this approach supports models of critique, decoding, analyzing, and reading of biased visual images.

APPLYING CRITICAL MEDIA LITERACY IN THE CLASSROOM: ANALYSIS OF TWO NEWSPAPER ARTICLES

Activities that help students to come to terms with or start to understand what I am talking about follow in this section to illustrate how one might go about investigating the insidious cultural pedagogy of the media, particularly in the daily press. I encourage students to explore a text from the daily press in order to find questions that are significant to the learner, and then systematically investigate and analyze critically the values embedded in those questions. In the following paragraphs, I provide a comparison of two newspaper articles: (1) "Study Angers Relatives of Dead Children" (*Philadelphia Inquirer*, October 27, 1994) and (2) "Malaria Vaccine Successful in Africa Test, Study Says" (*Center Daily Times*, State College, Pennsylvania, October 28, 1994). These articles have two things in common. They were published around the same time, and the stories tell about research on children. They revolve around the broader issue of life—particularly of little children—that is, how to enhance it and prevent death from trauma in victims of sudden infant death syndrome (SIDS) and from malaria infection. These two articles were used in my classroom setting with preservice students studying critical media literacy. Because of space constraints, I will outline the central themes of the two articles separately and present the comments and reactions of these students with a short discussion.

Eyes Taken from Dead Children in Study Here

[*Philadelphia Inquirer* Staff Writer
Relatives of the 19 youngsters, all under 3 at death, were not told. The city Medical Examiner's office removed the eyes.]

Without seeking permission from families of the dead, the Philadelphia Medical Examiner's Office permanently removed eyes and optic nerves from 19 deceased infants and young children—most of them abuse victims—as part of a study. According to a published scientific report, the study, which covered a 23-month period ending in August 1990, was a joint effort of the city Medical Examiner's office and the Scheie Eye Institute in West Philadelphia. The report was co-authored by two city medical examiners and two physicians from Scheie.

The study involved three categories of children: nine who died from blunt trauma to the head, four victims of shaken baby syndrome and six victims of sudden infant death syndrome, or SIDS. City officials declined to identify any of the children but the *Inquirer* was able to obtain records that identify some of them.

When one of the children's grandmothers was interviewed, she said that she had never been told about her grandchild's involvement in the study. "They asked me about transplanting his organs and I said definitely not," she said. "They never asked me about his eyes. Never." The reporter continued in the story to say:

The purpose of the eye study was to compare the brain and optic nerve damage suffered by the shaken child with the damage suffered by children who had visible head injuries. The study focused on intracranial damage and optic nerve hemorrhages in the three study groups.

An article published in March 1994 in *Ophthalmology* magazine, according to the *Inquirer* reporter, stated that the study concluded that the victims of shaken baby syndrome, despite the absence of visible injury, suffered fatal damage similar to victims of blunt trauma. Those injuries were not present in the six SIDS victims of the study.

Malaria Vaccine Successful in Africa Test, Study Says

[London, the Associated Press
Malaria kills between one million and three million children every year.]

An experimental malaria vaccine reduced illness among African children by about a third, offering a glimmer of hope that doctors may one day conquer the global killer. Malaria, caused by a parasite transmitted to humans by mosquito bites, kills one million to three million children every year, the vast majority in Africa. The bug bursts red blood cells and hobbles the immune system, leaving many survivors, particularly those who have suffered several bouts, chronically fatigued and highly susceptible to other infections.

The London-based AP wire service continued to provide details in this article of where in Africa this study took place and under what circumstances. The specifics included:

The trial included 586 children between ages 1 and 5 in Idete village in Tanzania. Scientists gave 274 children three doses of the vaccine. The rest got placebos. After a year, investigators found that the vaccinated children were 31 percent less likely to suffer from malaria. The results are encouraging, but further work is necessary to boost the vaccine's effectiveness, wrote Dr. Nicholas J. White, a researcher at the Oxford Tropical Medicine Research Programme in Bangkok, Thailand.

The writer of AP made sure that readers got some background information about malaria research worldwide, particularly in those places where malaria is rampant. The writer adds:

For decades, scientists have tried to create an effective vaccine. The research has been fraught with dashed hopes over test-tube experiments that did not pan out in animal or human trials. The new findings suggest that one experimental vaccine, called SPf66, is just as effective in Africa, where malaria is rampant, as it has been shown to be in South America. The vaccine reduced the rate of infection by nearly 40 percent in a South American study of 1,500 volunteers. Skeptics had

thought the promising South American results, first published in
March 1993, could be replicated because malaria is much more intense
in Africa.

The reporter concludes this story by adding that the results of the African
study were published in Saturday's issue of the *Lancet*, a medical journal. There were no details given as to the exact date or place of this
publication.

DISCUSSION

How might students begin to unravel the insidious cultural pedagogy embedded in these two articles? What kinds of global values are depicted?
Do these articles present an optimistic or pessimistic view of life? The
critical issues raised in the two articles reflect the standpoint of the social
context from which they were written and equally implicate the social
contexts of class, gender, and race of the audience for whom they were
intended. Readers of the *Inquirer* and the *Center Daily Times* (both owned
by Knight-Ridder Corporation) are typically residents of metropolitan
Philadelphia and State College, respectively, mostly working-class or
middle-class to upper middle-class Americans. For my students, the debate ensuing from the articles seemed to revolve around the larger issues
of doing research on children, the sacredness of life, objectivity in reporting, and misreporting about Africa and South America. Their critique was
informed and shaped by their views and attitudes about life, especially for
little children and consent issues. In the Philadelphia story, the students
noted these important issues of contention:

- Tampering with cadavers of nineteen children for medical science
  research seemed to bother students. Images from the movie *Sexist*
  were associated with this story.
- Parents/relatives of these infants were justified to be enraged because they did not give consent to the research objectives.
- The point of view of the journalist is biased in favor of medical research and seems to indicate that there were some benefits derived
  from such research. There was knowledge gained about the nature
  of trauma sustained by the infants as a cause of death.

By comparison, the malaria story seemed to raise more questions rather
than critical comments. Lack of details in the information given by the

story may have contributed to this kind of response. However, some of the specific comments and questions emanating from the malaria story were:

- The malaria study was *pure* research. In order to accomplish such research, a researcher must establish experimental and control groups.
- What happened to those infants who got placebos? Did they die? Were they treated after they contracted malaria?
- How can an experiment having a 40 percent success rate be claimed to be successful?
- Was Dr. White the principal investigator of this malaria experiment? What's the connection between the dateline (London), the research program where Dr. White is located (Bangkok), and Idete village in Tanzania? Were there no doctors in Tanzania or South America to comment on the results? Why are African doctors silent in this article? Wouldn't these doctors be more knowledgeable granted that they work in the countries where this fatal disease is prevalent? Why is a doctor in Bangkok being sought out as a spokesperson?
- What do estimates like "kills one million to three million children every year, the vast majority in Africa" mean?
- Do comments from the journalist such as "in Africa, where malaria is rampant," and "malaria is much more intense in Africa" build on the stereotype about Africa being the so-called "Dark Continent"?

Students were challenged to examine the reporting in these two articles, including the use of language, the descriptions of emotions, the value-laden statements (like "permanently removed eyes," "young children—most of them abuse victims"), and the lack of human appeal or human interest in the use of names of continents (Africa, South America) instead of specific countries. The malaria story did not seem to bother these middle-class students of central Pennsylvania as nearly as the Philadelphia story. Their comments about the "Africa" story were limited because, as they claimed, they knew little about malaria and about Africa. They admitted, however, that whatever they knew about Africa came from the media. When pressed, they did not have an answer to explain why they did not know much about malaria when it is a deadly disease, killing more that a million children every year—more than the AIDS epidemic.

Unfortunately, the malaria story must take its place within the continuum of many other disaster stories coming out of Africa and South America—continents seen as "jungles" by many Americans—that show us the "dark other" from the standpoint of whiteness. Notice that the reader is not told who invented the vaccine (it was, in fact, a doctor from Colombia) (Hoffman, 1996). Instead, the reader is left to wonder and probably wrongly guess the inventor to be the Oxford Tropical Medicine Center in Bangkok, European, or North American labs. As noted by Ukadike (1990), much of the image Americans have about Africa has come from the movies, and for most Americans there is no motive to challenge these images.

> It is amazing how, when films with exotic images reach Western screens, their hollow contents do nothing to diminish their anthropological value or rating. Nor is the audience inclined to seek detailed and accurate information for a true anthropological rendition of the culture or an attempt to point out when authors display latent prejudice abetted by careless research, poor writing, and inadequate editing (Ukadike, 1990, p. 42).

This point of view reiterates what we have known for quite some time and what Stuart Hall (1977) confirms in his analysis about the images of athletes of color, especially blacks in films. It is therefore true that the commercial cinema system has continued to stock its productions with themes and formulas dealing with black issues and characters that are reassuring to the sensibilities and expectations of an easy white audience. These filmic images tend to "mediate the dysfunctions and delusions of a society unable to deal honestly with its inequalities and racial conflicts, a society that operates in a profound state of racial denial on a daily basis" (Guerrero, 1993, p. 198).

Other scholars agree with Guerrero. Allen (1993), for example, states:

> The print and the electronic media, and especially cinema and television, have shown African people and other people of color in comedic stances and in degrading ways. The depictions have suggested that African peoples are not interested in and do not care about serious matters, are frivolous and irresponsible, and are unable to participate in the mainstream of U.S. society. Television has been notably powerful in implying, suggesting, and maintaining this myth. (p. 156)

These accounts simply confirm what many media executives' attitudes are: Americans have never paid much attention to news from Africa.

It is also important to note how interpretations of the two articles were framed by the context of the students' assumptions, general knowledge, and widespread beliefs about scientific research and about Africa. Their discussion quickly degenerated into U.S. "values" of life, posing contradictions—from rights of the unborn child, protecting minors, abuse of children, partial fetal abortions, to the death penalty. These two examples illustrate how "values" about life is a contested issue. Furthermore, their value for the lives of children in other countries, particularly far from home, was shaped by their Eurocentric view of holding to the tenets of science as more important than life. This view clouded over the fact that the Philadelphia children were dead corpses (19 of them), while the Tanzanian children (586 of them) were alive and their lives were threatened by both a deadly disease and medical science.

CONCLUDING COMMENTS

This chapter outlined how the mass media create global values. The author suggests applying critical media literacy as a form of curriculum inquiry into global values. In this context, curriculum inquiry simply means questioning the way the mass media construct, legitimize, and maintain values and ideologies in American society. By engaging critical media literacy across the curriculum, teachers will foster a multicultural curriculum where diverse values and attitudes can be accommodated. Such an approach conforms with a process of comprehensive curricular reform that challenges and rejects racism and other forms of discrimination in schools and society and accepts and affirms pluralism (ethnic, racial, linguistic, religious, economic, handicapping, and gender) that students and their communities and teachers represent. Within the complex interactions of students, parents, teachers, and the community at large, images and representations of the diverse viewpoints and cultural values manifest a rich curriculum of democratic principles and social justice.

This chapter also illustrated how a critical media literacy education employs a critical social theory that analyzes society as "a system of domination in which institutions like the family, schooling, church, workplace, media, and the state control individuals and provide structures of domination against which individuals striving for more freedom and power must struggle" (Kellner, 1995, p. 32). According to Kellner, and I concur with him, a critical media pedagogy is one that will enable students to make sense of their culture and society. It is one that will provide tools of criticism to help individuals to avoid media manipulation and to produce their own identities and resistance, and one that will in turn inspire media activism to produce alternative forms of culture and social transformation. Kellner urges us to adopt a concept of diagnostic critique that examines the insidious cultural pedagogy of American media culture to diagnose social trends and tendencies, and to read through the texts, the fantasies, fears, hopes, and desires that these media articulate. It is such diagnostic critique, I believe, that educators must foster in our students. This means cultivating the ability to ask difficult questions and the self-confidence to reject easy answers—the two fundamental goals of a critical inquiry and what it takes to be an educated person.

REFERENCES

Allen, R. L. (1993). Conceptual models of an African-American belief system: A program of research. In G. L. Berry, & J. K. Asamen, (Eds.), *Children & television: Images in a changing social cultural world.* Newbury Park, CA.: Sage.

Arnold, J. (1993). A curriculum to empower young adolescents. *Midpoints* (Fall). Columbus, OH: National Middle School Association.

Bagdikian, B. (1992). *The media monopoly.* Boston: Beacon Press.

Colombo, G., Cullen, R., & Lisle, B. 1989. *Rereading America: Cultural contexts for critical thinking and writing.* New York: St. Martin's Press.

Dines, G., & Humez, J. M. (1995). *Gender, race and class in media.* Thousand Oaks, CA: Sage.

Fiske, J. (1996). *Media matters: Race and gender in U.S. politics.* Minneapolis, MN: University of Minnesota Press.

Guerrero, E. (1993). *Framing blackness: The African-American image in film.* Philadelphia: Temple University Press.

Hall, S. (1977). *Africa in U.S. educational materials: Thirty problems and responses.* New York: Afro-American Institute.

———. (1997). *Representation. Cultural representations and signifying practices.* London: The Open University.

Hirsch, E. D. (1987). *Cultural literacy: What every American needs to know.* Boston: Houghton Mifflin.

Hoffman, S. (1996). *Malaria vaccine development: A multi-immune response approach.* Portland, OR: Book News Inc.

Kellner, D. (1995). *Media culture.* New York: Routledge.

———. (1990). *Television and the crisis of democracy.* Boulder, CO: Westview.

———. (1982). Television myth and ritual. *Praxis, 6:* 133–155.

Kimball, R. (1991). Tenured radicals: A postscript. *The New Criterion* (January 1991): 6.

Semali, L., & Pailliotet, A. (1999). *Intermediality: The teachers handbook of critical media literacy.* Boulder, CO: Westview.

Shor, I. (1993). Education is politics: Paulo Freire's critical pedagogy. In P. McLaren, & P. Leonard (Eds.), *Paulo Freire: A Critical Encounter.* London: Routledge.

Silverblatt, A. (1995). *Media literacy: Keys to interpreting media messages.* Westport, CT: Praeger.

Swanson, G. (1991). Representation. In D. Lusted, *The media studies book.* New York: Routledge.

Ukadike, N. F. (1990). Western images of Africa: Genealogy of an ideological formulation. *Black Scholar, 21*(12): 30–48.

CHAPTER 7

Reflection on Praxis
Media Literacy in the Classroom

What have we learned so far from the chapters of the this book? Most of the discussion has focused on media, schools, technology, curriculum, integration, and critical pedagogy. I outlined examples of analytical frameworks of critical media literacy teachers can use as a method of integrating critical pedagogy in their classrooms. I discussed the challenges that are likely to face teachers in the wake of a new millennium. Throughout this book, I raised many questions: How does a teacher teach reading or the language arts, science, or social studies to today's students—students who are constantly exposed to multimedia and technological advances in a world of virtual intelligence and electronic communities? What will it take for these multimedia technologies to be integrated in the K–12 curriculum? Are teachers willing to struggle and make the necessary reforms in the curriculum they teach to put critical content in democracy? This book traverses some uncharted territory and introduces alternative and oppositional ways to produce knowledge.

As I ponder over the questions I raised in this book and the questions several teachers have asked me in the course of my teaching, I cannot help but stop to ask: Have we learned anything new in these discussions? I constantly pose this question at the end of a course I teach at the university for preservice teachers, entitled: "Media Literacy in the Classroom." I am well aware that my students already practice media literacy outside the classroom. Mind you, many of them were raised with *Sesame Street*. My concern is how I can motivate them to bring the knowledge they have about the media outside the walls of the school to bear upon what they do and learn in the classroom. How can I become an instrument and guide for them as they try to produce knowledge on their own? How can I encourage them to take a critical stance as future teachers in their own teaching practice? When I reflect on these questions, I do not claim to come up with definite answers. The struggle inside me is a pull between my beliefs as a teacher and what my students expect me to do as a professional. I am constantly challenged in knowing that I must model for these preservice teachers methods with which to produce knowledge that reflects their own beliefs about education, teaching, and learning. As I guide them through the frameworks of critical media literacy in the classroom, I realize that the critical methods I espouse must convey an understanding of the unanticipated complications of classrooms. Just knowing that the examples that I give these students may no longer be valid for them when they step into their own classrooms, such understanding forces me to avoid the temptation to use generic methods applicable to all students in all contexts. With this realization then, one wonders what methods must a teacher apply to engage students so that they are able to produce their own knowledge?

Kincheloe and Steinberg (1998) remind us that teacher knowledge is created when teachers and students confront a contradiction, when students encounter a dangerous memory, when teacher-presented information collides with student experience, or when student-presented information collides with teacher experience. They insist that "a teacher who is willing to surrender his/her position as an expert and who is willing to help students produce knowledge on their own, this teacher begins to actually listen to his/her students. He/she is open to the stories of students, analyzing how the stories inform educational and social theory and how educational and social theory inform the stories" (p. 18). The cultivation of such abilities forms the core of critical media literacy curriculum. Critical media literacy helps students to become comfortable asking questions, deploying skills in inquiries about student experience; the ways dominant interests manifest themselves in schools, society, and individual lives, and in the ways individuals resist the domination of these interests. Such inquiry-based, problem-posed subject matter makes knowledge no longer appear as if it is immutable, a secret known only by the teacher, the elite, or the privileged.

My passion for critical education, as envisaged in a critical media literacy curriculum, is grounded in the belief that the theory and practice of media literacy extend my consciousness as a social being. Individuals who gain such consciousness understand how their political opinions, religious beliefs, gender roles, racial self-concept, or educational perspectives have been influenced by the dominant culture (Kincheloe, 1993). Upon self-reflection, these individuals will embark on alternative ways of pedagogy by becoming critics of their present teaching or learning experience and taking action to resist routine or hegemonic practices.

With a teaching practice conceptualized along these lines, I realize that I can no longer define curriculum in terms of the abstract categories of various isolated disciplines (such as history, English literature, social studies, etc.), but rather would incorporate themes and issues that address the concrete conditions and problems of adult life. In this new role, I am a guide and facilitator rather than manager and dispenser of knowledge. As a method of curriculum and instruction, therefore, critical media literacy challenges teachers and students to examine all media texts as objects of study by exploring their languages, codes, and conceptual frameworks and asks what sense students in classrooms today make of visual media as an object of study. Through the questioning of media texts, students engage in a process of learning the "deeper" meaning, and thus become empowered to form identities and worldviews that are their own, resisting the media spectacles that persuade and manipulate them to accept the interests of supposedly neutral formulations of science, mindless consumerism, and politics of illusion.

When I was researching the materials for this book, I visited an eighth grade class in our school district. The teacher, a former student of mine, asked me to talk to her class about gender roles and how the media shape our thinking about who we are as male or female (genderized) individuals. With my talk I presented Jean Kilbourne's videotape: "Killing Us Softly." At the end of my talk, two female eighth graders came up to me. They had a question for me. They asked: Where do gender roles come from? For how long must we endure such stereotyping of women? How can this be allowed in a democracy? Can we change this? At first, I did not know what to make of these questions. Briefly, I felt good about their understanding of the issues I raised. I was pleased that they came up with their own questions. But then, they did not stop with the questions. They presented me with an article they had clipped from *USA Today* (December 1997) on how media messages reinforce sexual stereotypes. The article listed the following findings:

- In TV programs, male characters were more likely (41%) to be shown working than female ones (28%). In the movies, men were almost twice as likely to be shown on the job as women (35%).

- Men in television programs also were more likely to talk about work than women (52%–40%). In the movies, women and men were about equally likely to talk about work (60%–58%).
- Women, on the other hand, were more likely than men in both TV shows and movies to be shown talking about romantic relationships: 63% of female characters compared to 49% of males on TV, and 38% of males in the movies.
- In teen magazines, 35% of articles focused on dating, while 12% discussed either school or careers.
- Women and girls in TV shows (34%) and especially in movies (69%) are shown actively using their intelligence and acting independently.
- TV programs (35%), movies (35%), and teen magazines (28%) also stress women's and girls' self-reliance to solve problems.
- Teen magazine articles include a focus on friendship (28%) as well as other important issues facing young people today, though with less overall frequency, such as self-confidence (19%); sexual issues (9%), including sexually transmitted diseases, contraception, and unintended pregnancy; and drugs and smoking (3% each).
- In movies, particularly, but also in TV shows and the accompanying commercials, women's and girls' appearance frequently is commented on: 58% of female characters in movies had comments made about their looks, as did 28% in TV shows and 26% of the female models in the accompanying commercials. Men's and boys' appearance is talked about significantly less often: 24% in movies, 10% in TV shows, and 7% in commercials.
- Of the articles in leading teen girls' magazines, 37% included a focus on appearance, and 50% of the advertisements used an appeal to beauty to sell their products.
- The commercials aimed at female viewers that ran during the TV shows most often watched by teen girls used beauty as a product appeal 56% of the time. By comparison, this is true of 3% of TV commercials aimed at men.

I could tell that these students were frustrated by the results of this study by Nancy Signorielli, a professor of communication at the University of Delaware, Newark. These students had discovered that the six types of media primarily used by teenage girls—television, commercials, films, music videos, magazines, and advertisements—present similar and consistent messages concerning gender roles. Why is this so? they wondered. Why does such portrayal of women persist in a democracy such as the United States? Perhaps, the reason why these sexual stereotypes continue to be so persistent is because of the demarcation (imaginary or real) and cultural assumptions Americans have between work and home. Even though this is changing as more people find it more efficient to work from home (immensely facilitated by computers, fax machines, e-mail, etc.), the cultural assumptions attributed to "work" are very "male" oriented—achievement, aggressiveness, single-mindedness, manipulation, intellect, competitiveness, strength, and autonomy. Home characteristics are considered very "female," perhaps focusing more on cooperation, patience, perseverance, multitalent, flexibility, and dependency.

Unfortunately, in the minds of many people these opposites are not equivalent in valuation in our society. Such demarcation forms cultural norms in our society. Following a work ethic, many people believe that anyone who is smart and ambitious will be out working in the world. Work is where you get ahead. Conversely, "home" does not allow you to get ahead. Thus, when we examine our cultural values about work, one explanation might look at how our society deliberately objects to women becoming more like men. This is a deep-seated fear in our society. And, as a result, some educators believe that these sexual stereotypes will be with us for a long time. How can this change? What can teachers do about it? In this chapter, I invite the reader—teachers and students—to reflect on these media messages and connect them with the discussions from previous chapters.

TOWARD AUTHENTIC QUESTIONING
IN CRITICAL MEDIA LITERACY

In my own teaching, I encourage students to examine more thoroughly the role that beliefs and values play in our "knowing" and "doing" as teachers, particularly those beliefs, actions, and values shaped by our media culture (biased or not). Specifically, in my course "Media Literacy in the Classroom," students examine how economic resources, advantages, and privileges are distributed inequitably in part because of power dynamics involving beliefs in racial, gender, and class divisions. Such analysis is not limited to TV and films only but is extended to other multimedia forms of representation including textbooks and other school-related materials. In this course, we seek to address issues such as the

destructive effects of hegemonic language forms borrowed and legitimated by the mass media, particularly when they become the sole lingua
franca of the classroom; the canonical provision of notions of knowledge,
truth, and beauty without regard to the grounds of their construction; the
violence perpetrated by an educational practice that inadequately addresses the reproduction of sexism and racism; the scientism of science
that constructs a powerful and excluding ideology regarding what it
means to do science; or the forms of work education that reduce valued
labor to that which fits existing economic arrangements (Kincheloe &
Steinberg, 1998).

This expanded approach to literacy with which I engage my students
to examine their own beliefs and their social practices has been referred
to by others as "genuine literacy" (Walmsley & Walp, 1990). Being gen-
uinely literate entails more than simply scoring well on a standardized
test, or learning a narrow range of reading and editing skills. Instead, it
entails actively engaging in literate behavior (Walmsley & Walp, 1990).
Rather than merely preparing students for eventual literate behavior,
teachers engage them in genuine acts of literacy right from the beginning
and throughout the school career. It also implies that the language arts
curriculum will not be fragmented into separate components for reading,
composing, and editing, but will integrate these in meaningful ways.
Further, it implies that skills will be taught within the context of genuine
reading, writing, speaking, and listening, rather than as separate or prerequisite components of the program.

Advocates of genuine literacy would have us pay attention to how
our society is marked by a multiplicity of cultures, meanings, and values.
By guiding students' attention to how powerful groups define their own
particular meanings, values, experiences, and forms of writing and reading as the *valued* ones in society, students will better understand the inequalities and violations of social justice the mass media continue to
peddle through its production of culture products. To guide such inquiry
and what to look for in the search of deeper meaning, social theorists
have developed key concepts of a critical media that move beyond "critical awareness" and understanding to "critical autonomy."

Critical autonomy implies a level of maturity of analysis of media
texts in which young adolescents can make meaning independently. According to Masterman (1985), such autonomy (1) does not degenerate
into stultifying and laborious accumulation of facts, ideas, and information about the media; (2) should not consist of dehumanizing exercises or
"busy work" on the media, designed primarily to keep students occu-

pied; nor (3) should it involve the dutiful reproduction by students of the teacher's ideas. I believe that to implement this vision of critical auton- omy in media literacy, students will be able to (1) analyze the hierarchi- cal positioning of individuals within the social order on the basis of race, class, gender, and sexuality, and (2) acknowledge the multiple and insid- ious ways in which power operates in the larger society "to reproduce the interests of the dominant culture" (Hammer, 1995, p. 79).

As future English instructors, preservice teachers grapple with the idea that English in all its forms and uses can never be a matter of neutral communication of factual information or fictional truths. The English textbook contains neither factual nor objective maxims valid for all times to be learned. In fact, many meanings evolve as readers/viewers interact with texts and construct meaning from them (Barthes, 1974; Derrida, 1990). Constructing textual understanding, therefore, is a recursive and ongoing process, not a linear or static one (Barthes, 1974). Through a cultural critique as represented in the multiple genres of the mass media, our students learn how forms of knowledge and the power they bring to the classroom are created in language and taken up by those who use such texts.

We broadly define "text" as beyond references to a verbal/written ar- tifact such as a story, play, or song lyrics. As used by cultural critics, a text can refer to any communicative or expressive artifact produced by media industries. Textual analysis, therefore, is a close examination of how particular media texts generate meaning. However, Kellner (1995) warns that audience reception and political economy approaches are also needed to locate texts in their social and political contexts. Through media literacy, therefore, students continually question how language might be put to different, more equitable uses, and how texts might be re- created in a way that would tell a different *unbiased* story.

The selected readings of the media literacy course I teach introduce the participants to curriculum inquiry methods and theories, critical media pedagogy, and analytical schemes and techniques of building bridges between school and society and between students and teachers. These bridges are key components of the holistic teaching and learning implicit in an integrated approach to education. The overall intent of the course is to seek ways to integrate the world of the classroom with the world of the student and society as a whole. Participants begin their in- quiry by exploring general questions: What is the role of critical teaching in a world in which culture can no longer be understood as providing the normative integration and common values that cement together democratic social life? Are there common or shared language, knowledge, history, and stories that identify us as "American"?

As contended by many critical theorists, there is no single, comprehensive monoculture in which all or even most of the citizens of this nation actually participate. Because the notion of national culture or what E.D. Hirsch (1987) calls "cultural literacy" cannot be applied to all Americans, students, particularly future teachers, must constantly question representational attempts to establish such monocultural visions of America. Are the visions of America represented in history books, in secondary English textbooks, in documentary films, in newspaper articles, in television genres, and so on, a fair, accurate representation of all Americans?

It is my desire that teachers use critical media literacy to interrogate the visions of America found in these texts and as a method of inquiry to initiate a process for their own learning and professional growth. I also hope teachers will commit to a critical pedagogy that promotes social critique, re-imagining the common good in a diverse culture, and creates classroom learning environments that support students in their inquiries. In this context, therefore, as I explained previously, inquiry involves immersing oneself in a media text or topic and taking time to explore the text in order to find questions that are significant to the learner and then systematically investigating those questions.

CONSTRUCTIVIST PERSPECTIVES OF CRITICAL INQUIRY AND OF QUESTIONING TEXTS

I have argued in previous chapters that critical media literacy would not only reestablish the adolescent as a learner but, more importantly, as a creator of knowledge. A key concept of critical media literacy encourages students to challenge or create oppositional meaning to mainstream or dominant knowledge (Berry, 1998). In her essay entitled "Nurturing the Imagination of Resistance: Young Adults as Creators of Knowledge," Kathleen Berry explains that such dominance is manifested extensively in textbooks, particularly those texts that privilege European white male history and ignore the accomplishments of women, African heritage, and the physically different.

According to Berry, the creation of knowledge through the *question* is an intrinsic part of being a learner. Because students are inserted into a world of knowledge and representations through predetermined curriculum content and structure, there is no opportunity for them to create knowledge since it is determined beforehand what knowledge is to be acquired and the order in which it is to be learned. Such an approach denies students the priority to ask questions. "Children at a very early age begin asking questions about their world—authentic questions in that there is not predetermined knowledge or answer to their questions" (Berry, 1998, p. 45). The media literacy movement has ignored this important aspect of critical inquiry. The nurturing in students to ask authentic questions has not been encouraged enough. Unfortunately, in a traditional school setting, students' questions are deemed inauthentic and merely asked as procedural, conformist, or intellectual capital. Berry (1998) explains that this attitude prevails because routine is more important to the schooling process, and it is conformist in that the teacher already knows the answer and the student is expected to guess what the correct answer is. Critical media literacy moves questions beyond the routine of testing, controlling, and determining students' acquisition of predetermined, preconstructed knowledge.

In this book I have emphasized that to teach students the intellectual habits of imagining new possibilities and valuing points of view different from their own, students must ask questions that raise further questions. Through such iterative questioning, students create their own knowledge from preexisting knowledge. They learn to challenge and oppose the status quo or mainstream thinking of the authoritative texts before them— all texts, whether visual, computer, media, printed, or otherwise. In this way students claim the knowledge as their own simply because they have produced the questions.

Berry (1998) warns that in a reductionist notion of questioning, knowledge is something to be acquired, developed, and tested instead of questions that permit students to create their own knowledge. In the traditional questioning format of schooling, students answer questions that require correct answers to preferred or mainstream knowledge. The nature of such questions is to circulate and maintain the status quo. Because of the important nature of questions, it is crucial for students, therefore, to receive and to learn a repertoire that creates and shapes knowledge instead of a technique that simply conforms to, develops, and furthers dominant and authorial knowledge.

In Chapter 4, I explained how traditional questioning of texts, for example, range from factual to analytical questions, from synthesis to evaluation, and at all times questions are to be answered in order to maintain the authority of the text and the concurrent subjection of the student. The knowledge contained within texts in traditional classrooms is not to be challenged or to be seen as inconsistent or contradictory to the knowledge or questions of the students. Some of the questioning methods found in reader-response techniques used by teachers in traditional class-rooms assume that the text is the authority and is legitimized through the educational system by people and policies. In other words, the text contains the universal, absolute, fixed knowledge, truths, values, and so forth. "Traditional questions find answers within the text, accept its knowledge and authority" (Berry, 1998, p. 47).

Berry outlines clearly what this confusion is all about. She believes that questions, even of the reader/personal response, embrace a mode of questioning that inhibits the creation of student knowledge. In this format, negotiated responses to the knowledge in the text are asked instead of authentic student questions. "The format tends to take the shape of 'What do you think?' 'How do you feel?' 'What is your opinion?'" In these examples, such questions only negotiate the representations of the text with those of the reader.

However, the kinds of questions a critical media literacy curriculum calls for aim to drive students to confront their own belief system and experiences. To truly return to the creation of knowledge, young adult students must seek out contradictions within the text relative to the social experiences. They must seek to oppose or resist the knowledge contained in whatever symbolic texts they are exploring. Authentic questioning means that the prepackaged knowledge that is in a text needs to be actively deconstructed before students can claim to re-create and reconstruct knowledge which is consistent with their questions. To illustrate the distinction between traditional types of questions and the authentic questions that might lead students to genuine literate knowledge and behaviors, Berry (1998) reminds us to look at the type of questions that were asked in traditional basal reading programs designed by publishing companies in a format that was fairly well teacher-proof and controlling of student knowledge. Some of these questions were:

- "Who is the main character?"
- "Where does the story take place?"
- "What happened when Fred's father left home?"
- "What is the main problem in the story?"
- "How was it solved?"
- "How is the setting related to the mood of the story?"
- "What is the atmosphere of the story?"
- "What happened to the main characters?"
- "What kind of animal is Oliver?"
- "Why did the pirate kidnap Grandma?"

As expected, in almost every case, these types of questions required a preferred reading of the text, and students were required to regurgitate the knowledge of the text. As will be recalled from previous chapters, the analytical frameworks I propose in a critical media literacy curriculum stand in contrast from a whole language or negotiated reading of text which requires that the students answer questions but not confront their beliefs and contradictions. According to Berry, questions in this category were framed as follows:

- "What do you think the story is about?"
- "Have you ever felt like Leora?"
- "What kind of person do you think the archduke is?
- "When you were reading the story, what events are similar to those that have happened to you?"
- "What do you think Princess Leora's father was thinking when he had to leave his daughter with the archduke?"

Berry believes that in each example, these types of questions ask for a negotiated reading of the text. In other words, the text has particular representations and meanings and the reader has a particular response to the text. The questions generate a negotiation between those of the text and those of the reader. Berry argues that framing the question with what "YOU" think/feel/know "is still a control of student knowledge in which the text holds a larger part of the authority/authorship of the knowledge."

In a critical media literacy approach, what changes when the students resist, oppose, or challenge the authority/knowledge of a text? How are the questions framed or produced that move the student into a position of power? Developing analytical habits in curriculum inquiry involves active, varied transactions of meaning-making, not as busy work, but as transactions that lead into action aimed at reshaping students' worldview relative to their own social context. For example, with critical media literacy, students learn to become critical consumers who are aware of visual manipulation and stereotyping as an important project toward being literate. This approach to curriculum inquiry aims to help demystify the nature of media culture by examining its construction, production, and the meaning-making processes by which media imagery and popular representations of people help shape students' personal, social, and political worlds. The analytical frameworks for examining media texts outlined in this book aim at the constitutive elements of power, knowledge, and representations of people, events, and desires.

Let us now compare the nature of the following questions to those asked previously in the traditional, basal, or whole language approach to literacy. In what ways are the characters in the story in a power position or oppressed by a dominant gender, race, class, age, and so forth? According to Berry, examples of a repertoire of questions that might complement what a critical media literacy analytical framework might do include questions like the following:

- What racial knowledge is present in this text?
- In what ways is race implied in the text?
- How has the author constructed men/women in this text that is consistent with or contradictory to mainstream knowledge of men and women?
- In what ways has the author constructed power/knowledge/relationships, representations/values, based on gender, race, class, and so forth?
- In what ways would you challenge the exclusions of certain cultures (race, sexuality, etc.) in this text?
- Who do you think created the representations and knowledge in this text?
- What do you oppose or resist about the representations/relationships based on age, class, history, dominance, privilege, marginalization, and so forth, in this text?
- In what ways has the author used mainstream knowledge to create a state of consent in the reader?

The discussions that might follow from this type of questioning nurture a critical inquiry/critical imagination. They are not oriented at answers or personal/reader responses to the text that extract preferred or negotiated readings. Instead, each of the questions require students to reformulate the knowledge and, in turn, return the responsibility to the students for creating the knowledge, not as mere restructuring, but as knowledge that is inclusive of new truths, values, relationships, and representations. Students create, produce, and shape knowledge and regain control of their initial entrance into the world of learning mainly through questions that challenge, resist, or oppose the dominant, exclusive, privileged, and legitimized status of established knowledge. When students consent to established knowledge (truths, relationships, and histories about gender, race, class, and so forth), they are gradually pressed into hegemonic practices. Critical media literacy demands counter-hegemonic questioning and a differently nurtured imagination.

EXAMPLES OF INTEGRATION

In the next section, I present two examples of unit plans that attempt to integrate critical media literacy across the curriculum. These unit plans are not finished products by any means. They are not meant to present "simplistic" notions of the correct way to teach. They are, however, an outline teachers developed as a guide of what might transpire in their classrooms. A continuous revision and adapting is still possible relative to the changing situations of the classrooms they were intended for. I invite readers to change these ideas, take from them, and add to them. They are not recipes. A daily reflection of what's going on in the lesson and overall unit is foreseen to be a daily practice of the classroom teacher.

English teachers Lisa and Jesse developed the first example of a two-week unit. The second example was developed by Alison, Leah, and Kathy. These teachers take up the notions of "utopia" (or mythical stories, dreams, etc.,) found in several novels read by high school students. Using the frameworks of critical media literacy, they designed their ten lessons to explore the visions of utopia as a critical exploration of a "perfect" society. The following shows how they described their goals:

EXAMPLE 1

Visions of Utopia: A Critical Exploration of a "Perfect"Society

Context:

"Visions of Utopia: A Critical Exploration of a 'Perfect' Society" will be taught to a predominantly white, twelfth-grade advanced English class comprised of twenty-five students: fourteen females and eleven males. Three students are African American (2 males, 1 female) and two are Asian American (both females). Our high school is set in a middle- to upper middle-class suburban Pennsylvania neighborhood flanked by six acres of mature forest. This unit takes place in the late spring.

Rationale:
Introduction

"Visions of Utopia: A Critical Exploration of a 'Perfect' Society" is an exploration through literature, of what so many have sought for so long, whether through religion, science, philosophy, politics, or daydreams: a more perfect society. Throughout the three-week unit (of which the latter two weeks are explicitly planned in these pages), students will continue to develop their ability to critically analyze texts ranging from novels to film and from essays to MTV, communicate their thoughts through verbal and written forms in an articulate, well-considered manner, and expand their understanding of a multitude of perspectives. By taking part in an array of class experiences, including a debate, Utopian Mural, group presentation, and solo reflection, students will explore the way in which difficult issues of race, class, and gender affect preconstructed utopian societies, student-constructed utopian societies, as well as our presently existing society.

Prior to Lessons Articulated in These Pages
Earlier in the fall, students read an excerpt from Henry David Thoreau's *Walden*. In the first week of the "Visions of Utopia" unit, the theme will be introduced through a brief overview of several examples of utopian (or potentially utopian) visions throughout history. Students will read and discuss Lois Lowry's *The Giver*. At the end of the week, the teacher will introduce James Redfield's *The Celestine Prophecy*, which students will begin to read over the weekend. By "Day 1," students will have reflected in their Insight Journals on the first four Insights—dealing with coincidences and energy—allowing us to begin on Monday with the outdoor Solo Experience.

The Importance of Relevance
Because we believe in a relatively student-centered approach to education, we have incorporated several methods to encourage students to bring their individual contexts into the classroom. Beginning with *The Celestine Prophecy*, students will keep Insight Journals that will allow them to reflect on issues raised in the texts as they relate both to utopia and to their own experiences. The Insight Journal provides the students with a more personal medium of forging connections among texts and between texts and their lives, as well as a sense of continuity throughout the unit by providing them with a comfortable place to document their evolving thoughts on utopia. The teacher will evaluate the journal to track individual students' progress.

Students will also frequently analyze and discuss texts in small groups: a forum conducive to sharing and considering personal contexts as they relate to the larger issues at hand. Importantly, through activities such as "A Mission to Save Our Civilization," which requires the selection of eight people from a list of thirty-one candidates, students will be challenged to question and critique their (cultural) assumptions and stereotypes.

In addition, because we feel that the classroom's layout has a significant impact on the way students participate and interact (and therefore, on the way students' contexts are either embraced or de-emphasized), the desks, including the teacher's, are always arranged in a circle to promote equality and to emphasize the importance of community. The exception to this format occurs during group work, when the students simply break the large circle into the appropriate number of smaller circles.

The Importance of Synthesis and Application
Because we feel that a critical aspect of learning is in the application of knowledge, we have designed a two-part culmination to the unit to encourage students to synthesize their experiences of the past weeks. On Day 9, the students will engage in a debate, entitled "Utopian Society vs. Presently Existing Society: Weighing the Arguments," which will require them to use textual evidence to support well-reasoned discussion not only about the utopias we have examined, but also about our own imperfect society. Students will focus on identifying and proposing solutions to the challenges posed by issues of race, class, and gender. On Day 10, students will theorize about ways in which elements described in Summerhill, an experimental school in England, could be integrated into the American educational system and, more specifically, into our own classroom. Finally, they will be working to construct a Utopian Mural that by incorporating concepts from the unit's texts, as well as from students' personal ideas, depicts our class community's vision of utopia.

DAILY LESSON PLANS (SELECTED LESSONS)

Day 1

Title: Energy Matters: A Connection to the Environment

Subject: Utopia and *The Celestine Prophecy*

Length: 50 minutes

Group Size: 25 students

Goals: To raise students' awareness of the energy flow between nature and humans, reflect on how this might parallel the flow between humans, and understand the value in solitude and reflection.

Materials Needed:

- Insight Journals
- Writing implement
- Something hard to write on
- Clear head
- Good weather (If inclement weather, Day 3 will be substituted for Day 1.)

Objectives:

Students will:

- Attempt to observe energy in nature and its effect on the student's well-being.
- Reflect in writing (poetry, essay, short story, or journal) on Solo Experience.
- Share thoughts with group on the effectiveness of the Solo Experience.

Procedure:

- In classroom, teacher will ask students if they would like to go into the woods to see if they can observe the energy fields they read about in the first four chapters of *The Celestine Prophecy*.
- If majority of students agree*, teacher will explain the need for this to be a Solo Experience (i.e., students will be "alone" for class period [no verbal contact with other students/teacher]).
- Teacher will ask each student to bring writing utensil, paper, and something hard to write on.
- Teacher will explain objectives: see above. Students should use their judgment, spending some time simply reflecting and some time writing, in their Insight Journals, the beginnings of a poem, essay, short story, or journal entry.
- Teacher will explain that, once in the woods, students will form a circle and then step outward (enlarging the circle) no more than 50 paces.
- Teachers will also inform the students that after 25 minutes, teacher will yodel (yodel-leh-hee-ho), signaling for students to return to original circle.
- Teacher will explain that, in time remaining, students will return to classroom to discuss their experiences.
- Teacher and students will go outside to the wooded area, form a circle, and proceed with Solo Experience.

- During time outside, teacher (remaining in the center of the circle) will be aware of location and activity of students and will also participate in the reflecting and writing process.
- After 25 minutes, teacher will yodel and class will return to circle and head back to the classroom.
- In classroom, with remaining time, teacher will ask students about their experiences in the woods: Was it enjoyable? Would they do it again? What is faith?
- Preview: Teacher will suggest that, when reading the next section of *The Celestine Prophecy*, students pay particular attention to the part of the text dealing with control dramas.

* If students wish to stay inside, teacher will facilitate open discussion on first four chapters of *The Celestine Prophecy*.

Homework/Evaluation:
- Read: *The Celestine Prophecy*, pp. 91–150, Insights 5 & 6.
- Insight Journal: Identify a published interpersonal interaction (in any medium: film, TV, plays, short stories, etc.) that demonstrates one or more of the control dramas; briefly summarize interaction and discuss how it portrays the control dramas.

Quote of the Day:
"The difference between loneliness and solitude is your perception of who you are alone with and who makes the choice."

—Anonymous

Day 3

Title: Government Influence: A Connection to Music

Subject: Utopia and *The Celestine Prophecy*

Length: 50 minutes

Group Size: 25 students

Goals: To expand students' understanding of government and corporate influence on media and to have them relate musical texts to written texts.

Materials Needed:
- Stereo
- John Lennon's "Imagine"
- "Imagine" poster
- The *Celestine Prophesy*

Objectives:

Students will:
- Brainstorm and compare notes on government control.
- Share ideas with class.
- Strategize ways to trace corporate influence on a given product/text.
- Begin to make connections between music and written texts.

Procedure:
- Teacher will have students pick groups (5 groups of 5 students) out of a hat.
- Teacher will direct groups to share their notes from the previous night on government control/censorship issue re the Peruvian government in *The Celestine Prophecy* and how the U.S. government controls or censors its citizens; teacher gives example of music labeling and censorship as a possible topic.
- Groups will choose one aspect of U.S. government control/censorship that they will brainstorm and then share with the class (25 minutes).
- Groups will take turns leading discussion on issue that was of particular interest to them (25 minutes).
- Teacher will introduce next project by discussing relationship between John Lennon's "Imagine" and *The Celestine Prophecy*, asking students to pay careful attention to the lyrics; teacher will also relate artifact ("Imagine" poster) to song and text as a visual connection.
- Teacher will play "Imagine" and point out any key points that were previously discussed (5 minutes).
- In their groups, students will brainstorm any songs they feel directly relate to any of the issues from *The Celestine Prophecy* that have been covered thus far.
- Students will choose one song per group they feel well represents one of the aspects/insights in the book (e.g., energy between people and people or people and nature, coincidences, control dramas, parental influence, government censorship, etc.) (5 minutes).
- Students will choose one group member to be responsible for bringing in their selection for tomorrow's class.

- Students will choose a second group member to type and hand in a copy of their selection's lyrics.
- Preview: Teacher will tell students that tomorrow they will be sharing their pieces as a group and discussing the connection they found between the piece and the text. Students may bring in any artifacts they feel would help to clarify the connection between the song and the text. In addition, teacher will remind students that tomorrow will be the final discussion on *The Celestine Prophecy*. Students should, therefore, brainstorm any final questions/comments they have regarding the text.

Homework/Evaluation:
- Read: The Celestine Prophecy, pp. 180–246, Insight 9.
- Insight Journal: Reflect on the ideal of a culture in flux. Toward what end might we be headed: Brainstorm any additional questions/comments you had about the text.
- One member of each group: Bring song (CD, tape, record, or computer Zip drive) that your group decided upon.
- All members of each group: Bring in visual artifacts to help make connections.

Quote of the Day:
"What good fortune for those in power that people do nothing."

—Adolf Hitler

Day 5

Title: Constructing Reality: A Connection to MTV

Subject: Utopia and Media Literacy

Length: 50 minutes

Group Size: 25 students

Goals: To continue to create critical media literacy by bringing analytical viewing frameworks into the classroom and, thereby, to encourage students to be skeptical about what they see, read, and hear.

Materials Needed:
- TV/VCR
- Tape of selected MTV music videos

Objectives:

Students will:

- Begin to question the construction of the media as it is presented to them, asking pertinent questions about race, class, and gender stereotypes.
- Develop a method to critically view media representations.
- Deep view selected MTV music videos.

Procedure:

- Teacher will introduce lesson by showing an MTV music video.
- Students will begin to deconstruct the video by discussing stereotypes (race, class, or gender) that they noticed.
- Teacher will show the same video again; students will identify messages they may have missed on the first run.
- Keeping the questions they just asked in mind, students (in groups of 5) will brainstorm a method for critically viewing media; teacher will facilitate/make suggestions based on the following method:
  1. The text and its context
     —who is the video's audience? (age? race? gender? class?)
     —what time was the video aired?
     —how was the video constructed? (what techniques were used?)
     —on the literal level, what do you see/hear, what happens?
  2. Drawing conclusions
     —based on your observations at the literal level, what were the stereotypes, biases, gender roles, distortions, etc., that were portrayed?
- Having established a rough draft of their methods, students will: "deep view" two additional music videos, looking for hidden media messages.
- Discuss all of the hidden messages: What does this imply about our consumer society? To whom are the messages directed? To whom do they appeal? How might these images be considered to be visions of utopia? Utopia for whom? Who is being silenced?
- Preview: On Monday, we'll have a read aloud and we'll continue our discussion of utopian societies.

Homework/Evaluation:

- Utopia/*Celestine* paper: Continue work—finish for Monday.

Quote of the Day:

"All the radios agree with all the TVs, and the magazines agree with all the radios."

—Ani Difranco

Day 9

Title: Bringing It All Together: Making Connections among Multiple Visions

Subject: Debating utopia

Length: 50 minutes

Group Size: 25 students

Goals: To have students reflect on all texts used throughout the unit to analyze the merits of a utopian society versus our society as it presently exists.

Materials Needed:
- *The Giver*
- *The Celestine Prophecy*
- *Summerhill*
- "The Diaries of Adam and Eve," "I Have a Dream," or "The Dream"
- Insight Journals
- Class notes regarding music, MTV, *Gattaca, Hamlet*

Objectives:
Students will:
- Participate on a randomly selected side of a debate.
- Identify strengths of their side of the discussion, as well as potential weaknesses, by predicting opponent's strengths.
- Articulate and defend their side of the debate by using evidence from any of the multiple texts studied during the unit.

Procedure:
- Teacher divides class into two sections for debate by splitting the circle in half; assigns sides: one to defend utopian society, one to defend presently existing society.
- Teacher gives guidelines for debate:
  1. Each side will have 10 minutes to prepare their opening statement and to otherwise identify their strengths, weaknesses, and arguments.
  2. Each side chooses one person to deliver 2-minute introductory argument (coin will be flipped to decide who goes first); same individual will also give closing remarks.
  3. Each side will take turns making a point to defend their side of the argument or to question the opposing side; teacher will act as

facilitator/mediator for the debate, maintaining a respectful atmosphere and keeping time (points must be 45 seconds or less).

4. Every point must be supported by one of the texts used in the unit (students are encouraged to use specific passages from the texts).

5. Each person must participate once before another can repeat participation on either side of the debate.

- Teacher has sides discuss their arguments (10 minutes).
- Teacher flips coin to determine which side will begin; debate begins.
- After 25 minutes, teacher asks each side for closing remarks (to total 5 minutes).
- Preview: Tomorrow, we'll be discussing selected texts from *Summerhill*, which describes a radically different approach to education (distribute copies): Through the creation of a Utopian Mural, we'll be considering ways in which we might incorporate some of Summerhill's philosophies and ideas into our own classroom.

Homework/Evaluation:

- Read: selection from *Summerhill*
- Insight Journal: What did you like about Summerhill's philosophy? What did you see as potential problems: How were issues of race, class, and gender discussed? Is this a utopian form of education? Would you attend? What ideas/philosophies can we incorporate into our own classroom?
- Bring in 2 to 3 two-dimensional utopian-related artifacts (photographs, magazine clippings, words, etc.) to be used for final project: The Utopia Mural.
- Bring completed Insight Journal to class to hand in.

Quote of the Day:
"Too often we enjoy the comfort of opinion without the discomfort of thought."

—John F. Kennedy

EXAMPLE TWO

Visions of the Future: Quantum and Speculative Literature (Two-week Unit Plan)

Background

Audience:

This unit is to be taught to a twelfth-grade English class comprised of twenty-six students who are of multiple cultures, races, genders, and social classes. There are ten girls and sixteen boys. There are six African Americans, three Hispanics, three Asian Americans, and fourteen white Americans. The class ranges in socioeconomic status from poverty level to upper class.

Rationale:

As the millennium approaches, our society is awash with visions of the future. Some are hopeful, full of ground-breaking technology and medical advances that improve the quality of life for everyone. Other visions are less hopeful. They predict environmental disaster, race or religious warfare, technological breakdown, demagoguery, and destruction. These representations of the future are everywhere in popular culture, in movies, books, magazines, and advertisements. Historians believe, as we do, that a majority of our future visions are marked by ambiguous emotions about the future, if not downright fear. Young people absorb these predictions and visions, yet are rarely asked what they think about the world they will inherit or the world their children and grandchildren will inhabit. Young people are often not encouraged to dream of the future beyond their immediate hopes for college or jobs, and rarely feel as though their actions have the power to change anything, much less shape their future.

Our unit is designed to introduce fiction, nonfiction, and media that present visions of the future through human history. Visionary literature and nonfiction pieces are not new concepts. From biblical times, to old-world France, to the 1960s and into the new millennium, people have tried to shape the future with their predictions, their dreams, and their visions. Every one of those visions was rooted in and shaped by the cultural and historical assumptions of its time period. What humans believed about the future in the 1500s is obviously a product of the cultural assumptions and values of the 1500s. In each case, this unit will ask: Who predicted the future? What issues did they address? How is their vision a product of the times in which it was created? How might it have challenged the times?

We believe important pieces of speculative literature and visionary nonfiction have provided, and continue to provide, challenges to the conditions of their present day. They point out problems and dare us to avoid them by changing our actions. In this complex information age, we believe education must empower students to think as problem solvers. They must be taught to recognize, analyze, reflect, and take action on issues that challenge our society's future. In this unit, students will look at past and present visions of the future within a framework that critically analyzes race, class, gender, and cultural context. This unit will help students critically analyze past and future visions in order to formulate their own visions of the future. We will emphasize that the visions of the future in this unit are a challenge to act in the present.

Through detailed analysis of Octavia Butler's *The Parable of the Sower,* students will grapple with a dark vision of their future. The students' final project will consist of the creation and presentation of their own alternative visions of the future, along with concrete actions that could make their vision a reality. Thus, through examination of both fiction and nonfiction writing, this unit will encourage students to discover their own ability to make positive life changing decisions that can shape the future.

DAILY LESSON PLANS (SELECTED LESSONS)

Day 1

Title: Quantum Leap

Subject: Introduction

Length: 50 minutes

Group Size: 26 students

Goal: Introduce the concepts of future visions and quantum leaps, while exciting our students about the upcoming unit.

Materials Needed:
(1) Video clip of television show *Quantum Leap*. (2) Materials needed for introduction activity. These materials include instructions for the

activity and character backgrounds written on note cards to pass out to the students.

Objectives: Students will understand the concepts of quantum leaps and future visions, the expectations for the upcoming unit, and will be able to relate quantum leaps to their own life experiences.

Lesson Steps:

1. The teacher will ask the students for a definition of a quantum leap. If unanswered, teacher will ask for a volunteer to look up the term *quantum* in the dictionary.
2. Class will discuss the term *quantum leap.*
3. Teacher will show clips from the television show *Quantum Leap.*
4. Teacher explains that the class will now participate in an imaginary quantum leap into the future.
5. Activity.
6. Teacher will explain how the quantum leap and future visions that they just experienced relate to their own cultural and historical contexts.
7. Teacher will help students to recognize that the choices that they make now shape their futures.
8. The teacher will explain that the class will be taking several quantum leap journeys throughout the upcoming unit. Within each leap and text, historical and cultural contexts will be analyzed, along with the concepts of race, class, and gender.
9. The teacher will explain the final project for the unit and hand out the project packet.
10. The teacher will go over the rubric and project ideas sheet and answer any questions the students may have.
11. The teacher will explain homework assignment.
12. Teacher will provide personal examples of a potential quantum leap essay topic.
13. Teacher will play CD that will hint toward the quantum leap that will be taken in tomorrow's lesson.

Final Project:

Students will create a representation of their own quantum leap into their future, incorporating issues of race, class, and gender within their own historical and cultural contexts. This representation can take the form of any media representation. Examples: essays, video, artwork, computer-generated images, or music representations. Students must be able to explain how their project generates meaning and their reasons for choosing their selected medium.

Homework:
Students will write a two- to three-page essay about a quantum leap that they will take back to an event in their past. The essay must include a description of the event, the reason behind choosing that particular event, and how their lives would be different had the chosen outcome occurred.

Leap Hint:
You are a young man named Daniel being held captive in a foreign land. You feel little hope in ever seeing your homeland again. Although you are a prisoner, you have earned the respect of the ruler of the nation you are being held captive in and you have been able to live comfortably. You have even been given an education and hold a position of respect. As much as you are thankful for being treated well, your greatest longing is to be able to return to your homeland. Where are you and what is the date?

Day 3

Title: Astrology and Horoscopes

Subject: The writings of Nostradamus and how horoscopes predict the future.

Group Size: 26 students

Goal: Students should see a connection between the ancient visions of the future and their own lives through the horoscopes. Visions were a part of sixteenth-century France just as they are a part of our world today, but the contents of the predictions of each time period were based within their historical and cultural contexts.

Materials Needed:
1. Seven copies of the local paper.
2. An old local paper situated around a significant event in the teachers' life.
3. A handout with some of Nostradamus's predictions.
4. French music CD.

Objective: Students will evaluate the horoscopes and predictions (using the framework) and analyze the validity of the claims in order to draw conclusions about the relevance of such claims in their own lives.

Lesson Steps:
1. Teacher will have the music playing as the students enter the room.
2. Students will form their literary groups.
3. Teacher will do a short historical synopsis of sixteen-century astrology and Nostradamus.
4. Teacher will pass out a copy of the newspaper and handout with Nostradamus's predictions to each group.
5. Groups will apply the framework to both the horoscopes and the predictions.
6. Groups will share their interpretations with the class.
7. Students will each write a short horoscope of their own that connects to their unit project and future vision.
8. Teacher will remind students that they should have a concrete plan for their unit project and ask for any questions or discussions that may be needed.
9. Teacher will hand out Day 3's leap hint while playing the 1960s music for the next quantum leap.

Leap Hint:
A copy of Martin Luther King, Jr.'s "I Have a Dream" speech without the title or the author.

Day 4

Title: Quantum leap to 1960s–1970s: Study of Martin Luther King, Jr.'s "I Have a Dream" speech.

Subject: 1960s–1970s Martin Luther King, Jr.'s "I Have a Dream" speech

Length: 50 minutes

Group Size: 26 students

Goal: To give students insight into American life in the 1960s and 1970s. Within that historical context, they will learn about Martin Luther King's life, and his famous speech, "I Have a Dream."

Materials Needed:

Music segments from the 1960s and 1970s, information of Martin Luther King, Jr. biography, printed copies of "I Have a Dream."

Objectives: Students will gain an understanding of the historical and racial context in America during the 1960s and 1970s. By using our framework, they will be able to understand why Martin Luther King, Jr., wrote and delivered his speech in the manner and time in which he did, and will see the relevance of the material to visionary literature.

Lesson Steps:
1. Teacher will begin class by playing a music clip from the 1960s and 1970s (from previous day).
2. Teacher will ask the students when in American history was the particular music popular.
3. Teacher will give historical background of 1960s and 1970s, focusing on racial, class, and gender issues.
4. Teacher will then ask students if they can name the visionary speech that they were to have read the night before ("I Have a Dream").
5. Teacher will then have students divide into four groups of four, and two groups of five to complete their frameworks.
6. Students will discuss the speech in relation to their frameworks for the remainder of the class period.

Homework:
Teacher will hand out sci-fi survey and will remind students that their project proposal is due the next day.

Day 9

Title: *The Parable of the Sower* and Race: Different People Frightened Her in Some Deep, Hard, Ugly Way.

Length: 50 minutes

Group Size: 26 students

Goal: Students will consider racial demographics/issues today such as projected racial demographics, interracial statistics, and a sixteen-year-old's opinion of race relations to Butler's 2025.

Materials Needed:
 1. Copies of *The Parable of the Sower*.
 2. Race packet.

Objective:
Students will share their opinions of race relations in today's historical/cultural context. They will consider projected racial demographics and implications of these numbers for their futures. Students will compare their opinion/articles concerning race today to the vision of race in *The Parable of the Sower*. Based on the articles and novel, students will evaluate how important race relations could be to a vision of the future.

Lesson Steps:
 1. Teacher plays gunfire. Teacher points out link between race and violence in the novel by asking students to recall the two reasons Lauren dressed as a man to make the trip north. (One reason was because a group of two men and one woman would appear stronger than a group with two women and one man. The other reason was so she and Zahra would appear to be a black couple with a white man, instead of a mixed group.) Ask students to turn to p. 153. Point out the quote, "Mixed couples catch hell whether people think they're gay or straight. You'll piss off the whites and Harry will piss off the blacks. Good luck." Note that this quote is Butler's future, and now we're going to look at race in the present.
 2. Teacher will ask students for their opinion of race relations in this historical/cultural time period based on what they know and the race packet they read.
 3. Teacher will write down student-generated list of racial/religious issues on the board.
 4. Students will break into small groups and look for racial issues in the novel. If certain groups are stuck, teacher might suggest certain pages to search (pp. 19, 77, 150, 153, 182, 186, 196, 258, 271).
 5. Students will create another listing on the board of race issues in the novel.
 6. Teacher will ask students to draw a connection between the two lists. Do they see any similarities? What are the differences? Why do they think Octavia Butler made the Earthseed community such a racially mixed group? Do they think race relations are better or worse in 2025?

7. Teacher will stress that race is the final component that students must address in their final project. They must discuss how people will deal with difference or diversity of race or religion in the future. Will things improve or worsen? They must be prepared to justify their opinions with facts from our present historical/cultural context.
8. Teacher will play music from 1999 and announce the final leap.

Leap Hint: You are an eighteen-year-old student in the United States. Technology is exploding around you and the possibilities for the future are immense. The people are worried about the future as well. Violence, war, poverty, the environment, and other issues are all concerns. What do you think? What will the future be like? What should it be like?

Framework:

Who predicted the future?

What issues did they address?

How is their vision a product of the times in which it was created?

How might it have challenged the times in which it was created?

What Is the Issue?
1. What sense do the representations make of the world?
2. What are the visuals representing to us and how?
3. What are typical representations of groups in society?
4. What does this example of visuals represent to me?
5. What do the visuals mean to other people who see them?
6. How is the issue/event defined?
7. What is the source of the information?
8. What form does the event take?
9. How does the form shape my understanding of the event?
10. How does the form serve or not serve my purposes?
11. What information is left out?

Who Is Involved?
1. What point of view is present?
2. Who is the target audience?
3. What are the arguments?
4. Why is a particular visual image selected?
5. What information presented in the image is factual?

6. What portion of content is inaccurate?
7. Why is shot/camera work arranged that way?
8. Do visual images match narration?
9. How does sound affect visual images?
10. How is repetition of visual images and texts used?
11. How do graphics affect the message?
12. What is left out?
13. How is the message affected by what is left out?

What Is Taken for Granted?
1. What attitudes are assumed?
2. Whose voice is heard?
3. Whose points of view are assumed?

INDIVIDUAL LEARNING PROJECTS

1. Create a shoe box diorama of a favorite scene.
2. Develop a time line or story map to indicate events of your vision.
3. Make a collage by cutting out letters, words, and pictures from old magazines.
4. Record a part of your vision on tape and make the recording available for others to enjoy.
5. Tell your vision with musical accompaniment.
6. Create a meaning between a kid today and one from your vision.
7. Create a mural to tell the vision.
8. Create a scrapbook of interesting facts and information based on your vision.
9. Create a TV news report dealing with a special event in your vision.
10. Create flannel-board characters and tell your vision using them.
11. Create a story and map by sketching the main events of your vision.
12. Create a cartoon, comic book, or comic strip based on your vision.
13. Invent a mock interview with someone in your vision.
14. Write a sequel book and share it with other students. Solicit their opinions.
15. Invent a new character and create some dialogue between him or her in the future.

16. Design a "book of quotations" listing important sayings spoken by (one of) someone in your vision.

17. Present an oral summary of your vision (but must have a visual also).

18. Dramatize your vision.

19. Build a scale model of an object of the future and tell the vision around it.

20. Draw a clock showing the time an important event occurred.

21. Make a "picture book" of your vision.

22. Illustrate the most important part of your vision.

23. Do a watercolor picture.

24. Compare your vision with another you read on a similar subject.

25. Produce a "movie" of your vision.

26. Put together a three-dimensional scene from your vision.

27. Give a pantomime of an important part.

28. Present a pantomime as a guessing game.

29. Read from your book orally while other students pantomime.

30. Give a chalk talk.

31. Conduct a scientific experiment associated with your vision.

32. Do a soap or balsa wood carving.

33. Design and make stand-up characters.

34. Compose a poem about your vision.

35. Send a letter to a friend about your vision.

36. Categorize stories with similar themes.

37. Make up jokes or riddles about your vision.

38. Make a picture book version of your vision.

39. Make a report card for issues to be covered (race, class, gender) with descriptions of why the grade is given.

40. Describe a scene from your vision as if you are an on-the-spot reporter.

41. Make up a board game or physical game based on your vision.

42. List the tests the main character of your vision has to face. The tests may involve a physical challenge or hardship, emotional troubles, or some kind of conflict. Describe one test in detail.

43. Imagine that you have to explain your actions to reporters. Write a paragraph that gives you a chance to explain these actions from your point of view.

44. Compose a song or write a poem about your vision. Recite your poem for the class.

45. Build a diorama of the setting of the story or of one scene from your vision.
46. Draw a map of the story's settings. Include important geographical features, such as lakes, rivers, and so on. Explain the events that took place at the various locations.
47. Create a game related to your vision. Make up your own rules and game cards. Teach other students how to play the game.
48. Write your vision in cartoon strip form. Create your own cartoon version of characters and write their dialogue in bubbles. Share your completed cartoon with some younger children.
49. Construct a time line to show the sequence of events in the story. Tape $8\frac{1}{2} \times 11$ inch sheets of paper together in a long row. Write and illustrate one event per page. Display your time line on a classroom wall.
50. Make finger puppets depicting scenes of your vision, and with a friend, act out some parts of the story.
51. Make a ten-page picture book showing the most important parts of your vision. You may choose a classmate to help you stage your performance.
52. Create a script for a puppet show based on an exciting part of your vision. Each page should include an illustration and several sentences.
53. List the sights, sounds, smells, tastes, and feelings (physical and emotional) to convey your future vision.
54. Write a journal as if you were living in the future.
55. Write about or draw a picture with an example of what makes your vision noteworthy.
56. Make a newspaper with stories based on your vision. You might draw pictures to go with the stories, and you could add other parts to the newspaper, like a weather report and cartoons.
57. Design a poster to advertise your vision. Write a blurb, a short statement on your vision highlights, and compose an advertising jingle.
58. Think of advertising slogans (from other products or an original one) that could be used in your future vision.
59. Turn the vision into a play. Write a script and act it out.
60. Write character dialogue for two people of your vision.
61. Write about the parts of your vision that were the funniest, saddest, happiest and most unbelievable.
62. Write original play.

The teacher will be open to students' suggestions; however, the project must include representations of race, class, and gender. It must also show signs of student action. Descriptions of an optional project topic must be turned in to the teachers by Day 5.

Project Expectations:
The final project is an accumulation of everything learned throughout the unit. Through your own piece of futuristic literature, you will demonstrate power and influence over your future. It is important to remember that everything you foresee in the future is based on the historical context in which you now live. You will display your future vision using a particular format, as given on the "Individual Learning Project Sheet," or from developing your own format, clearing it with me well in advance. This project must include portrayals of race, class, and gender, using your own knowledge of these areas to share your hopes and fears for the future. Once you have decided upon your future vision, you must demonstrate signs of action. You must show that you believe in making your vision a reality, and that you are empowered to influence the world in which you live. There are no outrageous ideas, as the future is yours. Make a difference now and allow this world to become a better place to live.

DISCUSSION

These unit plans are similar in several ways. They both deal with visions of the future—the dream, predictions. They were both designed for the twelfth-grade in an English class. Some of the readings selected overlap. But the choices these teachers made on how to go about integrating media literacy are different. In the first example, the teachers make explicit their overarching rationale of taking up this thematic topic. Thematic topics are a creative way to introduce students to real-life situations and engaging them to learn a topic from multiple perspectives as well as from their own experiences. For example, Lisa and Jesse state their intentions: "students will continue to develop their ability to critically analyze texts ranging from novels to film and from essays to MTV, communicate their thoughts through verbal and written forms in an articulate, well-considered manner, and expand their understanding of a multitude of perspectives. By taking part in an array of class experiences, including a debate, Utopian Mural, group presentation, and solo reflection, students will explore the way in which difficult issues of race, class, and gender affect preconstructed utopian societies, student-constructed utopian societies, as well as our presently existing society." These teachers make it their objective to explore multiple texts as a creative way to gain multiple perspectives. Critical pedagogy is employed as an analytical method to examine all texts—not limited to mass media texts but including classroom texts.

In the second example, the teachers put together a packet of readings that introduce students to the complex topics of race, class, and gender from the mass media. These texts are blended together with literature texts. The analytical framework they presented the students with which to read the texts critically heightens their media literacy moment. Then, the teachers encourage students to engage in creative projects that force them to think on their own in real-life situations. They are presented with over sixty topics to demonstrate their creativity, critical mindedness, and critical thinking skills. In education, these two examples show an attempt of what teachers can do to create classroom environments where students and teachers are alive with creative ideas, imaginative interpretations, and a passion for understanding—a clear attempt of integrative practice.

LESSONS

I must now return to the question I posed at the beginning of this chapter. What have we learned from the discussion of this book? First, we learned in Chapter 2 that through critical media literacy students engage in a "process" of curriculum inquiry that seeks to employ analytic habits of thinking, reading, speaking, or discussing, which go beneath surface impressions, traditional myths, and mere opinions. When students apply these analytical frames, they wish to refine or reshape their worldview relative to their own social context. This process is part of constructing knowledge, which is learning. Central to this process is critical, careful analysis of the meanings media texts transmit and the meanings viewers construct for themselves. The questions generated through this inquiry process to get to the deeper meaning of texts are not complete or accomplished by one round of questioning. The questioning is iterative, that is, one set of questions leads to new questions. As students compare the media text in question to their own social context and notice contradictions, they are motivated to pose further questions. For these students, therefore, questioning becomes part of learning, producing knowledge for themselves. Questioning enables these students to produce knowledge on their own.

As discussed previously, teachers and students can no longer take the texts they read in classrooms for granted. They must take a hard look at what any media text is telling them and pose questions that resist hegemonic practices. Critical media literacy demands counter-hegemonic questioning and a different method of inquiry that goes beyond the preferred meaning or negotiated reading to enable students to create their own knowledge of or from the text. The rationale for counter-hegemonic questioning is driven by the belief that: (1) media messages are constructions; (2) media messages are representations of social reality, (3) individuals construct meaning from messages; (4) messages have economic, political, social, and aesthetic purposes; and (5) each form of social communication has unique characteristics. By recognizing these basic concepts of critical media literacy, teachers and students gain power to read, view, and think critically and engage in the social struggle over meanings and assume a critical stance and a reflective perspective that avoids generalizing a "masculinist conception of the self" and legitimating a "Eurocentric and patriarchal" worldview dominant in the mass media, schools, and the workplace (Hammer, 1995, p. 79).

Critical theorists are convinced that critical media literacy is an appropriate response to hegemonic practices. As such, it is part of a process of critical pedagogy that teaches individuals how their culture, society, and the polity are structured and work. Critical media pedagogy involves teachers to mobilize students and citizens so that they can learn to "more effectively create their own meanings, lives and society" (Kellner, 1995, p. xiv). Since children are immersed in the television experience, everyday schooling or parenting that omits an examination of TV's curriculum also ignores the world that children experience. The challenge of American education therefore is to help young people navigate consciously/actively the sea of messages flooding into their lives daily through TV, movies, radio, music, video games, magazines, newspapers, even billboards, bumper stickers, and T-shirt logos. The complexity of the relationship between what we see and hear, what we believe and think, and how we interact with one another underscores the need for across the curriculum teaching of critical reading, critical thinking, and critical viewing skills.

The second lesson is that teachers and students must not see these activities of viewing and thinking about media as *technical* skills to be acquired in isolation and limited to the classroom. Since the media themselves form a day and night curriculum and instruction for many youth in America, critical media literacy needs to counter the daily bombardment by teaching individuals how to "read" and "criticize" the media, and how to "produce" alternative media and culture. It is true that many youth in America today are part of a large consumer society targeted by toy industries, car manufacturers, fashion designers, and other large corporations for their products and a society that has sold wholesale to a media frenzy completely supported by a capitalist ethic based on the profit motive and economic gain. Media products, including the advertising of consumer articles, cultural artifacts, emotions, ideals, or values are presented as a form of entertainment. Because of the economic imperative (i.e., media corporations are in the business of making money and advertising is a major component of the media business), media products often are packaged without any warning about the intended manipulation, overt bias, and distorted perspectives imbedded in the media messages in order to "make money," to sell a product, or to persuade the public politically, socially, economically, or educationally. The ultimate message orchestrated in the media products may well be an intentioned device to legitimize, maintain, or peddle a hegemonic culture or ideology.

As explained by Kellner (1995), a hegemonic ideology is not a system of rigid ideological indoctrination that induces consent of existing capitalist societies, but instead, it is the use of "the pleasures of the media and sound, and the spectacle to seduce audiences into identifying with certain views, attitudes, feelings, and positions." Thus, media consumer culture works hand in hand to generate thought and behavior that conform to existing values, institutions, beliefs, and practices. However, the counter-hegemonic questioning that critical media literacy aims to model for students is not meant to deny or deprive them of the pleasures they might experience from a TV program, film, or novel. Rather, by questioning routine practices they gain insights that open up those locked up spaces of bias, manipulation, and distortion, which might otherwise have been concealed from them by intentional or unintentional actions of the producer, writer, or webmaster.

The third lesson is that critical viewing is a process rather than an analytical skill of decoding content. Critical media literacy challenges educators to extend their contributions to students by designing curricula that draw on the full range of human ways of knowing. This implies that instead of preparing students for eventual literate behavior, teachers engage them in genuine acts of critical literacy right from the beginning and throughout the school career. It also implies that the language arts curriculum will not be fragmented into separate components for reading, composing, and editing, but rather integrate these in meaningful ways while valuing students' experiences, particularly mass media experiences. Further, it implies that skills will be taught within the context of genuine reading, writing, speaking, and listening activities, rather than separate or prerequisite components of the program.

This means, therefore, that the traditional practices of teaching reading as separate from writing, and of isolating grammar usage, spelling, and vocabulary, and teaching them as if separate subjects are in large part misguided and counterproductive. However, this is not to suggest that content is not important. Rather, content is important for a different reason. It is an ongoing developmental process on the part of the learner. I suggest that teachers strive to make content relevant to the experience of the learner. This is to say that larger process-related considerations should govern the selection of content. Content is so important because it demands to be studied in sufficient detail to allow us to make meaning around it. We need to "understand the conditions of its production and validation, who benefits from it and who does not, and how it relates to knowledge and information" (Kincheloe & Steinberg, 1998, p. 14). Applying this kind of critical mindedness in tackling texts and making this the object of critical media literacy alters the central tenets of the dichotomous arguments of content perspective on curriculum. Thus, the goal of the language of criticism proposed in critical media literacy is to generate among teachers and students the habits of questioning until they question all information every time they encounter it regardless of source.

The fourth lesson we have learned is that a major source of knowledge in schools is the textbook, in which is found prepackaged, preordered, legitimized, objective knowledge. Teachers find such knowledge in the texts of the sciences, arts, humanities, and the growing number of "how to" books, including the technologies of media, computers, and the Internet. Knowledge in these texts is selected, ordered, and produced by authorities who control the discourse in the disciplines, to be consumed by the reader—students (Berry, 1998, p. 45). Even at university level, the authority of textbooks controls thoughts and knowledge—just visit a campus bookstore and you will see what I mean.

It seems that the first location for students to create their own knowledge would be at the university. Yet, the textbook has become the dominant source of knowledge for students and in no way are they given the opportunity, encouraged to, or evaluated on their abilities to challenge, resist, or oppose that authority. Instead, they are evaluated and judged on their ability to consume without negotiation or resistance the prepackaged knowledge. Students have told me how professors of their college courses simply read from the textbook or have the students recall verbatim information from the textbook.

In my own teaching experience, I have found that heavy reliance on the use of prepackaged knowledge is not only attributable to actions of omissions of professors. For a variety of reasons, students themselves seem to resist creating their own knowledge, even at graduate level. I hear complaints such as: "Just tell me what I have to study or give the questions I need to prepare for the examination," or "I prefer a final exam instead of a research paper," "I'm not ready to write my thesis, I need to take more courses." Students do this for lack of confidence to learn on their own. Thus, they resist the opportunity to create their own knowledge, draw their own plan of study that matches with their interests or research questions. Students tell me of professors whose lectures draw crowds of students. These numbers look good to administrators who are in the business of bean-counting credit hours, not what knowledge students produce on their own. I am equally frustrated by the pressure students put on me to lecture to them. Few questions are asked about how students made use of the data, theories, or even how long they remembered it. The methods I have outlined in this book begin to shift away from the position of advocates of less deeper and more analytical coverage of content. I suppose students have been molded this way since the years of high school to expect the teacher to be the authority of the subject matter, to spoon-feed them with doses of prepackaged knowledge. Those of us who have begun to introduce critical pedagogy into classrooms understand that force-feeding students massive amounts of data wanes their interest in a subject and their appreciation of the meaning of the material. As we learn to make meaning to search for connections between subject matter and student-produced knowledge, and to relate students' worlds to the lived reality of scholars, our methods and curriculum-making begin to change. As argued previously, these incremental changes will motivate students to adopt new research methods that not only enhance their learning but also encourage them to produce knowledge on their own.

The fifth lesson is that assumptions, "common knowledge," common sense, "general" knowledge, myths, widespread beliefs, and popular attitudes are all part of the *context of meanings* within which cultural norms or values are enhanced and circulated. That is to say, power intervenes in (a cultural discourse) the process of shared cultural codes to guarantee that meaning remains stable forever. For example, to keep meanings stable, authorities in society use ordinances or sanctions to regulate or ensure that meaning remains stable. Definitions of words of social practice or language use as explained in dictionaries play similar functions in society to control meaning.

Sixth, we learned that the message in social communication is always complex in structure and form. It always contains more than one potential "reading." Messages propose and prefer certain readings over others, but they can never become wholly closed around one reading. In other words, they remain polysemous. Also, often overlooked in this perspective, however, is the fact that society is marked by a multiplicity of culture, meanings, interpretations, and values. Thus, individuals construct the contexts of meanings out of their experiences within specific social contexts of institutional structures, race, gender, class, and so forth. Rather than one abstract psychological process, contexts of meanings are historically defined social practices that are subject to political, academic, and cultural hierarchies. This sociopolitical context and our individual ranges of knowledge, values, and attitudes are governed in turn by asymmetry of power that enables powerful groups to define their own particular meanings, experiences, ideas and conventions as well as forms of writing and reading as valued ones in society (Aronowitz & Giroux, 1991). It is in this hierarchy, therefore, that some values or meanings come to be dominant and others marginalized.

Seventh, the dominant knowledge (which includes more than just facts and logic, but also values, attitudes, institutional structures, history, etc.) of the modern era, is assumed to be structured and validated by Western, European, white, middle-class males. Excluding all other knowledge, Euro-American knowledge systems have permeated every aspect of late, modern consciousness, including postcolonial nations in varying stages of development, such as some African, Asian, and Latin American populations.

The eighth lesson is that the mass media are a major constructor of knowledge in late modernity. Their place of prominence has been due to the influence of media and computer technologies. Whatever the influence, students, especially those not privileged by the status quo, are eventually robbed of their participatory consciousness.

CONCLUDING COMMENTS

I would like to conclude this reflection on praxis by borrowing from Patrick Slattery and Rebecca McElfresh Spehler's response to the cliché: "The youth are our nation of the future." These scholars believe students today are the past, present, and future of the world all at once— not just of the future of our nation. Thus, the future will continue to be elusive if it is not thought of as part of the present and the past. I am optimistic that the analytical frameworks I have described in this book will empower students when they find themselves able to ask questions about the contradictions they see in their present lives and what they learn. Such questioning must begin now as they read texts in classrooms as well as out of school. They need not wait for some future date when they will mature to do so. When they engage in this kind of inquiry, they will be led to seek right-probing questions rather than the correct answers. This enterprise in turn leads to critical consciousness of self—an active consciousness that motivates them to take up, instead of ignoring, the gaps that persist in their education. This will mean legitimizing their unique contribution to the global community in the present moment. An inquiry that leads to reflection and leads to taking action produces a long-lasting knowledge. When the analytic habits of such inquiry become part of daily life, students and teachers will be armed with a renewed sense of their possibilities and be able to exercise their imaginative, intuitive, and transformative powers in the educational process. It is only with such renewal that our vision of a just, caring, and ecologically sustainable global community is possible.

REFERENCES

Aronowitz, S., & Giroux, H. (1991). *Postmodern education: Politics, culture and social criticism.* Minneapolis: University of Minnesota Press.

Barthes, R. (1974). *S/Z* (R. Miller, Trans.). New York: Hill and Wang/The Noonday Press

Berry, K. (1998). Nurturing the imagination of resistance: Young adults as creators of knowledge. In J. Kincheloe, & S. Steinberg (Eds.), *Unauthorized methods. Strategies for critical teaching.* New York: Routledge, pp. 43–55.

Derrida, J. (1990). *Le probleme de la gentese dans la philosophie de Husser.* Paris: Presses Universitaire de France.

Hammer, R. (1995). Rethinking the dialectic: A critical semiotic meta-theoretical approach for the pedagogy of media literacy. In P. McLaren, R. Hammer,

D. Sholle, & S. Reilly, *Rethinking media literacy: A critical pedagogy of representation.* New York: Peter Lang, pp. 33–85.

Kellner, D. (1995). *Media culture: Cultural studies, identity, and politics between the modern and the postmodern.* New York: Routledge.

Kincheloe, J., (1993). *Toward a critical politics of teacher thinking: Mapping the postmodern.* Westport, CT: Bergin & Garvey.

———, & Steinberg, S. (1998). *Unauthorized methods. Strategies for critical teaching.* New York: Routledge.

Masterman, L. (1985). *Teaching the media.* London: Comedia Books.

Slattery, P., & McElfresh Spehler, R. (1998). Teachers and administrators: A vision of prophetic practice. In J. Kincheloe & S. Steinberg (Eds.), *Unauthorized methods. Strategies for critical teaching.* New York: Routledge, pp. 254–263.

U.S.A. Today. (1997). Messages reinforce sexual stereotypes. December 7, p. 4.

Walmsley, S. A., & Walp, T. P. (1990). Integrating literature and composing into the language arts curriculum: Philosophy and practice. *Elementary School Journal, 90:* 251–274.

Index